Karachi's
Public Transport

ORIGINS, EVOLUTION, AND FUTURE PLANNING

T0002669

Karachi's Public Transport

ORIGINS, EVOLUTION, AND FUTURE PLANNING

Arif Hasan, Mansoor Raza, and
Urban Resource Centre

OXFORD
UNIVERSITY PRESS

OXFORD
UNIVERSITY PRESS

Oxford University Press is a department of the University of Oxford.
It furthers the University's objective of excellence in research, scholarship,
and education by publishing worldwide. Oxford is a registered trade mark of
Oxford University Press in the UK and in certain other countries

Published in Pakistan by
Oxford University Press
No. 38, Sector 15, Korangi Industrial Area,
PO Box 8214, Karachi-74900, Pakistan

ISBN 978-0-19-070639-5

Typeset in Adobe Garamond Pro
Printed on 68gsm Offset Paper

Printed by Kodwavi Printing Services, Karachi

Acknowledgements
Cover photograph by Zahid Hussein

Contents

List of Appendices

Appendix

Acronyms

BRT	Bus Rapid Transit
CBD	Central Business District
CDGK	City District Government Karachi
CNG	Compressed Natural Gas
EFI	Electronic Fuel Injection
IUCN	International Union for Conservation of Nature
KBCA	Karachi Building Control Authority
KCR	Karachi Circular Railway Rickshaws
KIBOR	Karachi Inter Bank Offer Rate
KMC	Karachi Metropolitan Corporation
SITE	Sindh Industrial Trade Estate
URC	Urban Resource Centre
IIED	International Institute for Environment and Development
JICA	Japan International Cooperation Agency
KTIP	Karachi Transportation Improvement Project
OPP	Orangi Pilot Project
RTI	Research and Training

Acknowledgements
Arif Hasan

Much of this book consists of papers written by the authors and supported and published by the International Institute for Environment and Development (IIED), UK as working papers and articles in *Environment & Urbanization*, the IIED Journal on Human Settlements. The authors are thankful to the IIED for having given permission to use this material.

The authors are also thankful to Hamza Arif for having helped to put this book together and to have added material to a number of chapters, which given the diversity of the chapters, was not an easy job. A number of other individuals also need to be acknowledged; the interviews of government officials and transporters along with those of community members in the low-income settlements were carried out by Zahid Farooq and Rizwan-ul-Haq (social organiser and manager documentation, respectively at the URC, Karachi). These interviews were transcribed from Urdu to English by Dr Qamar-uz-Zaman Yousefzai (Urdu faculty member at the Benazir University, Karachi), Saima Shivejee and Ravina Anthony (students of Social Science Department, ZABIST University, Karachi), and by Rizwan-ul-Haq. The interviews of women commuters were carried out and transcribed by Anadil Iftekhar (a school teacher who had interned earlier with the URC). She also located and identified the respondents. We are also thankful to Faisal Imran and freelance writer, Asifya Aziz for converting the raw data from interviews into case studies. The questionnaire survey employed in Chapter 3 was supervised by Mansoor Raza and Humayoon Waqar (a freelance researcher). Those who participated in the survey are URC staff members: Zahid Farooq, Adnan Farooqui, Mukhtar Yousuf, Shakeel Gill, Rao Nasir Ali, Seema Liaquat, Muhammad Jamil, and Shazia Perween. Others who assisted in the survey are Rana Sadiq and Shakeel (both community activists). The data feeding of the survey through SPSS was done by Rozina Imtiaz and the analysis was carried out by Mansoor Raza who also helped me in putting the initial document together. URC Director, Younus Baloch, monitored the URC part of the work.

Introduction

Arif Hasan

This book is about Karachi's public transport, or the lack thereof, in a city often referred to as Pakistan's economic 'hub'. It is also one of the largest in the world, with an official population of 16 million and an unofficial figure that varies between 20–25 million. The city has only 20,000 buses for such a large population and most of these are small 35-seaters and are in poor condition. As a result of their small numbers and limited seating arrangements, people are forced to travel on the rooftops of these vehicles. Women have no option but to choose their work locations according to the availability of transport. The better-off travel by Careem, or Uber and there is also Bykea (a motorbike service), which is comparatively affordable, but a smart phone is required to use it, which the poor do not always have access to. Increasingly, the population depends on rickshaws (4-seaters three-wheelers), of which there are over 230,000. These too are expensive for the low-income groups, but are, nevertheless, easily available.

To overcome the problems of inadequate and uncomfortable transport, the private sector has developed a number of innovations. One of these was the Qingqi: a motorbike pulling a carriage that carried up to nine passengers. Capital expense, operation, and maintenance of the Qingqis was relatively low and the commuting public, especially women, were happy with it. However, Qingqis were banned by the Supreme Court of Pakistan. Their design did not meet the safety regulations for three-wheeled vehicles and also because the police insisted that the 50,000 Qingqis operating in Karachi, were responsible for the city's traffic jams. The loss of Qingqis removed over 300,000 transport seats per day. In addition, there are now an unspecified number of Suzuki pickups that operate as buses, although they are not registered as such and have no route permits.

However, the most important investment in transport has been of motorbikes, of which there were 1.2 million in Karachi in 2011 and 2.8 million today. They are now available through hire purchase, at rates affordable to Karachi's lower-middle class. Motorbikes have changed the lives of the families that possess them, because of their flexibility and savings in commuting time and costs. But, Karachi has paid a price for this, as it has led to massive traffic jams and fatal accidents on its streets.

Yet at the time of independence—when Karachi was a city with a population of 450,000—it had a reasonably efficient transport system, consisting of a tramway, 10–20 buses and about 30 taxis. After independence, the state made considerable investments in providing Karachi with a bus-related transport system. The system passed through various stages, from government- to privately-owned, from private–public partnership to the establishment of corporations, and also included a Pakistan Railways-operated circular railway. But for a host of reasons, most of these initiatives were shut down because of enormous losses and non-availability of the state (some say unwillingness) to deliver.

The closing down of the government-owned Urban Transport Services (UTS) in 1997 as well as the circular railway, was the last nail in the coffin. The UTS had a vast fleet of large buses, considerable real estate in the form of depots, terminals, workshops, and arrangements with the automobile industry in Karachi, for maintenance of the rolling stock and training of the UTS maintenance staff, and considerable support from other transport-related governance departments. Because of its large losses, the World Bank advised the government to sell off UTS and since there were no buyers, it was closed down and its staff given a golden handshake.

The initial two chapters of the book provide the context with respect to Karachi and details of what has been mentioned in the paragraphs above, along with their causes and repercussions. Chapter 3 deals with the responses of different stakeholders to the transport crisis, such as: the response of the market, technical innovations, views of transporters, commuters, and comments and proposals of transport-related government officials. These views are about different physical, socio-economic, administrative, environmental and planning issues. Chapter 4 discusses Karachi's ride-hailing culture and its socio-economic repercussions. Chapter 5 consists of the perceptions of users of different modes of transport; the infrastructure they use, and the causes of different problems, such as traffic jams, parking, and of the issues related to car maintenance, security, health, attitudes of the government and the public, and road traffic injuries. Chapter 6 consists of individual interviews of persons involved in the transport drama, including taxi drivers, mechanics, traffic police officers, male and female passengers, spare parts dealers, bankers who provide loans for the purchase of vehicles, ambulance drivers and environmentalists. Chapter 7 consists entirely of women's transport issues, described through a series of interviews with women commuters.

If putting this book together is of some help to Karachi's planners, civil society and citizens, in better understanding the issues involved in designing, maintaining and operating public transport in Karachi, then its purpose will have been served.

1

Karachi: The Changing Urban Landscape

Arif Hasan

K arachi is Pakistan's largest city and has the only two functioning sea ports of the country. Pakistan's official census figures[1] document almost a 60 per cent increase in the population of Karachi with the population increasing from 9,339,023 in 1998, to 14,910,352 in 2017. In addition to this, there are two million immigrants officially classified as 'aliens'. As such, a little over 8 per cent of the country's total population and 22 per cent of the country's urban population resides in Karachi.[2]

In addition to population, there are other reasons for Karachi's importance. It is Pakistan's only port city. It contains 32 per cent of the country's industrial base, generates 20 per cent of GDP, 25 per cent of federal revenues, and 62 per cent of income tax. It houses powerful federal institutions, such as the Karachi Port Trust (KPT), the Civil Aviation Authority (CAA), railways, customs, and military cantonments. All these federal institutions own land, carry out developments on it (including residential and commercial real estate), and employ a large number of people. In addition to the provincial government (which also owns land), they all have a say in Karachi's development. The city government controls only 31 per cent of Karachi's land, mostly through ownership.[3] Coordination between the different landowning agencies is almost non-existent.

Karachi is also the capital of Sindh province. It accommodates 62 per cent of Sindh's urban population and 30 per cent of its total population. This figure is interesting since the second-largest city of Pakistan, Lahore, the capital of Punjab province, accommodates only 7 per cent of the population of the province.[4] Karachi's large-scale industrial sector employs 71.6 per cent of the total industrial labour force in Sindh; the city produces 74.8 per cent of the province's total industrial output and provides 78 per cent of its formal private sector jobs.[5]

Due to migration from India after 1947 and continuous migration from other parts of Pakistan, Karachi is a multi-ethnic city. Even though it is the capital of Sindh, according to the 1998 census, only 14 per cent of the population speak local languages as their mother tongue, whereas 48.25 per cent speak Urdu. The Urdu-speakers are the post-1947 migrants to Karachi. As such, a predominantly Sindhi-speaking province has an overwhelming majority of non-Sindhi speaking ethnic groups in its capital city.

The Pakistan Peoples Party (PPP), popularly known to represent the Sindhi-speaking population of the province, can only control Karachi's enormous resources through a centralised province-controlled system of governance for the city. Meanwhile, the MQM (Muttahida Qaumi Movement) asserts that it represents the Urdu-speaking population of the city and can only control Karachi's assets if there is a decentralised form of local governance. Since the two parties cannot arrive at a consensus, local governance and its related institutions have been in a flux for over a decade.

Traffic and transport are one of the most serious problems faced by the city. This seriousness can be judged by the fact that in 2011, only 0.85 per cent of its vehicles were buses, and 4.04 per cent were three-seater motor rickshaws (three-wheeler vehicles), whereas cars constituted 38.21 per cent and motorcycles constituted 49.59 per cent (for details *see* Fig. 1.1). Statistics show that conditions have not improved since then, yet 60 per cent of the 24.2 million trips generated in Karachi every day are carried out using the existing public transport sector consisting of buses and motor rickshaws.[6] To overcome this crisis, the informal private sector had introduced about 50,000 plus Qingqis[7] (motorcycles with six-seater carriages attached). These were registered as motorbikes and not as six-seater carriages and as such were considered illegal by the police. As Karachi expands spatially, the problem of commuting increases. At present, the lengths of commutes for the working class are in the range of 20 to 40 km.

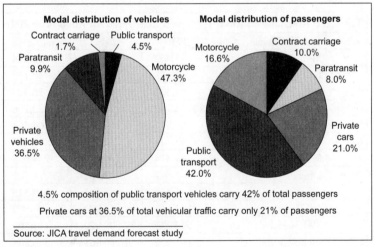

Figure 1.1.

The situation has been summarised by the Karachi Metropolitan Corporation (KMC) as follows: (i) internationally accepted ratio is of one 100-seater bus for a population of 1,500; (ii) population of Karachi is 20 million; (iii), as such requirement of large buses is 13,333; (iv) existing equivalent of large size buses in the form of 35-seater minibuses: 4,657; thus (v), the shortfall (immediate requirement) for Karachi is 8,676 large buses.[8]

The situation described above exists despite the fact that since independence, both the federal and provincial governments (and more recently, the city government) have made large investments in the transport sector and have experimented with different models from owning and running (both federally and provincially managed), to supporting the private sector, to public-private partnership (both provincially and local government managed) and promotion of the build-operate-transfer model. The government, in its various attempts, has also developed, at a considerable cost, transport related infrastructure, including depots, terminals, workshops and office spaces required for their management and operation, and invested heavily in the purchase of transport vehicles. Fig. 1.1 gives the modal distribution of vehicles and passengers. Table 1.1 gives the number of vehicles registered in Karachi, in 2013, and illustrates the transport crisis in Karachi, where motorcycles account for 58 per cent of all vehicles. Their rate of growth is also phenomenal. Between 2011 and 2018, they increased by more than 100 per cent, from 1,296,481 to 2,856,704, while minibuses decreased from 15,807, to 12,264, in the same period.

Table 1.1: Mechanised Road Transport Registered on Road June 2018

S. No.	Type of Vehicles	2010	2011	June 2018
1.	Mini Bus	15,452	15,807	12,264
2.	Buses	6,458	5,506	10,132
3.	Mini Truck	11,876	12,624	16,529
4.	Truck	14,759	15,588	22,196
5.	Van/Pickup	99,077	104,097	304,463
6.	Taxi	47,170	47,165	29,065
7.	Rickshaw	74,334	105,684	234,675
8.	Lifter	2,812	2,901	1,187
9.	Tractor	3,364	3,535	9,523
10.	Oil Tanker	2,663	2,876	879
11.	PVT Vehicles	946,733	998,920	1,143,509
12.	Motor Cycles	1,105,232	1,296,481	2,856,704
13.	Ambulance	1,728	1,832	1,055
14.	Coffin Carrier	69	71	15
15.	Disable Person	98	99	0
16.	Catholic Trust	113	113	0
17.	School Bus	244	246	0
18.	Church	38	35	0
	Grand Total	**2,330,220**	**2,614,580**	**4,642,196**

Source: Excise and Taxation Department, Government of Sindh

Different plans for mass transit light rail and Bus Rapid Transit (BRT) systems, have been prepared following detailed studies since 1972. A circular railway was also established in 1964 but was closed down in 1998. Various attempts at its revival have been made but have not been successful. (For a list of important studies and proposals, prepared since 1980, *see* Box 1.1.)

According to the 2017 census, the city population was growing at a tremendous growth rate of 5 per cent.[9] This growth rate is attributed to the perennial rural–urban migration. Moreover, according to a survey conducted in 2011, there are 2.5 million 'aliens' in Karachi.[10] (*See* Table 1.2).

Table 1.2: Per annum growth rates in Karachi, 1941–1998	
Year	Per Annum Growth %
1941–1951	11.50
1951–1961	6.05
1961–1972	5.00
1972–1981	4.96
1981–1998	3.52
1998–2017	2.40

The figure of 16 million, recorded by the 2017 census, is not accepted by the political parties of Karachi and the city's civil society, who insist that the city's population has been understated and is well over 20 million. Meanwhile, the secretariat of the United Nations Department of Economic and Social Affairs (UNDESA) puts urban Karachi as the twelfth-most populous urban centre in the world. In 1990, Karachi had occupied the 22nd position and by 2030, it is projected to be seventh most populous city of the world.[11] It is important to note that the UNDESA estimates were made on a growth rate of 3.3 per cent,[12] which is low compared to the 2017 census figures.

Table 1.3 highlights the staggering growth patterns of Karachi. The population added to city between the census periods of 1951 and 1981, over a period of thirty years, is 4.139 million, which is almost the same as the total population added between the census period of 1981 and 1998: in seventeen years, the addition is 4.06 million, with a mere difference of 79,000. Statistics from the census reports tell us that in 1951, for every male, there were 3.2 females, while in 2017 for every male there were 1.05 females; so, the gender gap is narrowing.

Table 1.3: Increase in Karachi's population over the last 150 years	
Year	Population
1856	56,875
1872	56,753
1881	73,560
1891	105,199
1901	136,297
1911	186,771
1921	244,162
1931	300,799
1941	435,887
1951	1,068,459
1961	1,912,598
1972	3,426,310
1981	5,208,132
1998	9,269,265
2006	13,969,284
2007	14,500,000
Source: Government of Pakistan Census Figures	

The spatial distribution and spread of livelihood opportunities for a city of between 16 to 20 million people, is strongly correlated with the health of its transport system. To give an idea of the geo-concentration of employment opportunities in the city, 56 per cent of employment in manufacturing is in the Sindh Industrial Trade Estate (SITE) area and Landhi and Korangi industrial areas. More than 80 per cent of business services are located in the central area. Additionally, 50 per cent of the employment in wholesale and transport is in the central area. Trip lengths are in the range of 20 to 40 km for working class commuters. Moreover, Karachi has to generate 3.5 million jobs at every five-year interval, for the rapid population growth.[13]

Karachi has an area of 3,780 km² (almost four times larger than Hong Kong) and low-income groups constitute 68 per cent of Karachi's population. Density is 6,000 people per square kilometre. Between 1998 and 2011, the average household size has increased by 6.7 persons to 7.3 persons. This increase is due to the shortage of housing and not to an increase in fertility rates.[14] That Karachi is a city of low-income communities, is highlighted by the fact that 88 per cent of houses are built on 120 square yards or less and only 2 per cent of total houses are built on 400–800 square yards.

In addition, 62 per cent of Karachi's citizens live in informally developed settlements on 23 per cent of the city's residential land. Many of these have densities of more than 4,500 persons per hectare (1,821 per acre) with more than 6 to 10 persons per room and up to 20 persons sharing a toilet. As such, they face serious overcrowding problems, of which the main victims are family cohesion, women, children, and the elderly. These settlements, in the absence of housing options, continue to densify. Conversely, 36 per cent of Karachiites live in formally planned settlements on 77 per cent of the city's residential land. Here, densities can be as low as 84 persons per hectare. Such low-density settlements continue to increase.[15]

Previously, the *katchi abadis* were on the periphery of a small city and hence nearer to places of work and social infrastructure. Today, however, the city has increased from an area of 2,103 km² in 1951,[16] to 3,780 km² in 2010.[17] The periphery today, is very far from places of work and social amenities, and it is the only place where affordable land in the informal sector is available for low-income groups. Living on this periphery means increased transportation costs, associated discomfort, and time spent commuting. It also means that women who have to look after families, have to forego certain job opportunities, as they cannot afford to commute for longer hours.

Added to this are some major social changes that are taking place. According to the Karachi Strategic Development Plan 2020 survey,[18] 89 per cent of families in Karachi are nuclear, whereas the 1989 survey showed the same indicator at 54 per cent. The family institution is in transition, fuelled by the desire to: educate their children, be independent of in-laws, have different lifestyles, and upward social mobility. Affordability, security and availability of transport to commute to places of work, education and recreation, are, unfortunately, dictating the choice of residence for couples moving out of homes belonging to their parents/in-laws. The transport system has to respond to these changing realities. Added to this is Karachi's traffic congestion and mismanagement, of which the main victims are the lower and lower-middle income groups, who have to travel long distances in uncomfortable conditions and in a degraded physical environment. Karachi's transport sector does not have the capacity to deal with the existing or changing realities.

As per data collected by the Urban Resource Centre,[19] in 2011, the number of registered vehicles in Karachi was 2.6 million. In 2018, this number grew to 4.6 million vehicles. According to a news report by *Pakistan Today* in 2014, a massive 900 new vehicles are registered on daily basis.[20]

Table 1.4: Registered Vehicles in Karachi, 2011		
Types of Vehicles	Numbers	Percentage
Minibuses	15,807 (8,773 in 1998)	0.60
Buses	6,506 (14,854 in 1998)	0.25
Taxi	47,165 (13,613 in 1998)	1.80
Rickshaw	105,684 (23,337 in 1998)	4.04
Motorcycles	1,296,481	49.59
Cars	998,920	38.21
Others	144,017	5.51
Total	2,614,580	100.00
Source: Raza 2014.		

Table 1.4 indicates that public transport (including para-transport) accounts for only 7 per cent of the total number of registered vehicles. Individual vehicle ownership dominates, as motorcycles and cars cumulatively accrue to 88 per cent of registered vehicles. 'Others' include trucks, lifters, ambulances, and oil tankers etc. It is also evident that from 1998 to 2011 (a period of 13 years), the number of buses has been reduced by 65 per cent. A press report claims that in the year 2000, 140 new minibus routes were approved, out of which only 60–65 are operational. Also, in 2000, sixty routes for buses were approved, but only 20 are currently operational. No new investments are being made by transport companies and many vehicles have been manufactured since 20–60 years.[21]

Karachi has a rapidly growing middle class. At present, there are over 200,000 apartments under construction.[22] Many of them are gated neighbourhoods on the fringe of the city. In addition, *katchi abadis* are densifying, because it is cheaper to rent places nearer to work, than to live on the fringe. Unless a comfortable transport system can be created, the middle class will keep buying cars and motorcycles, thus congesting the roads further. Also, unless an affordable system is put in place, the inner city *katchi abadis* will keep densifying, creating all physical and social negatives that contribute to overcrowding. To achieve such a transport system, political will is required as well as support from the federal government, which is not always forthcoming, and the creation of an effective municipal government, which has eluded Karachi so far.

Box 1.1: List of Important Studies on Karachi's Transport Issues

- Japan International Cooperation Agency, 'Feasibility Study on the Electrification of Karachi Suburban Railway and Preliminary Feasibility Study Report on Mass Transit System,' Government of Pakistan, March 1997.
- Karachi City Transport Shortages, Causes, Accidents and Suggestions,' prepared by the Karachi Bus Owners' Association at the request of the Transport Minister, Government of Sindh, 1993.
- Karachi Development Authority, 'Environmental Impact Assessment of Corridor-1,' Government of Sindh, 1994.
- M. Sohail and the URC Karachi, *Urban Public Transport and Sustainable Livelihood for the Poor: A Case Study of Karachi, Pakistan*, WEDC, Loughborough University, UK, 2000.
- Mass Transit Study 1990: Final Report on the Evaluation of Alternatives,' prepared by the Karachi Development Authority and Maunsell Consultants Limited, London and Parsons Brinckerhoff International Incorporated, New York and Llyassons and Associates, Karachi, 1990.
- 'Person Trip Study of Karachi City,' prepared by Exponent Engineers/Japan International Corporation Agency (JICA) for the CDGK; December 2005.
- Railway Constructions Pakistan Limited, 'Proposal for Upgradation of the Karachi Circular Railway,' Railway Constructions (Pakistan) Limited, Islamabad, 1996.
- 'Report of the Committee on Proposed Metropolitan Transport Authority,' by the Transport Commission Working Group, investigates the shortages of transport and making recommendations, included improved bus designs, prevention of road accidents, public transport discipline, mass transit fares and acts, rules and regulations relevant to them, 1982.
- 'Report on the Transport Sector: Karachi Strategic Development Plan-2020,' prepared by the Master Plan Group of Offices, City District Government Karachi (CDGK), February 2007.
- 'Revival of Karachi Circular Railway,' prepared for the Karachi Urban Transport Corporation by Environmental Management Consultants; 2009.

Source: Detailed study on a *Private-Public Partnership based Environmental Friendly Public Transport System for Karachi*; prepared by the Karachi Mass Transit Cell of the City Government for the Karachi Strategic Development Plan-2020, February 2006.

2

Transport Sector in Karachi:
Post-Independence History

Arif Hasan and Mansoor Raza
with URC

In 1947, there were 20 to 50 large buses operating in Karachi,[1] which were owned by three private sector companies. Most of the commuting public, however, relied on the tramway. The tramway connected the port to various important locations in the city, such as the wholesale markets and the cantonment railway station. It was also within easy walking distance of the city railway station, which handled both passenger and port-related intercity cargo. At any given place in the city, one was never more than 3 km from the tramway (for the location of the tramway, *see* Fig. 2.1). The importance of the tramway can be gauged from the fact that the number of tram cars increased from 37 in 1918, to 64 in 1954, and to 157 in 1955. However, the tramway was closed down in 1974. The reason for its closure was that it was blocking traffic on the main corridors of the city, thus resulting in accidents. Another reason for its discontinuation was that the Karachi Master Plan 1975–85 had developed elaborate plans for a mass transit system—the main underground corridor that was under the existing tramway's right of way. (*See* Box 2.1 for a history of the tramway).

At the time of independence, Karachi had a population of 450,000 and its spatial spread was only 25 km² as compared to 3,780 km² in 2010.[2] As such, the buses and tramway were more than adequate for its needs. In addition, about 30 taxis[3] were also available and so were horse-drawn carriages for the

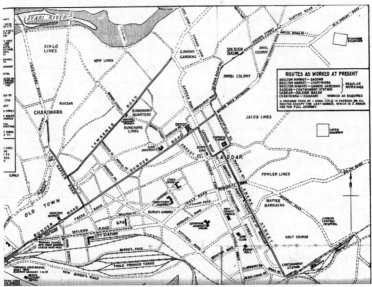

Figure 2.1: Tramway Routes at the time of Partition.

richer sections of the population. Most of the cargo-handling between the port and the rest of the country, was by railway. Intra-city cargo from the port to the wholesale markets in the city and to the railway stations, was by camel and donkey carts.

However, 600,000 refugees from India moved into the city in the last three months of 1947 and in the 1951 census, Karachi's population had increased to 1.37 million.[4] This occurred despite the fact that over a 100,000 Hindus and Sikhs were forced to leave the city. The migration from India resulted in the densification of the city and the creation of settlements on its immediate fringe. As a result, the transport issue became crucial.

The demands for transport increased considerably as a result of the 1959 Karachi Resettlement Plan. Under this plan, two satellite towns—New Karachi in the north and Landhi–Korangi in the southeast—were created about 20 km from the city centre back then. Industrial areas were an integral part of these plans; the concept being that the residents of these towns would work in the industrial areas and would not have to travel to the city. Health and education infrastructure were also provided. However, the industry did not materialise, and the working population of the towns had to commute long distances on bad roads to the work areas in the city's business district, port and adjacent industrial areas.

The 1959, Karachi Resettlement Plan converted a dense city into a sprawl. In addition, it segregated rich and poor areas and since the vast majority of the population that were shifted to the satellite towns consisted of Urdu-speaking refugees, it also created ethnic-based segregation.[5] The various initiatives of the government to tackle the transport issue between 1948 and 1977, are listed in Box 2.2. The failure of these initiatives has been attributed to financial issues.

A major initiative taken by the government was in 1977, with the creation of the Karachi Transport Corporation (KTC). The corporation was owned by the federal and provincial governments and it inherited the Karachi-based assets of the Sindh Road Transport Corporation (SRTC), an earlier provincial level government initiative. These assets consisted of six depots, central stores, transport training institute, buses, and a staff of over 5,000. Under the KTC, a number of initiatives were undertaken. Links with the recently nationalised automobile industry were created and they undertook to develop technology, in order to build large buses. As a result, 550 large new buses were introduced. New premises for the transport institute, central workshop, and stores were built along with a central bus terminal capable of handling 200,000 passengers daily. The head offices of the KTC were also established at the Civic Centre, where the Karachi Development Authority (KDA) was located.[6] This added to the importance of the KTC and it was integrated into the planning required for the implementation of the Karachi Master Plan, 1975–85.

But the KTC ran into hurdles. By December 1996, it was running at a loss of Rs 10 million per month, and of its 303 buses, only 100 were operational. Amidst the political violence, which gripped Karachi during 1994–6, 24 buses were destroyed and 184 were irreparably damaged. This damage was evaluated at Rs 55.5 million, but the KTC received no compensation from the government. Because of the losses, KTC's performance was evaluated and it was agreed between the Sindh government and the World Bank to privatise KTC, after twenty years of operation. The remaining KTC buses were dumped in its depots and 3,400 of its employees were given a golden handshake of Rs 1.1 billion while Rs 3.75 million were required to pay the benefits of those who had retired earlier.[7]

Various reasons are given for the failure of the KTC. One view is that a leakage of fare revenue and the failure to maintain the buses properly were the real reasons for the problems that the organisation faced. The maintenance issue was a serious one, since the technical staff was not properly trained and the spare parts used were of low quality. As a result, there was a sharp increase in the number of buses that could not be used. The rising cost of diesel, without the government's approval of a proportional increase in fares, or the provision of subsidies, also had a negative effect on the functioning of KTC.[8]

Today, the property of KTC, which is worth billions of rupees, is being used as part of the infrastructure requirements for the BRTs (Bus Rapid Transit) that are currently under construction. Some portions of it have been grabbed informally, for commercial purposes. The government has also established police-monitoring check-posts in some of the depots.[9] Attempts by the government to sell off these properties were stopped by a judgement of the Sindh High Court, on a petition made by an NGO that argued that these properties were amenities and as such their land use could not be changed.[10] The most important repercussion of the failure of the KTC was the change that took place in the thinking of government and transport-related professionals; they came to believe that only the private sector can manage transport.[11] This thinking suited the neoliberal lobby that was increasingly dominating development philosophy in Pakistan.

Free Transport Policy and the Emergence of the Minibus

In 1971, the government introduced what is known as the 'free transport policy'. This policy was introduced because there was an increasing demand for transport from the various *katchi abadis* developing on the then periphery of Karachi, while government transport only functioned on the main corridor of the city. Under the free transport policy, any individual who purchased a bus could apply for a route permit. A route permit was for a particular route identified by the Regional Transport Authority (RTA) of the government of Sindh. This process has created what is known in Karachi as the 'minibus'.

Individuals—sometimes more than one—acquire a bus. Since most of those who purchase a bus are not well-to-do, they go to a moneylender; the moneylender takes a down payment and then recovers the cost of the bus in monthly instalments. If the purchaser defaults, the bus is taken away from him and he loses his investment. The moneylender is officially the owner of the bus until the purchaser has made the full payment. Most of the moneylenders are from the Khyber Pakhtunkhwa prvoince, so they prefer to lend to people from their own region, or its adjoining areas. As such, most minibus owners are Pathans, or Hazarawalls. Motor rickshaws were also purchased through loans from moneylenders, most of whom were from Khyber Pakhtunkhwa. Most of the informally-financed public transport vehicles are owned or operated by a single ethnic group.[12]

The cost of a 35-seater minibus in 2000, was Rs 1 million. However, the purchaser had to pay twice this amount over a two-to three-year period. Minibuses were purchased as opposed to large buses, because the cost of a large 100-seater bus, at Rs 6–8 million, would be unaffordable to the purchaser and also the fare, as a result, would be unaffordable to the commuter.[13] Yet all the formal and informal players in the transport 'drama', who were interviewed for this study, agree that large buses are the adequate solution to Karachi's problems. Large buses are comfortable, there is room for people to stand in them and they can carry up to 82 passengers; they are cheaper to run per passenger; and occupy less road space per passenger. The minibus has a 32-person capacity, standing in it is quite difficult, because of its low-ceiling, and it is very hard to get on to it as well, because of the height of the footrest from the ground.

The process of operating a minibus is as follows: (i) the purchase of the minibus; (ii) its registration as a commercial vehicle with the excise department; (iii) the acquisition a fitness (roadworthy) certificate from the police; (iv) the acquisition of a route permit from the RTA; and (v) the operation of the bus. In this process, over 20,000 minibuses have been registered in Karachi over the years.[14] To operate a bus, the bus owner, or driver/conductor has to join one of the transporters organisations; the one that embraces all of them is the Transport Ittehad. This organisation protects the commercial interests of the transporters and through it, they present their claims, guard their gains and negotiate the rate of informal payments they have to make to a corrupt police force. Because of continuous conflict with the state on fare-related issues, and with the public on their 'poor service and unreasonable attitude', the transporters are often referred to as the 'transport mafia'.

The system has many different arrangements among various actors in this drama. One of the actors is the individual who has a route licence from the RTA and makes an arrangement with the bus-owner to operate a route. Very often, the owner of the vehicle operates it himself. The owner carries a high risk since he has to pay the route owner, the moneylender, *bhatta* (extortion) payments to the police, and all the running, maintenance and repair costs. To meet these requirements, he has to work long hours, maximise profits, and cut costs. This results in overloading and poor levels of vehicle maintenance.[15]

There are some cases where bus owners have both a route permit and a number of buses. They acquire the services of a driver and conductor team to operate their buses. This is not formal employment as the driver and conductor team are paid a percentage of the daily revenue they bring in. In this arrangement, the owner often hires an illiterate staff to operate his bus in order to save costs.[16] This lowers the quality of service.

The method of operation of transport described above, is legal. However, there is also an illegal system that the government agencies allow to operate. This illegal sector comprises buses operating without a route permit. The origins of the illegal sector go back to 1985, when a speeding minibus crushed a university student to death under its wheels. The driver was from the Pathan community and the victim was an Urdu-speaker. The accident resulted in ethnic riots between the two communities and a number of minibuses were burnt. As a result, the government decided not to register any more minibuses. However, the ban has to a large extent been overcome by slight adjustments in the design of the minibus and the renaming of it as a 'coach'. It is estimated by bus owners that the number of illegal operators is less than 200 buses. It is also important to mention here that although there are 329 minibus routes in existence according to the RTA,[17] only 67 are in operation, according to the Urban Resource Centre.[18] The reason for these inoperative routes is that they are not considered lucrative by the transporters.

It is generally considered that the informally financed transport sector in Karachi is anarchic and disorganised. However, the drivers have a strict timetable, implementation regulations, fixed locations for parking their vehicles, and an organised regime that determines the relationship between different actors in the transport drama and with the police.[19]

The Karachi Circular Railway (KCR)

An important mass mode of travel has been the Karachi Circular Railway. It was made operative in 1964, mainly for the transportation of goods. It was extended to a full circle of 44 km in 1970, to connect the four important industrial areas of the city: the port, the Sindh Industrial Trading Estate (SITE), the Central Business District (CBD), and the Landhi Industrial Area. As it also passed through a number of dense residential areas, it soon started to serve commuters as well. In the 1980s, it operated 24 trains per day, for the full circle. The operation from the CBD to the Landhi Industrial Area, consisted of 80 trips per day. Approximately 6 million passengers used this facility per year.[20]

In the mid-1980s, the service started to decline due to a lack of maintenance and replacement of rolling stock and the lack of maintenance of tracks and stations. By 1998, the KCR was making only twelve trips a day and was losing Rs 6 million annually. In December 1999, the operation was stopped. An unsuccessful attempt was made to restart it from the CBD to the Landhi–Korangi industrial area, in March 2005.

There are several other reasons, in addition to those cited above, for the failure of KCR. One is that Karachi expanded well beyond the KCR's reach (see Fig. 2.2). As a result, a new network of minibuses and motor rickshaws started serving commuters, and those living within the route of KCR also started to use it. There are also allegations that the 'transport mafia' informally pressurised the government not to upgrade KCR and developed bus routes that were parallel to the KCR corridor, to facilitate its demise. Additionally, no attempt was made to integrate KCR into a larger transport plan for Karachi.

Although officialdom abandoned KCR in the 1994 Transport Plan, civil society has constantly fought for its revival. Because of the pressure—both from outside and within government circles—a plan for its rehabilitation, financing and implementation has been developed and is discussed later in this book.

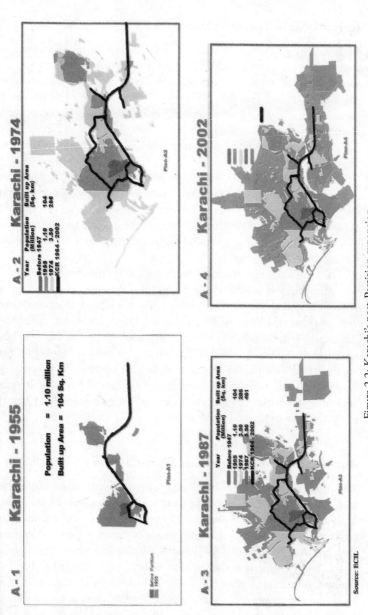

Figure 2.2: Karachi's post-Partition expansion.

Karachi Public Transport Society (KPTS)

In 1997, the government invited the public sector to invest in transport. It promised the investors that it would provide vehicle depots and they would have full support of the traffic police. This led to the creation of the Karachi Public Transport Society (KPTS), the chair of which was the transport secretary the government of Sindh. The society has twenty-seven members, eighteen from the government, including the DIG traffic police. Nine members are from within the 'public' and are prominent citizens of the city.

An entrepreneur, Javed Chaudhry, who purchased 200 buses, was invited by the society on the following terms: (i) that the buses would operate on a route and be available every five minutes at the stop; (ii) no one would be allowed to stand inside the bus; (iii) the conductor would be in uniform and there will be no screaming on his part to attract passengers; (iv) there will be no races with other buses.

The society negotiated security from the 'transport mafia' for these buses, with the police and rangers, who also supervised their operation. The fare was higher (Rs 7) than the minibus (Rs 5). Daily, monthly, and seasonal tickets were available at a discount. The facility was hugely successful. When Javed Chaudhry died, his wife, the sole inheritor, sold the business and the buses were taken to different cities and provinces. At present, some 150 buses are registered with the KPTS but only 100 are operative.[21] This example illustrates how difficult it is to maintain and replicate successes, which often depend on the nature of negotiations and political compromises particular to the time, situation, and actors involved.

Attempts at Developing a Mass Transit System

The first serious attempt at developing a light rail mass transit system was made during the 1970s and in keeping with the proposals of the Karachi Master Plan, 1975–85. It consisted of upgrading the Circular Railway and pushing it into the suburbs through a number of spurs. A partly underground (through the CBD and Old City), partly elevated and partly at-grade metro was to bisect the circle of the Circular Railway.[22] By 1977, plans had been finalised, funds were available, and rolling stock was being negotiated. It was a government project and was to be completed in stages, within a five-year period. However, the political conflict of 1977 led to the dismissal of the government of Zulfikar Ali Bhutto, which had developed these plans. The subsequent military government abandoned the scheme.[23]

The next attempt was made in 1990, after a detailed study by the Karachi Mass Transit Programme, with the help of World Bank consultants, as part of the Karachi Development Plan 2000. The study concluded that both for economic and technical reasons, a light rail system was not feasible for Karachi and that buses would perform best while affording the necessary capacity to meet Karachi's expanding needs. The study proposed six bus transit ways (a total of 87.4 km) and identified priority Corridor-1 which was mainly elevated and passed through the Old City and the main artery on which Karachi's heritage buildings are located.[24] The project was to be built on a build, operate, and transfer (BOT) basis.

Civil society and academic institutions, including trade unions, objected to the heritage-related environmental damage that the elevated expressway would cause.[25] They created the Citizens' Forum on Mass Transit (CFMT), a large network of civil society organisations. Adjustments were made to accommodate some of the concerns of the CFMT. However, the project never took off because politicians turned the bus-way option into a light rail project. It is said that because of this, no investment was found and no contractor placed a bid for the project.[26] It is important to note here that subsequent to the failure of the bidding process, a former chief engineer of the railways and a consultant to the Karachi Mass Transit Programme suggested the revitalisation of KCR and related projects through rolling stock manufactured locally at the Pakistan Railways workshops in Mughalpura, Lahore.[27] According to his conversations with the author,[28] this would reduce costs to a level that the Government of Pakistan could easily afford without taking out a loan. Another former chief engineer of the railways held similar views.[29]

In 2005, the city government undertook a number of studies with the help of Japan International Corporation Agency (JICA). These studies led to further research, which became a part of the Karachi Transportation Improvement Project (KTIP) 2010–12 and resulted in the preparation of the Transport Master Plan (TMP), which has a vision for 2030. The studies have proposed six BRT corridors and the revival of the KCR, including a rail corridor bifurcating the circle of the KCR and extending it to the Super Highway, the main exit leading out of Karachi and to the rest of the country.

The JICA proposal is outlined in Table 2.1. Detailed paperwork for the JICA revival of the KCR was completed. It is supposed to cater to 0.7 million people per day and is considered to be cornerstone of the KTIP Plan. It was argued that if the KCR was revived, then the other corridors would be completed in fifteen years. For the KCR project, JICA agreed to provide

. 93.5 per cent of the cost through a loan with a 0.2 per cent mark-up, payable over forty years.[30]

However, the KCR revival project has been delayed for a number of reasons, the most important ones being the lack of political will and absence of administrative and institutional ownership of the project because of an absence of proper local government system and lack of clarity due to ever-changing institutional arrangements. In addition, there is also the failure to develop an acceptable resettlement policy for about 5,000 *katchi abadi* households that are to be relocated from the KCR corridor. So far, they have been offered a relocation at a considerable distance from the city centre and their work areas, children's schools, health, and recreational facilities, are at an easy distance from their present homes. The KCR Affectees' Action Committee (KCR-AAC) has offered two alternatives. Firstly, they have identified government-owned railway land for their relocation. This land is nearer to their places of work. Secondly, they are willing to move if they are paid the market price for the land they occupy and they will find their own alternative accommodation. The second alternative will raise the cost of the rehabilitation project from 1.6 per cent of the total project cost of the KCR rehabilitation, to 2.5 per cent. The office bearers of the KCR-AAC also point out that a majority of the households have legally acquired water and electricity connections and a larger number also have gas connections. Many of the houses have reinforced concrete roofs.[31]

As a result of delays, the cost of the KCR Project increased from Rs 147 billion in 2009, to Rs 246 billion in July 2012.[32] In addition, without a subsidy, the service will not be affordable to the poorer sections of the commuting public. For reasons unknown, the project has been taken away from JICA and is now to be constructed as a CPEC project. Meanwhile, the government had decided to go ahead with the BRT-2 Corridor, which is now in the process of being implemented. The corridor was partly elevated through M.A. Jinnah road and was affecting the view to fifty-nine heritage buildings but the government stated that there was no option but to elevate the corridor at certain locations until it was pointed out that the elevated corridor would also affect the view to the Mausoleum of the Father of the Nation. As a result of this 'discovery', the entire length of M.A. Jinnah road on the axis of which the mausoleum is located, was brought down to grade.

Table 2.1: Estimation of Available Budget for Mass Transit Development in Karachi (Rs in Million)

Year	Annual Investment Amount				
	CDGK	GOS	Federal	Loans	Total
2010	700	790	490	7,920	9,900
2011	732	827	513	8,292	10,364
2012	766	865	537	8,681	10,849
2013	802	905	562	9,089	11,358
2014	839	947	588	9,516	11,890
2015	878	991	615	9,963	12,447
2016	919	1,037	643	10,431	13,030
2017	962	1,085	673	10,921	13,641
2018	1,007	1,135	704	11,434	14,280
2019	1,054	1,188	737	11,971	14,950
2020	1,103	1,243	771	12,533	15,650
2021	1,154	1,301	807	13,122	16,384
2022	1,208	1,362	844	13,738	17,152
2023	1,264	1,426	883	14,383	17,956
2024	1,323	1,493	924	15,059	18,799
2025	1,385	1,563	967	15,766	19,681
2026	1,450	1,636	1,012	16,507	20,605
2027	1,518	1,712	1,059	17,282	21,571
2028	1,589	1,792	1,108	18,094	22,583
2029	1,663	1,876	1,160	18,944	23,643
2030	1,741	1,964	1,214	19,834	24,753
2013-30	**21,859**	**24,656**	**15,271**	**248,587**	**310,373**

Source: Estimation by the JICA Study Team.
Note: Annual investment is assumed to increase by 4.7 per cent a year.

The CNG Crisis

The introduction of CNG (Compressed Natural Gas) as fuel for transport was initiated by the Government of Pakistan in 1990. There were two reasons for this: (i) CNG was available in Pakistan and if used, would considerably reduce the import of petrol and diesel; this would reduce foreign exchange spending; (ii) the use of CNG would reduce pollution. Today, Pakistan is a country that uses CNG most in proportion to its population. The use of CNG received a big boost when, in 2005, the Supreme Court ordered all those vehicles running on diesel to convert to CNG. The transport sector complied immediately. An added benefit of converting to CNG (per unit cost Rs 6–7) is its cheaper cost than diesel (per unit cost Rs 40) or electricity (per unit cost Rs 17).[33] CNG is also used by domestic users; fertiliser and cement factories; and for power generation. In winter, the demand for gas increases by about 300 per cent.[34]

A crisis occurred in 2008–10, when the price of oil rose substantially, and it was during those years that power outages increased in Pakistan. In Karachi, because of the outages, electricity was out for an average of more than six to seven hours a day. As a result of this, people, especially the elite, installed gas generators, as did industrialists and shopkeepers, to run their industries and businesses. Since using gas generators was cheaper than getting electricity from the grid, a number of homes and industrial establishments have continued to use gas even though electricity is available. In December 2013, the Supreme Court passed a judgement in which it ordered that CNG used for the generation of electricity should be charged so that the cost of producing electricity from gas was the same as that of acquiring it from the grid, except for those industries who used boilers, or need gas for their processes.[35] This Supreme Court order has not been implemented because of weak government institutions and a refusal by CNG users to obey the court orders.

Pakistan has substantial CNG reserves. However, it opted for importing CNG from Central Asia and then from Iran, since it was cheaper than developing new CNG extraction sites. The Central Asian project did not take off due to the Afghan war and the Iran pipeline option fizzled out because of the UN-imposed sanctions on trade with Iran.[36]

As a result of the government initiative and the court order, 4.5 million private cars and public transport were converted to CNG, while CNG use for power generation also commenced. The cost of conversion from diesel to CNG varies between Rs 40,000 for a small car and up to Rs 200,000 for a bus. Once converted from diesel to CNG, the vehicle cannot be converted back to diesel. The only option is to change its engine. Many school vans and university buses transporting students also converted to CNG.[37] Because of these issues, there is now an acute shortage of CNG in Pakistan. As Pakistan's industrial hub, Karachi is home to the largest public commutes in the country and as a result, has suffered the most. The government response has been to permit CNG stations to function only four days a week in the city. Due to this, CNG buses, which account for 70 per cent of the registered buses,[38] stay off the roads during the non-CNG days, causing immense problems for the commuting public and losses for the transporters and CNG stations. It is now common to see long queues of vehicles at CNG stations, waiting for the CNG station to start functioning. People can wait for up till five hours or even longer to get their vehicles filled.[39]

Banning the use of CNG, as has often been suggested in the media, is not possible because it substitutes for 2.3 billion litres of petrol/diesel. If it is shut down, Pakistan will have to import 2 billion litres, for which foreign exchange of approximately $1 billion per year will have to be spent. In addition, the CNG sector employs more than 400,000 persons in the city.[40] They will become unemployed.

In addition to the lack of comfortable transport, there is the problem of Karachi's growing traffic, which is becoming increasingly unmanageable; congestion and air and noise pollution have become detrimental to the health of commuters. There are a number of reasons for this—the most important of which is the rapidly increasing number of vehicles. In 2013, Karachi registered 776 vehicles per day, of which 71 per cent were motorbikes.[41] In 2018, this number has increased to 907.[42] The lack of police officers is also given as a reason. There are a total of 3,200 police officers (half of them per shift) on traffic duty, whereas there is a need for an additional 5,000 to regulate traffic.[43] To help the police force control traffic, the elected city government (2001–7) inducted 1,575 wardens. They were members and/or supporters of the MQM. Once the 2001 local body regime was dissolved, the provincial government sent these wardens home. It also is alleged that driving licences are often issued on the payment of bribes, without driving tests. Drivers are also known to drive without a licence and when confronted by a police constable, they make an informal payment to him and get away.[44]

Government departments often react to these malpractices by taking action against individuals, but no reform in the police force has been implemented, despite many being proposed.

In theory, no public transport vehicle can operate without a roadworthy certificate from the Vehicular Emission Control (VEC) programme, which is a programme of the Sindh Environmental Protection Agency (SEPA). The

Sindh chief secretary issued a notification ordering the police department to help the VEC programme to fulfil its duties. This notification was issued in October 2009, only after the Sindh High Court took *suo moto* notice of the environmental pollution caused by public vehicles.

However, in the absence of any coordination between the VEC programme, SEPA and the Sindh police, this notification has yielded no results. The deputy inspector general (traffic) police responded by saying that if the order is implemented, most of the public transport vehicles will be off the roads and the poor will suffer. So, buses without proper seats, with deformed bodywork, no window panes, and emitting pollution, continue to operate in the city.[45] Due to noise and air pollution and travel in stressful conditions, environmental-related diseases have increased considerably. These diseases include asthma, angina, anxiety, emotional instability, sexual impotence, hysteria, and psychosis. All this can lead to social conflict and domestic violence.[46]

There are also infrastructure issues. There is an absence of proper terminals and depots for buses and rickshaws—and previously, Qingqis. So, road space and roundabouts serve this function, increasing congestion. Many of the roads are in bad condition and slow down traffic movement, increasing travel time for commuters and substantially increasing fuel costs for the transporters.[47] In many locations, such as transport terminals, or where transport picks up large volumes of passengers, hawkers occupy road space. This is because of a close economic interdependence between the poor, commuters, and hawkers. This link has not been recognised and hence has not been catered to by politicians, professionals, and city planners whose only solution is to evict the hawkers.

This has never been done successfully because of the negotiating power of the hawkers, who are backed by payments of *bhatta* (extortion) to the concerned authorities and representatives of political parties.[48]

Another cause of congestion is double parking on the roads in all the commercial areas of the city. The government has provided multi-storey parking plazas but they are used to less than 10 per cent of their capacity. The double parking is managed by informal persons who charge a fee for identifying parking space for the vehicles and for shifting them around. In many locations, receipts in the form of slips are provided for the payments made. Many open spaces and pavements are also used in a similar manner for motorcycles. The local government and cantonment board also collect parking fees from vehicle owners, but it is difficult to clearly identify whether it is local government or mafias backed by political parties who are collecting, at any given location.[49]

Because of ethnic conflicts and since 9/11, the use of drones by the US army against the militants in Khyber Pakhtunkhwa, in the northwest of Pakistan—resulting in fairly large 'collateral damage'—strikes and shut downs are common in Karachi. During such days, there is no public transport and people, especially daily wage labour, suffer considerable economic loss. There is also a serious threat to the lives of important government functionaries and politicians from these 'Islamic' militants and criminal gangs and also from kidnappings for ransom. So, traffic is held up so as to facilitate 'VIP' movement. This causes large gridlocks, which are resented by the Karachiites.

During the monsoon season—which in Karachi is seldom more than three to five days—the city also floods and traffic comes to a halt. The flooding is the result of encroachments by elite housing on the outfalls of the natural drainage system to the sea and by encroachment on the natural storm drains by formal and informal housing.[50]

The government's response to traffic congestion has been to build signal-free roads and flyovers wherever traffic congestion takes place. Between 1993 and 1999, the government built only six flyovers. However, since decentralisation was instituted in 2001, the elected government and the present province control system have built thirty-seven flyovers (as of 2013)[51] and six signal-free roads. At non-rush hours, they have reduced travel time, but during rush hours exit points are clogged. Many government officials feel that this was not a solution to Karachi's traffic problems.[52]

Karachi's bus fares increased from Rs 6, to Rs 10 per trip in 2004 and Rs 15, to Rs 20 per trip in 2014.[53] Meanwhile, the cost of diesel increased from Rs 22.78 per litre in January 2004, to Rs 120 in September 2014.[54] The incomes of low and lower middle income groups have not increased proportionally. In addition, travel time has increased due to congestion. As a result, it is becoming cheaper and more comfortable for the poor to rent within the city's low-income settlements than to live on the periphery.[55] In this way, transport problems are shaping the form of the city as well.

Due to the situation described above, the number of fatal road accidents in Karachi is very high. They were 1,719 in 2009 but have slowly dropped to 1,352 in 2013. Motorbikes were involved in the majority of these accidents. Most of them could have been avoided if the riders had been wearing a helmet, which is compulsory under law. However, the law cannot be implemented because of corruption within the police force and a lack of interest of police officials and politicians in implementing the law. It is interesting to note that animal-drawn vehicles and push carts were involved only in 0.12 and 0.92 per cent of cases.[56]

A number of decisions taken by the Sindh government, which have now become law, will add to the traffic congestion in Karachi. One is the establishment of the Sindh High Density Board, which can declare any area, or even a single plot, as high density and increase its FAR (Floor Area Ratio) by whatever it thinks is appropriate. Another law—The Sindh Special Development Board Act, 2014—gives the board the right to bulldoze *katchi abadis* and turn them into multi-storey apartments.[57] The decisions of both these boards (whose members consist of politicians and government officials, with only two representatives out of twenty-seven members from professional bodies on the Sindh development board) are ad hoc in nature, since they are being taken without carrying out a larger urban design exercise, in the absence of which thousands of vehicles will be added to the business and elite districts of the city.[58]

The Urban Transport Scheme

The Urban Transport Scheme (UTS) was initiated by the city government in 2001 and implemented in 2002. The government invited investors and offered facilities and subsidies which it did not ultimately provide. About 364 large buses were introduced by thirteen investors. The operation of eight companies and 221 buses failed due to losses and they shifted the vehicles to other locations in the country, where fare structures were better. The fate of the other 143 is unclear although twelve are operating on one major route in Karachi.[59] The problems that led to the failure of the scheme surfaced within three years of the launch and are detailed in Box 2.3.

In 2007, the federal government approved a project of 4,000 CNG buses for Karachi. Eventually, the number was reduced to 2,000. The terms were similar to those of the UTS. The banks were instructed to extend loans to the operators. They refused because of the past experience of UTS of non-payment of instalments on time. Then, a 'pilot project' for the introduction of dedicated CNG buses was launched to demonstrate that such a model could work.

Seventy-five CNG buses were put into operation in July 2009, by the outsourcing of contracts for two years, to three operators. Contracts consisted of: (i) operation, management, and maintenance of buses; (ii) supply of CNG fuel; (iii) an e-ticketing system linked to a centralised computer network, rendering it possible to make a choice among different types of tickets—a day, a trip, or a week.

The deficit between revenue and expenditure was to be met by the City District Government Karachi (CDGK). After the expiry of the contract, on

30 June 2011, all three contracts were merged into one and the operator was made responsible for all operation and maintenance expenses. The e-ticketing system was discontinued to reduce operational costs, so that the project could be self-financed. The operator faced serious difficulties due to the CNG crisis, an increase in CNG costs, and the Karachi law and order situation. The contract expired in April 2013 and no operator participated in the next bidding process, as a result of which seventy-five large buses stopped operating. Seventy-three of them were lying at the depot before they were sold and because of vandalism, would require extensive maintenance to become operable.[60]

The government also considered bringing back these buses on roads after carrying out essential repairs and replacing their tyres and batteries and other necessary parts. Given the CNG crisis, it also considered the conversion of these seventy-three large buses to diesel. The total cost of repair and maintenance worked out to Rs 39.583 million, whereas the cost of conversion to diesel was Rs 265.388 million. This worked out to Rs 304.971 million. The project planners understood that the project would need a subsidy to the tune of Rs 2.729 million per month—for each twenty-five-bus package—to make it viable.[61] In 2018, only twelve renovated buses are plying on the Landhi to Mereweather Tower route.

CNG Rickshaws

In 2004, the President's Rozgar (livelihood) Rickshaw scheme was introduced by a fund from the federal government. At that time, the MQM was in power in Karachi. As part of the scheme, loans for CNG-fuelled rickshaws were introduced in keeping with the Supreme Court decision to convert all public transport to CNG. The majority of the rickshaws went to MQM supporters. As such, for the first time a sizeable number of Urdu-speakers entered the transport business (Urdu being the mother tongue of the Muhajirs, migrants from India at Partition and their descendants, who form the core support of the party). The scheme still continues, but as the MQM is not in power, other ethnicities are also accessing loans. By 2014, 60,000 CNG rickshaws were operating in the city.[62]

In 2007, as a result of a Sindh High Court ruling that government must curb pollution, the Sindh government decided to phase out the older two-stroke rickshaws in a period of three years; the owners could either replace them or convert them to ones with four-stroke engines.[63] As a result of this, the price of the two-stroke rickshaws fell from Rs 150,000 to Rs 40,000.[64] For this reason, the decision was resented by Karachi Rickshaw, Taxi, Yellow and the Black Cab Owner's Association, all of which blocked Karachi's streets in protest. Since most of the members were from Khyber Pakhtunkhwa, the Awami National Party, representing the Pashtun population, supported the protest.[65] The conversion to four-stroke engines had not yet taken place and as such the Sindh High Court decision had not been implemented.

* * * *

The history of Karachi's transport shows that many important public sector interventions were initiated. However, because of an absence of political will and constantly changing local government policies, they were abandoned at crucial stages in their evolution. The failure of most of these systems was because of corruption, which was the result of an absence of monitoring and accountability process. Although, it was clearly understood by the planners and policy makers that without a subsidy the systems were unsustainable, no subsidy was guaranteed. After the transport system was handed over to the private sector, no support—such as bank loans—were provided, as a result of which substandard minibuses came to dominate the transport scene in the city. A detailed analysis of this has been provided in Chapter 9.

Box 2.1: A History of the Karachi Tramway	
1879	John Brunton, Railway Engineer devised a special rail of 4 feet gauge which was later used for the tramways in Karachi.
1881	Plans for a tramway were made by Municipal Secretary and Engineer James Strachen.
1881	Edward Mathews of London submitted the tender for construction of the tramway tracks.
1883	Formalities for construction were finalised.
1884	Work started in October.
1885	Tramway inaugurated in April. The first track was from Napier Mole to Keamari. The trams were steam locomotives and also carried freight. Locomotives functioned at every 15 minutes.
1886	The locomotives were replaced by horses because the locomotives were noisy and let out smoke. They disturbed the animals which were used in carts and for travel purposes. The tramway was managed by the East India Tramway Company.
1905	Petrol trams were inaugurated in March and by 1918, there were 37 trams which increased to 64 in 1954.
1911	Frere Road was added to the network in September and Soldier Bazaar in 1916.
1928	Kerb Side loading for freight was introduced at Boulton Market.
1945	New Diesel operated cars were introduced.
1949	The East India Tramway Company was purchased by the Mohammad Ali Transport Company.
1955	Cars increased to 157.
1974	Tramway closes down.
Source: www.siasat.pk	

Box 2.2: Government Transport-related Initiatives 1948–77	
1948	Government began to provide transport to and from new settlements created as a result of mass migration from India. This was a federal government initiative. Karachi, at that time, was the capital of Pakistan.
1950	This initiative was handed over to the Karachi Improvement Trust (KIT) which was created to plan the expansion and management of the city.
1957	The KIT initiative proved to be quite inadequate and so in December the Karachi Transport Syndicate (KTS) was created with a fleet of 280 buses.
1958	The KTS failed for financial reasons. It was disbanded in December.
1959	As a result of the Greater Karachi Resettlement Plan, transport requirements increased substantially. To meet these demands, the Karachi Road Transport Corporation (KRTC) was established in January as a joint venture of the central government and the public, who were invited by shares. 324 buses including 24 double-deckers started operating. Adequate depots and workshops were provided for these buses.
1964	The KRTC was wound up in February for reasons that are unclear. The government's share was bought by the Gujrat Transport in February 1964 and the operations were taken over by a consortium of Commerce Bank and Valika Group under the name of Khalid Riffat Transport Company. Due to financial reasons, the organisation collapsed in December 1967.
1968	The preparation for the Karachi Master Plan 1975-85 with UN involvement was undertaken by the Karachi Master Plan Department.
1968	The government initiated the Karachi Omnibus Service which was a subsidiary of the West Pakistan Road Transport Corporation (PRTC). Over 600 buses were inducted and a sub-depot was established for them. This was in addition to the depots and workshops which had been developed earlier for the KRTC.
1973	West Pakistan was subdivided into provinces and so the PRTC was subdivided province-wise and as a result, the Sindh Road Transport Corporation (SRTC) was established and 2,000 buses were inducted into the system. A number of depots and workshops were commissioned for these additions.
1977	The SRTC losses continued to grow and finally in 1977 February, the SRTC was divided into the Karachi Transport Corporation (KTC) for the city and SRTC for the rest of the province under the provincial government.
Source: Aquila Ismail, Transport (URC Karachi Series), City Press, 2002.	

Box 2.3: Reasons for the Failure of the UTS

The UTS failed for a number of reasons which have been documented in a stakeholder meeting report. The reasons are following:

- An increase in price of diesel by 100 per cent raising operational costs by 50 per cent;

- The CDGK allowed increase in fares but this did not help the UTS operators as the minibuses did not increase their fare. So, the UTS operators could not compete with the minibuses;

- The CDGK had promised preferential routes but instead they overlapped with many minibus routes. Even other UTS operators were allowed to compete against other UTS operators (legally and illegally) and the CDGK took no action;

- The CDGK and provincial government committed to give all the routes of minibuses to UTS as the old minibuses started plying without route permits on the same routes;

- According to contractual commitments, the CDGK had promised to acquire depots from the provincial government for the operators but this did not happen;

- Partial compensation for the interest on the loans that the operator had taken from banks was promised as part of the agreement but was never delivered;

- There was also police harassment; strikes and demonstrations; frequent VVIP movements; hampering traffic; and related insecurity for the vehicles and their operators;

- There were other issues as well such as the buses used 58 per cent more fuel than the manufactures had promised, lack of skilled persons to conduct the business and lack of maintenance because of the use of low quality lubricants and spare parts so as to save costs; and

- For many of the operators, this was a wrong business option—they thought it would result in massive profits.

Operators concur that in spite of the increase in fuel costs they would have survived if illegal competition with the minibuses had been curbed and if the government had paid the subsidy as per agreement. Source: KMTC, 2006

3

Responding to the Transport Crisis in Karachi

Arif Hasan and Mansoor Raza with URC

The methodology of the research for this chapter consists of: (i) a literature review extending to press clipping, compiled by the URC on transport, over the last five years (*see* Appendix 3.1); (ii) open-ended interviews with transporters, transport-related government officials, women commuters and residents of low income settlements (*see* Appendix 3.2); and (iii) questionnaires served to 150 men and women commuters[1] at different locations in Karachi (*see* Appendix 3.3).

A list of different stakeholders in the transport sector and transcripts of interviews with them are also provided in appendices 3.4 and 3.5. It can be observed in Appendix 3.4 that many institutions that previously carried the suffix 'Karachi', now carry the suffix 'Sindh'. This is because of a move by the PPP-run provincial government to take control of Karachi's local institutions.

There have been different responses from different stakeholders to the transport crisis in Karachi. These responses have come from the market, from commuters themselves, from innovation by small workshops, and also from medium-sized engineering establishments.

The Market Response

The most important market response has been the introduction of the Qingqi (pronounced *chingchi*), which has now been banned by the Supreme Court. The Qingqi is a Chinese motorcycle manufactured in Pakistan that has a six-seater carriage attached to it. It originated in Punjab, where it substituted the tonga (a light horse-drawn two-wheeled vehicle). It was introduced in Karachi in 2002. The number of Qingqis in Karachi grew to over 50,000; 40,000 of these were registered with the Karachi Qingqi Welfare Association. The association would allocate routes, determine fares that the Qingqi drivers received, identify the locations for their stands, and negotiated the informal payments that had to be made to the police and to political parties in whose areas their stands were located. The association also maintained a database with photos and details of the Qingqi drivers and owners.

A Qingqi owner would have to apply to the association to get a route. The association had a special committee which managed the routes and saw that there was no 'overlapping'. The body agreed that there were a number of Qingqis operating that were not members of the association and that some of their members had hired underage children as drivers of these vehicles. The association also had a system that was decentralised to the district level and enabled the registration of complaints against its members and drivers and of taking action against them if they violated traffic regulations, or misbehaved with the public, and of dealing with accidents and police on the members' behalf.[2]

According to the association, it had provided the government with its proposals for regulating the Qingqi routes and developing rules and regulations for operation. The association had also suggested a separate lane on the main roads for these vehicles and stated that if any of their members violate the lane, their vehicles could be confiscated. These proposals were made in 2010, but no meaningful negotiations with government departments had taken place after that; it seemed that the government was not interested.[3]

Transport-related government officials agreed that the Qingqis had helped overcome some of the problems that many commuters faced. However, they felt that the vehicles were unreliable and unsafe and should not be used on the main corridors of the city.[4] The traffic police was also against them, since it was not the Qingqi that was registered with them, but the motorcycle that pulled it. Also, the police believed that Qingqis were one of the major causes for traffic jams in Karachi. Because of pressure from the police and from the transport lobby (who were anti-Qingqi since they took away business from the buses), the government banned the operation of Qingqis in October 2013.[5] However, the Sindh High Court removed the ban and granted a stay to the association,[6] but in 2017, the Supreme Court banned the plying of all Qingqis because they were unregistered and did not meet safety standards under law. As a result, an estimated 360,000 transport seats per day were removed from the Karachi transport system. The annual turnover of Qingqi activity was Rs 8.64 billion and as such, it added substantially to Karachi's economy.[7] In addition, commuters found them more comfortable, affordable and more easily available than the minibuses.[8]

Technical Innovation

Sensing the demand for transport and reacting to court decisions, transporters and the workshops that manufacture rickshaws and Qingqis, have made a great deal of innovations. Four-seater CNG rickshaws and Qingqis are being converted to fulfil the demands of the regulations that govern rickshaw design. This is being done in spite of the fact that it is not permissible under law. To overcome the non-availability of CNG on certain days, the capacity of rickshaws for storing CNG has been increased from 2 kilos, to 7 and 8 kilos. A recent trend is to change the shape of the old two-stroke rickshaw to look like a CNG rickshaw, while the two-stroke engine remains unconverted. This is to prevent police harassment, which the old two-stroke design rickshaws have had to face. The workshops that continue to carry out these innovations are, for the most part, small establishments and function on the roadside. The expertise that these workshops have can be judged from the fact that they were, with the advice of operators, able to convert a two-stroke engine into a CNG rickshaw, to show the government that it can be done.[9]

The Motorbike Option

In the absence of a reliable transport system, Karachiites have purchased motorbikes. The number increased from 450,000 in 1990 to 500,000 in 2004. In July 2018, this number had increased to 2,856,704. The motorbike owners say that aside from the capital cost, the bikes are cheaper and faster than public transport, they are flexible and with an enlarged seat, a family of four can travel easily and cheaply to places of entertainment, recreation, and to family gatherings. The problem is that women do not ride motorbikes in Karachi; 70 per cent of males interviewed at bus stops in Karachi said that they would like to buy a motorbike but they could not afford it. Fifty-three per cent of women said that they would like to use a motorbike if permitted by their families and if women-friendly bikes could be introduced.[10] Now, a few women who are increasing in number, can be seen driving motorbikes on the streets of Karachi.

However, all motorbike users mentioned that they have to deal with high levels of air and noise pollution. They also complained about an absence of proper traffic control systems, bad road surfaces, police harassments, and an absence of a physically segregated lane for motorbikes, in addition to the absence of parking space.[11] Meanwhile, the number of establishments dealing with providing motorbikes on hire purchase is increasing and the terms are growing increasingly attractive.[12] In addition, the manufacture and import of cheaper models and those that are women-friendly, are also being studied by the suppliers and one such initiative has been launched.[13]

Arrangements Commuters Make

Although no figures are available, commuters and institutions in Karachi make arrangements to overcome transport problems. Many schools have transport vans that pick and drop their students for a fee. Universities have what is known as a 'point'. The point picks and drops students at given locations in the city. The corporate sector, some government sectors, and other organisations also pick and drop their employees, especially women. Vehicle-owning households arrange to pick and drop school children in turns. Motorbike owners offer to carry members of their neighbourhood at a pre-arranged fee.[14] Women domestic workers employed in the elite areas of Karachi commute long distances daily—an exercise that becomes unaffordable to them if they use conventional transport modes. Instead, they make arrangements with truckers to transport them in groups.

Transporter's Issues

Transporters are of the opinion that they know best how to run transport and manage its various aspects, such as routes, timings, coordination with each other, and operating economically viable solutions.[15] Government reports endorse these statements.[16] The main complaint of the transporters is that in spite of this knowledge, they are not meaningfully consulted by the government and except in a few cases in the 1990s, have not been taken on board by government when it develops its plans and policies.[17]

Transporters also put up a strong case about the transport sector no longer being economically viable for them, given the low fares that are decided upon by the transport department so as to make them affordable to the commuting public. They feel that if they are to invest in transport, then the fares will have to be doubled.

An important issue is the torching of buses during strikes and political conflicts around various turfs. Government compensation for torched buses—which cost between Rs 1.5 to Rs 1.8 million—is only Rs 200,000 and is dispensed after a great deal of hesitation and only when prolonged efforts are made to emphasise the need for the same. No insurance company is willing to cover a private sector public transport vehicle, nor is any bank willing to provide a loan for the purchase of such vehicles. They claim that if loans from banks were available, they would purchase large buses, instead of ending up paying Rs 2 million in instalments for a small bus that costs less than Rs 1 million.[18]

Transporters also point out that fares in Karachi are low as compared to fares in Punjab (Rs 28 per 20 km, as opposed to Rs 14 in Karachi) and Khyber Pakhtunkhwa. This is because the government 'is afraid of the people of Karachi', who are anti-transporters. Not only has the cost of fuel increased considerably, but so has that of spare parts and tyres. The old bus manufacturing companies have wound up and the product of the new companies costs much more. Apart from main corridors, the roads are in a terrible condition and reduce the life of the vehicle. To reduce operation costs, the bus owners' organisations had to do away with the ticketing system, as a result of which it has become difficult for them to have an accurate calculation for their profits and losses.[19]

Ethnic issues also take a toll on the functioning of the system. Most of the minibus drivers are from the Khyber Pakhtunkhwa and are reluctant to go into areas that are strongholds of the MQM. Two years ago, a large number of Pashtun drivers were killed. Their opponents think that they do not care about following the law, since they pay *bhatta* of Rs 2,000 to Rs 3,000 per month to the local police. In addition, they have the support of their organisations, which provide them with protection.[20] It is alleged that the emergence of MQM supporters as owners of rickshaws and Qingqis, was resented by the Pashtuns. The Qingqi owners believe that Pashtuns who own the minibuses were responsible for the ban that was imposed on the Qingqi.

There are other issues as well. The city police force is corrupt and Transporter Ittehad believes that this is because they are paid a low salary, ranging between Rs 15,000 to Rs 20,000 per month. They point out that the motorway police, meanwhile, are not corrupt because they are paid Rs 40,000 to Rs 50,000. Additionally, owing to low profits, good drivers can no longer be afforded by the transporters, so the quality of service has declined.[21]

Due to the issues mentioned above, a lot of transport vehicles have shifted from Karachi to Hyderabad and a number of them have converted to cargo-carrying trucks and inter-city buses. Many of the bus owners have sold their businesses and moved to operate from Dubai, Saudi Arabia, and South Africa.[22]

Currently, the main issue that concerns the transporters themselves is that they converted the majority of their buses to CNG at considerable expense. Converting them again to diesel means more expense, which they will not be able to recover because of low fares, high costs of maintenance, the law and order situation in the city, and an absence of credit at normal rates from banks. (As mentioned earlier, when buses are burnt by angry mobs, an inadequate compensation is provided by the government). Also, since no insurance company is willing to cover these buses, the transporters have no security.

Commuters' Point of View

The questionnaire handed out to 150 commuters is provided in Appendix 3.3, along with an analysis showing different ways in which men and women view the transport issue in Karachi.

The combination of preference and availability of transport varies between normal days and those that are perceived as unusual by the respondents. The latter occur on occasions such as those when the city closes down because of strike calls, or the blocking of roads due to demonstrations by various political, religious, and ethnic parties and groups. Days when there is CNG closure are also considered as unusual. On normal days, a combination of bus and rickshaw is used, while 48.7 per cent of commuters do not go to work on unusual days. In addition, the majority (86.7 per cent) find it difficult to get a bus on non-CNG days. On such days, the dependence on rickshaws—and Qingqis before they were banned—increases.

More than half the respondents consider a motorcycle as a cheaper, more flexible and faster means of commuting. In addition, the majority (60 per cent) considered the emergence of the Qingqi favourably, since it was cheap, could stop anywhere, did not have to limit itself to specific stops, and offered zero waiting time. A majority of respondents claim that they cannot find transport easily at night and that this limits their movement after sunset. The majority (82.7 per cent) also feel that it is not safe for women to travel at night.

The difficulties mentioned by respondents range from excessive time spent travelling in and waiting for buses, standing inside the bus due to a lack of space, sitting on the roof top, suffering injuries, being forced to get off before arriving at their destination, the harassment of women commuters, damage to attire, non-standardisation of bus fares, and the fear of the gas cylinder (which is placed inside the bus) exploding.

The largest number of commuters (35.3 per cent) spends between 41 to 60 minutes one way on the road each day while commuting and 13.3 per cent spend 81 to 90 minutes commuting one way. Waiting time at bus stops, however, is reasonable and can vary from 5 to 20 minutes. It is often longer outside of rush hours, when drivers wait for a long time so that their buses can be filled up.

Overcrowding is an issue, as only 13.3 per cent of the respondents said they got a seat in buses while commuting. Six per cent, on the other hand, claimed that they have travelled on buses' roof tops. A small majority (54 per cent) said that there are often disputes over fares. Moreover, buses sometimes fail to reach their destination or change their routes because they run out of CNG, either because of mechanical faults in the bus, or because of the law and order situation in the city.

Getting on and off buses also causes injury, according to 47.3 per cent of the respondents, 60 per cent of whom blame this on the footrest from which one enters the bus and/or the damaged body of the minibus. The most serious issue identified by the questionnaire analysis is that persons are often robbed while travelling on a bus. Sixty per cent claimed that they had been robbed once or more than once. As mentioned earlier, CNG cylinders are placed within the bus, often adjacent to the women's compartment, 79.3 per cent of respondents consider this a safety hazard. In addition, 46 per cent of respondents are of the opinion that women face harassment while travelling. Finally, 82 per cent believe that a better transport system would increase their options for job opportunities.

The respondents made a number of recommendations. Eighty-six per cent are of the opinion that there is a need to increase seating arrangements for women on buses. Seventy-seven per cent are of the opinion that there should be buses exclusively for women, although there was an understanding that this would make it difficult for families to travel together. An overwhelming majority (92 per cent) think that senior citizens should be given a discount in fares.

From the questionnaire analysis, one can conclude that with a reported average monthly income of Rs 13,482, the respondents spend, on average, Rs 1,500 per month (Rs 18,000 per annum) and an approximately 120-minute daily round trip (624 hours per annum) while commuting, which is much higher than world-average commuting hours. The time spent in commuting by the respondents in a year, is equivalent to 78 working days (assuming eight working hours in a day). According to a study,[23] world average commuting time is 80 minutes a day. Thailand is considered to have the longest commuting in the world, while Malawi has the shortest. A 2007 Gallup Survey (in the USA) indicated that on a typical day, workers' average round trip took 46 minutes. Similarly, according to the UK Office of National Statistics (2011), 75 per cent of the workers took around one hour for a round trip, from home to work.

There is also a difference between men and women commuters in their responses to certain questions. These differences are highlighted in the gender analysis table in Appendix 3.3. Women have more complaints against the system than men. Their complaints are largely against the condition of buses, the non-availability of seats in the absence of which they are forced to stand, the speeding and reckless way in which the vehicles are driven, the failure to stop at a bus stop, the absence of consideration being provided to the elderly, women and children when disembarking, the government's plans for transport, and the traffic police.

There is a difference between men and women commuters on other issues as well. Fewer women (7 per cent) than men (38 per cent) have been robbed more than once while commuting. Also, 89 per cent of women, as opposed to 78 per cent of men believe that a good transport system facilitates securing a better job. A larger percentage of women (68 per cent) as opposed to

57 per cent of men, believe that a motorbike is a better form of commuting. Although the margin is very small, a larger number of women than men are against banning of music played by all drivers while commuting.

Despite all the difficulties of travelling, a majority of respondents travel by minibus, although they consider motorcycles and Qingqis as better modes of conveyance. Besides all perceived misgivings on transport governance, the respondents' recommendations about scaling up the transport system reflect their pinned hopes on a viable mass transit system and/or on an increase in the number of buses.

Government Officials' Comments and Proposals

All government officials interviewed, have either clearly stated or implied that Karachi's transport problems cannot be solved without the induction of large buses and some sort of a rail-based mass transit system.[24] They have also indicated that one of the major reasons for non-induction of large buses, is the absence of bank loans and subsidies—not only to the private sector, but the public transport sector as well.[25]

It is also agreed that if public sector or public-private partnership sector's fare is related to the price of diesel, then the public will not be able to afford the service.[26] It is pointed out that the UTS service was stopped because the contractors were not making enough money to pay back bank loans so they abandoned their vehicles.[27] It is for these reasons that public transport has diminished and where it has continued, the quality of service has deteriorated. For instance, to save costs the UTS contractors removed the e-ticketing system, in the absence of which they were overloading and experienced difficulty in controlling the entry point of the buses.[28]

There were other reasons given for the failure of the various private and public-private partnership initiatives. It was stated that strikes, protests, and demonstrations (both religious and political) not only disrupt traffic, but force transporters to take alternative routes to the ones assigned to them, disturbing the entire system.[29] It is also felt that the government does not consider transport as a 'service' as it does education and health, which it subsidises heavily.

It is also pointed out that the Karachiites have become very individualistic and have lost all civic sense. They burn buses if a bus is involved in a fatal accident, instead of letting the police handle it.[30] Additionally, many are of the view that without the involvement of the CDGK, there cannot be an appropriate transport system in the city. As long as there was an elected mayor, subsidies were paid to the UTS scheme. Subsequently, the mayor had to appear in court; because in spite of everything being done transparently, the authorities believed that there had been an element of corruption. Rivalries between political parties have disrupted continuity in policies and have resulted in allegations and counter-allegations.[31]

The KCR is considered as an important element in developing a mass transit system. However, it is pointed out that it will require a system for the repayment of loan required to build it; the process for this to be achieved is unclear. In addition, all projects where a loan is involved, require sovereign guarantees to the contractors and/or the governments from whom the loan is being received. The government of Pakistan is not in a position to provide such guarantees because of the enormous cost of the project.[32]

Government officials have also commented on the flyovers and signal-free roads, the emergence of the Qingqis, the energy crisis, and the conversion of Karachi buses into trucks and carriers. It is felt that flyovers and signal-free roads are not a solution and they have not solved the problems of traffic, or transport.[33]

On the question of Qingqis, opinions were divided long before the vehicle was banned by the Supreme Court—and still are. The traffic police was of the view that Qingqis should be banned on the main roads; that they should be stopped from using roundabouts as terminals. Unless these actions were carried out, they argued, the problem of traffic (and hence of road transport) would not be solved. However, the court decided that Qingqis could only function with major alterations to guarantee safety and existing standards. This change meant too big of an investment for Qingqi owners, hence the Qingqi has disappeared altogether, apart from the peri-urban areas and *katchi abadis* of the city and in the process, as mentioned earlier, Karachi lost about 360,000 transport seats per day.

The business of coaches and vans has increased due to the ban.[34] There is also a perception that administrative measures were biased and only the operators of Qingqis were targeted, while the other actors (such as manufacturers) in the Qingqi chain were spared. 'If the administration does not want Qingqis, why have they allowed them to be manufactured in the first place? The assemblers, marketers, and police officers who allowed Qingqis to ply on the road also need to be taken to task.'[35]

The problem is that if a court has granted a stay, action against the Qingqi cannot be taken.[36] Then there are the officials who feel that there is no solution at present, but there can be one if the existing systems are integrated within a larger plan.[37] For this, there is a need to talk to the existing private sector operators and develop a plan that includes them.[38] Regarding energy issues, there is a proposal that CNG should be provided for public transport seven days a week, while non-CNG days can apply for all other transport modes. Meanwhile, the commissioner of Karachi has placed a ban on the conversion of buses into carriers and trucks.[39]

Institutional arrangements were also discussed in interviews. By describing the changes that constantly happen, officials have implied that the absence of continuity is an issue.[40] The problem of coordination between different agencies has also been raised. This in spite of the fact that the transport and communication department, the KMC director, the secretary of RTA and the traffic police, along with their staff, all sit in the same building. It is felt that there could be better coordination if all these facets were unified under 'a higher authority'.[41] Corruption has been considered the 'worst enemy' and played an important part in the failure of the KTC, the SRTC, the KPTS and the UTS.[42] There is also a perception that traffic jams will increase if the present system is allowed to continue.[43]

The officials place their hope on the JICA Karachi Transportation Improvement Project and are of the opinion that the BRTs being implemented now will ease the situation. There is also a sense that the federal, provincial, and city governments will arrange for the required subsidies.

An ex-official of the CDGK, not wishing to be named, says that Karachi's transport plans have not been executed because of an absence of political will and interference; an absence of a promoter for the Karachi plans at the federal level in Islamabad; conflicts between different ethnic groups in power in government; and a weakening of local and provincial government institutions due to constant changes in them; and non-merit political appointments in the relevant agencies and departments. He also feels that the government's flyovers and signal-free roads will be a hindrance to the building of a light rail and/or a BRT service.

Transport Study: Postscript, 28 May 2015

On 20 March 2015, in a meeting at the Pearl Continental Hotel in Karachi, the government of Sindh unveiled its strategy for Karachi Mass Transit Programme and announced the creation of a Sindh Mass Transit Authority that would oversee and guide it. The meeting was attended by Sindh government officials, consultants to various mass transit proposals, the media and some civil society invitees. Also present, was Enrique Penalosa, who had been appointed as a consultant to one of the corridors (Blue Line) being built by the largest real estate development company in Pakistan. A synopsis of the proposal is provided in Table 3.1.

Table 3.1: Karachi BRT Corridors

Line	Financing	Length in km	Cost in billion PKR	Ridership Daily	Status
Yellow	Public-Private Partnership	26	12–14	150,000	Bidding complete
Orange	Government of Sindh	4.7	2.364	50,000	Under construction
Green	Government of Pakistan funding	21	27	400,000	Under construction
Red	Government of Sindh funding	21.5	12–15	350,000	Feasibility study completed by ADB
Blue	Private developer	41.7	187	450,000	Feasibility study completed
Circular Railway	JICA loan and government of Pakistan + government of Sindh funding	43.24	265	600,000	JICA funded. JICA conditionalities completed by Government of Sindh

The proposal that was considered as the most appropriate in economic and technical terms, was that of the Red Line, which has been proposed by the Asian Development Bank consultants. The Red Line BRT is all at-grade, including the stations and as such is far more economical and environmental-friendly. As per the proposal, twenty-three existing bus routes were also planned to feed into the BRT Corridor, thus increasing ridership considerably. Since then, the routes that were supposed to feed into the Red Line Corridor have been deleted. The proposal also consists of upgrading the physical environment of the roads through which the BRT passes, including those that will link up with the BRT Corridor. The ADB proposal also includes public transport reform and parking and non-motorised transport improvement.

On 21 March, a meeting was held at the NED University, between Enrique Penalosa, local consultants of the Blue Line BRT, university professors and a representative of the Urban Resource Centre, Karachi. It was decided that for heritage and environmental reasons, the Blue Line would be at-grade through the city centre. However, since then, the real estate development company financing the Blue Line has also backed out.

The local media's response has been one of scepticism. Journalists have raised the question as to why four separate entities are building four different routes. Consultants of the ADB held similar views and emphasised the need to integration the various routes and the necessity of uniform vehicles, signage and ticketing.[45]

* * * *

The BRT corridors proposed are being built at an enormous cost and with borrowed money, which has to be returned with interest. They are also expensive to maintain and operate and will require increasing subsidies to make them affordable to the commuting public. Even after the entire corridors are complete, they will cater to no more than 7.5 per cent of the 24.227 million rides that are generated per day in Karachi on weekdays.[46] This gap will have to be catered to by buses, for which so far there is no comprehensive programme.

4

The Ride Hailing Culture: The Widening Gap between the Haves and the Have Nots

Mansoor Raza

In the absence of an affordable, efficient and decent mass transit system in Karachi, ride-hailing culture has taken the city by storm. To cater to the needs of commuters, the city has at least six ride-hailing services. These include: Uber, Careem, Paxi, Bykea, Limofied, and Uride.

Ride-hailing ventures are redefining the taxi experience. It is interesting to note that an absence of a formal mass transit system in Karachi has generated two stratified responses for commuting by the market; motorbikes and Qingqis for low-income segments and smart phone app-based ride-hailing for upper and middle-income segments.

In 2017, rozee.pk, a private job placement company, conducted a survey on ride-hailing culture in Pakistan. It surveyed 7,391 respondents, all of whom owned smart phones. Out of those 7,391 respondents, 73 per cent reported using a ride-hailing app, between one and three times in a month.[1] According to the same survey, commuters' preference between various ride-hailing choices is dictated by a range of factors. These include: waiting time for the vehicle to arrive, the user friendliness of the app, the condition of the vehicles, the cost of the trip, the security factor (particularly for women), the behaviour of the drivers, and discounts by service providers. The survey is reflective of changes in the users' mindsets. Besides concerns about the cost, the new consumers demand comfort and hence subscribe to the notion of achieving maximum value for their money.

One of the reasons for the popularity of ride-hailing services is the ease with which young girls in groups can use these and travel together. Besides the sense of security, it also proves to be economical. Young male and female professionals whose participation in the corporate sector is constantly increasing, also prefer travelling in new, air-conditioned, and well-maintained cars. This is because these cater to their class aspirations. However, these comforts come with their own repercussions, which are elaborated upon later in this chapter.

A few years ago, cabs operated without meters, and dilapidated black and yellow taxis were the only option available to relatively well-off commuters. These were not able to survive the onslaught of app-based competitors backed by huge investments of global financial giants. The range of services offered by app-based ride-hailing services is only possible with huge financial investments. Fare calculation, route tracking, driver profiles, and a door-to-door service without the stress of fare and route negotiation, is made possible only through capital intensive technology which is unthinkable for small-scale entrepreneurs.

Despite all the benefits of ride-hailing services, they have garnered some critique which merits discussion. The spread of these services may be a good idea for those who can afford it, but it makes majority of the population (55 per cent of Karachi population lives in *katchi abadis*)[2] uncomfortable as well. The classes for whom these privately-owned ride-hailing services are affordable seem to be forgetting that public transport is a great equalizer. As money is spent on these private services, public transit loses revenue and this is detrimental for the city, society, and environment. Proposing private ride-hailing as a viable alternative to mass transit, in order to remedy commutation woes, is like a doctor treating cancer patient with a sedative: widening further the gap between the rich and poor. The initiative of Bykea is an exception to this as it is relatively affordable, though it still requires a smartphone and only offers motorbikes.

Sociologists are of the view that the app-based gig economy, of which the ride hailing service is a part, creates an illusory employment bubble and promotes a culture of underemployment.[3] A considerable number of university graduates have opted for the designation of 'captain' (taxi driver) on the basis of how the position provides a higher income than they would otherwise earn in the early stages of their careers. It provides temporary relief to state institutions responsible for providing the youth with employment, while underutilizing workers' skills and the country's economic capacity.

The dwindling rate of commissions is another factor that puts a considerable number of investors-cum-drivers in trouble. One of the respondents, who operates a cab from Hyderabad to Karachi on a daily basis, mentioned that he purchased a new car on lease from a bank to join the app-based service. In the first few months of the debut of the respective company, bonuses were lucrative and targets easy. In his opinion, with each passing day, the company was maximizing on its profit by tightening the noose around drivers' necks—cutting down on bonuses and making it difficult to achieve targets. It is tough for this respondent to exit the market as he has to pay instalments to the bank while his earnings dwindle.

Another issue is that consumers of these services are probably safer than the drivers. One of the drivers mentioned that he was mugged twice by the riders and he could not do anything as this is a risk associated with the job. The company directives are clear that he cannot let down the customer and once the ride is booked, he has to be very customer-friendly, as the latter, at the end of the ride, is supposed to provide online feedback about the driver, which is one of the factors considered for the driver's bonus. He stated, in a bitter voice, that if he got killed one day, the company would not provide any benefits to his family.

The 'peak factor' charges are also a point of irritation for the users. One of the female respondents who is a frequent customer, reported that she sometimes ends up paying 2.5 times of the actual fare. This happens mostly in traffic jams and rush hours. The term peak factor is applied to the augmented tariff of app-based rides on the pretext of increased fuel consumption and the opportunity cost for the service provider in traffic jams and slow traffic movement.

The consolidation of ride-hailing culture is detrimental to walking habits, as it provides a door-to-door service. The traditional practice of walking to the bus stop, waiting (usually by standing) for a bus to come, and then again walking from the bus stop to the destination, is not applicable to millennial ride-hailers. According to research, the walkability index of Karachi is 50, whereas Bangkok stands on 121.[4] It is reported that 21 per cent of Karachi's population walks for livelihood, social, and recreational activities. Sixty-six per cent of the commuters are multi-modal, using public transport as well as walking for their daily commute. This entails walking to a destination, or to another mode of transport.[5]

The penetration of ride-hailing services in the transport circuit is also said to be cannibalising public transit. As mentioned above, app-based ride-hailing is no alternative to mass transit. And the danger associated with mass transit not developing soon, only increases the prospects of an inequitable ride-hailing culture. This will make it much more difficult to establish social and economic equity in mass transit.

A key point to understand about ride-hailing services is that while their affordable fares makes them lucrative, their business models are ones that offer heavily subsidised fares in order to aggressively increase their market-share. Rickshaws and black and yellow taxis in Karachi have already started going out of business because of the cheap fares ride-hailing services offer. The question to be asked here is: what consequences will the city's transit system and its stakeholders face when ride-hailing service providers decide to remove subsidies in order to make profit on their investments? This price increase is inevitable as even the largest of these ride-hailing companies are yet to make profit. For example, Uber reported losses of $4.5 billion in the year 2017. These losses were borne by its wealthy venture capital investors. What can, however, be learned from ride-hailing services is that they are addressing a gap in the market, i.e. door-to-door services, and that public transport planning can and should incorporate door-to-door services as well. Some countries have already started doing this.

Urban planning, at any given point in time, is a political process with power groups dominating the discourse and setting the direction for it. Also, urban planning is, most of the time, a response to the crisis created by capitalism. The absence of mass transit in Karachi is a reflection of the fragmentation of government responsibility in planning, leaving gaps for private enterprises to fill. The diffusion of ride-hailing services in mainstream transport is yet another case of the private sector catering to middle and upper segments of the population. The looming question—for planners—is that after huge investments on mass transit infrastructure of Karachi and with plans for further investments, will the affluent classes of the city use mass transit and give up the culture of door-to-door ride-hailing services?

Box 4.1: Safe and On-Time

Aasma Jabin, a 20-year-old female student living in a hostel in Karachi, far from her home in Chakwal, gets an interview call for an exchange program. The interview is in Marriot Hotel, Karachi, on the coming Monday. She is currently pursuing her bachelors in computer science from the Institute of Business Administration and has no transport of her own. Belonging to a conservative family, she never travels alone, especially not in public transport. Aasma Jabin decides to use Careem (a ride-hailing app) for the first time. What further convinces her to go for it is the service's 'Share Tracker' feature, which lets her share her location with a friend in real time. A white Corolla pulls up outside the university's campus minutes after she books a ride and she reaches her destination with a good half an hour to spare. Her first experience in a ride-hailing service leaves her feeling happy, satisfied, and secure.

Source: Ahmed, R., 2020. *How Ride-Hailing Services Are Changing The Way College Students Commute In Pakistan.* Propakistani.pk. Retrieved from: https://propakistani. pk/2017/03/27/ride-hailing-services-changing-way-college-students-commute-pakistan/.

Box 4.2: Independence and Concerns – Interview with a Woman Commuter

She uses ride-hailing services for their ease and security. In her late twenties, Hunza is single and belongs to the upper-income segment of Karachi. Her father is a businessman and she is one of four siblings. She earned a Masters in Sociology from a local private university and is now working as research assistant at a public university. Hunza says that the ease of access, the detailed information of Captain, and his picture and car details create an aura of security and that's the biggest reason for her to use the service often. She also mentioned that her parents often refuse to let her commute in the home car on the pretext of high fuel costs and so she uses ride-hailing services which prove to be cheaper. She was of the opinion that ride-hailing is in vogue amongst female students as it comes cheap to the girls' students travelling in groups from the same locations or routes. Group travelling through ride-hailing services is also popular amongst young female professionals. 'I think that women are using it more and don't need a male to accompany them now, as Careem has the 'share tracker' option so you can track your ride. I can tell you that my *phuppo* (paternal aunt) who didn't think of travelling without her siblings now uses Careem to come to our place'. She mentioned that late night travel is also safe because of the responsiveness of the service provider, 'Careem's call centre is very alert when you are on a ride', she said. 'Once I was with one of my friends at Do Darya and his car's tyre got punctured. It was 11 p.m. in the night and I got nervous as the road was deserted and it is known to be unsafe. As a last resort, he called a ride-hailing service and sent me home.' However, in her opinion everything is not very rosy about ride-hailing culture. The radical increase in the number of private cars on the roads of Karachi which are already filled to their capacity, contributes to severe congestion. 'When I find a decent captain, I do chat with him. Once I asked him about the number of cars that are registered with Careem, the response of the captain was quite astonishing: approximately 1 million. You know what that means, 1 million cars and one million drivers', she mentioned. She never came across a female captain although she believes that there are a couple of them operating in ride-hailing services. The venture also provides part-time driving and encourages drivers to enhance their incomes. 'Once I spoke to a retired man and he said to me that it is better to earn some money through this service than to flip channels at home. Not only him, I also met a software engineer who was not paid well by his employer so he used to drive for a ride-hailing service, part-time, to enhance his earnings.' When asked whether she would use mass transit, if available to the residents of the City, she replied, 'I will use mass transit if it is cheap and provides the same level of security.'

Source: Interview by Mansoor Raza, 15 September 2018, unpublished.

Box 4.3: Solving a Financial Emergency

Driving a new Toyota Corolla with the air-conditioning at full speed, a lit cigarette, and music playing in the background, he continued his conversation. This young captain is the son of a deceased businessman who died recently after falling ill, leaving behind a widow, a young son, and two daughters. This captain is a graduate of visual studies from a prestigious local institute, whose interests lie in documentary filmmaking and entreprencurship rather than 'office jobs'. 'I spent several days in and out of hospitals with my father. We lost a substantial amount of money and after his death my mother and sisters are my responsibility'. He had left some savings that the young man used to buy a car and invest in Careem in order to earn a sufficient income. He starts late in the day and continues till 2 a.m. in the morning. He is happy and thinks that more such ventures will bring prosperity to the city. For him, the day and the celebrations of the moment are more important than heavy notions of being underemployed.

Source: Interview by Mansoor Raza, 5 April 2018, unpublished.

Box 4.4: Social and Financial Mobility

Mr X is a Careem 'Captain'. He is not well-educated by any urban standards. Although he wanted to enroll himself for higher education, he had no option but to work to earn a sufficient income for his household right after passing his intermediate examinations. He got a job as a record keeper for a factory but at an insufficient salary of Rs 14,000 per month. He came to know about Careem and decided to sign up as a Captain. He did this by selling his motorcycle, his only asset, and borrowing money from a moneylender at a 30 per cent markup for purchasing a new Suzuki Wagon R for Rs 1.1 million. This initiative brought a significant change in his monthly earnings. On an average, he now earns Rs 2000 per day. Due to these earnings, he was able to save up and get married. He drives 10 hours a day and doesn't work on Sundays which in his words, is a family day. He is planning to buy another car for his younger brother so that he can also walk in his footsteps. In his estimation, approximately 14,000 young people are employed by Careem.

Source: Interview by Arif Hasan, 5 June 2019, unpublished.

5

Exploring Karachi's Transport System Problems: Diverse Perspectives of Stakeholders

Mansoor Raza

Karachi's traffic situation can be summarized through the following sights: gridlocked main road corridors and arteries, pedestrians struggling to cross fast moving signal-free corridors, oil tankers and cargo carriers being driven in the wrong lanes, the persistent high-pitched sound of ambulances, VIP movements for whom all traffic is brought to a halt, and commuters crowding around legal and illegal bus stops.

Besides braving health and environmental hazards, Karachi loses Rs 663 million (£4.171 million) collectively every day due to traffic jams and gridlocks.[1] Various newspaper articles, media reports, research discussions suggest that the transport issues of the city have linkages with demographic changes and the social and economic life of its city dwellers.[2] These issues also partly define and dictate major decisions of a person's life, which include housing and preferences for livelihood opportunities. In 2006, the Karachi Strategic Development Plan 2020, by the then City District Government Karachi (CDGK), cited that there are 24.2 million persons' trips generated in the city every day, out of which at least 60 per cent are realised through the existing system of public transport.[3] It would not be unreasonable to state that with the growth of the population, those are bound to increase in number.

The purpose of this chapter is to provide additional case study material on transport issues in Karachi, which present the genesis of the crisis and its impact on various stakeholders. It aims to understand these traffic issues and their impact, by exploring the diverse perspectives of those who travel on Karachi's roads—from minibus, rickshaw and ambulance drivers, to mechanics, spare-parts dealers and commuters. It is assumed that these respondents have a deep understanding of the issues that define transport and traffic management in Karachi. For this purpose, twenty-three interviews with a diverse range of relevant stakeholders were conducted and the following sections summarise the results of those interviews.

The interviews were conducted over 1,080 hours, at different locations of Karachi: North Nazimabad in District Central, Pakistan Employees Cooperative Housing Society (PECHS), Clifton and Saddar in District South and Orangi Town in District West. The interviews took place in both formal and informal settings—in offices and on the streets and footpaths. Before interviewing the subjects, the objectives of the study were explained to them as a procedural prerequisite of research ethics.

Stakeholder Perceptions: Major Findings

This section presents a summary of major findings of the study that relate to the perceptions of various stakeholders of the transport system and associated facilities and services of Karachi. Drawing on qualitative results, it considers how urban stakeholders confront common challenges of everyday life in ways that shape their relationships with the transport circuit. The specific findings are outlined in Table 5.1. For further details on the sections on motorbikes and pedestrian bridges, see Appendices 5.1, 5.2, and 5.3.

Table 5.1: Major findings: Stakeholder perceptions of Karachi's transport system	
THEME	PERCEPTIONS
Modes of Transport	• Buses/Minibuses: buses are preferred to minibuses but the former are disappearing as they are becoming economically unfeasible, increasingly. • Motorbikes are becoming more and more popular but they are a nuisance as well. • Qingqis are more attractive to low-income groups but a source of irritation to car owners. • CNG rickshaws are more lucrative for owners than the petrol-driven rickshaws. They are also more environmental-friendly, but only if well-maintained. • Peddle power—is the use of bicycles—has become less popular.
Infrastructure	• Poor infrastructure encourages traffic to flow in the wrong direction. • Bus and minibus drivers rarely stop at designated bus stops. • Signal-free corridors have promoted speeding and are running out of capacity. • Pedestrian bridges are mostly unutilized.
Reasons for traffic congestion	• The increase in traffic volume due to irresponsible lending by banks. • Ill-planned infrastructure. • Uninformed and unplanned rallies and protests. • Violation of traffic laws. • Ageing vehicles block the roads.
Parking space	• Escalating land prices discourage the creation of additional parking space in the city. • There are no designated parking spaces for roadside mechanics and other relevant service providers' vehicles, forcing them to park on the roads. • Unchecked illegal parking creates disruption in traffic flow.

Table 5.1 (continued)

THEME	PERCEPTIONS
Lack of availability of vehicle parts	• Smuggled vehicle parts have flooded the markets, suffocating trade in legally imported parts. • Devaluation of the rupee against the yen has caused an inflation in prices and popularized the use of 'kabuli'* (used vehicle parts). • Trade in salvaged vehicle parts is not officially recognized but does make spare parts affordable.
Role of the police	• There is endemic corruption within the Karachi police force. • The cost of bribes are arbitrary; there are no fixed rates. • Instead of educating the public about the law, police personnel prefer to exploit the ignorance for monetary gain.
Obtaining documents	• Except for vehicle registration certificates, most vehicle documents can be obtained with ease by bribing the relevant personnel. • As a result, the validity of such documents is lost in the eyes of the public.
Health and environment	• Spending a lot of time travelling on Karachi's roads results in altered psychology and physical illness. • Besides affecting health, the loss in environmental quality has financial repercussions as well.
Gender issues	• Public transport systems are failing to respond to the changing status of women. • Harassment is an everyday occurrence for women in public spheres.
Attitudes	• The ease of access to car loans has made drivers more careless.
Security	• High levels of street crime put the lives of commuters at risk. • Transport operators are wary of going to some areas after dark, thus making life difficult for commuters.
Causes of accidents	• Lack of respect for the law. • Lack of sleep of drivers on highways. • Delays due to traffic congestion encourages drivers to speed elsewhere to make up for the time lost. This causes further accidents and in turn more traffic jams; a vicious circle.

*Kabuli (i.e. imported from Kabul in Afghanistan) here referred as to second-hand spare parts for vehicles.

Modes of Transport

Buses and Minibuses

According to the respondents, although congested, buses are perceived as spacious in comparison with minibuses: 'I had to use 7C (route number of a bus) as well. The advantage of the bus is that it is spacious…the other disadvantage of a minibus is that the passengers' clothes get dirty and crumpled. The little space forces passengers to lean against each other or the walls and seats of the bus. Also, because of the lack of space, passengers belonging to certain professions, like mechanics and plumbers, also leave their marks on one's dresses.[4] As mentioned above, over a span of thirteen years there has been a 65 per cent reduction in the number of buses. The respondents cited various reasons, including the rising cost of spare parts.[5]

Another reason is that bus fares are considered insufficient, which makes bus operation less lucrative. The fares are on the lower side. The distance from New Karachi to Kemari is 35 km and the fare is between Rs 17 to Rs 18.[6] In Kashmir, the fare for a 10 km journey is Rs 150 and one has to pay an extra Rs 50 for luggage. In Faisalabad, for a distance of 35 km, Rs 100 (£0.62) is charged.[7] The reduction in the number of buses has an impact on affiliate businesses as well. 'If the number of buses is becoming less, then our businesses are also affected'[8] stated a mechanic.

Few new investments are made in buses, but Table 5.1 shows a 44 per cent increase in the number of minibuses in Karachi over thirteen years. According to one respondent, the cost of a vehicle has also increased. In 2003, when a Mazda (mini-bus)[9] was assembled in Pakistan, the cost was Rs 350,000 (approximately £2,204). The entire production has been shifted to India and now a vehicle costs Rs 1.4 million (approximately £8,820). It is difficult to get a zero-meter Mazda these days and the Chinese vehicles are not so powerful to be able to take the load and are unable to ply on the streets for long.[10] Had this price hike not happened, the number of minibuses would have been more. 'W-11 (a minibus route number) used to have 450 minibuses and now it has 150–170 minibuses. Earlier, 2–3 minibuses departed from the terminal per minute and now one bus leaves the terminal every 2 minutes.'[11]

Motorcycles

To overcome the problems of commuting by public transport, an increasing number of Karachiites are purchasing motorbikes. The number of motorbikes increased from 450,000 in 1990 to 500,000 in 2004, to 2,856,704 in 2018. In 2010, their number was one million. This means that there are 57 motorbikes for every 1,000 persons. It is estimated that at the present rate of increase, the number of motorbikes in 2030 will be 3.64 million—or 115 motorbikes for every 1,000 persons. However, until recently, women did not ride motorbikes in Karachi. Many feel that gender discrimination prevents them from opting for a better mode of commuting.

To understand the motorbike increase phenomena and the commuting preferences of Karachiites, a small research was carried out.[12] One hundred male and sixty-eight female respondents were interviewed at nine different bus stops at different locations in the city. Almost all the respondents belonged to the lower-income areas. In addition, 25 motorbike users and 25 dealers were also interviewed. A web search for motorbikes available in the international market was also carried out. The results of the interviews are interesting

Seventy per cent of the male respondents said that they would like to purchase a motorbike but do not have the means. The reasons given for wanting to purchase a motorbike are its flexibility, cost, and time-saving in commuting. Eighteen per cent of the respondents do not wish to use a motorbike because they, or their families consider it an unsafe mode of commuting. The average commuting time (varying between 30 minutes to 6 hours) is 2 hours from home to work and back.

Fifty-three per cent of the female respondents would like to commute by motorbike if given an option. Sixteen per cent of the respondents felt that motorbikes were not suitable for women. Seven per cent said that using a motorbike was 'against their religion', as compared to 64 per cent of the men. The rest said that although they would like to ride bikes, their parents, or guardians hesitated to give them permission. Like their male counterparts, the average commuting time of the respondents is 2 hours from home to work and back. In addition, the respondents also pointed out that women required 'women-friendly' scooters, since straddling a motorbike seat is culturally not acceptable.

All motorbike users mentioned high levels of air and noise pollution on the road as major problems encountered by them. Other problems identified were the absence of proper traffic control systems, bad road surfaces, police harassment and an absence of a physically segregated lane for motorbikes. Forty per cent of the respondents also mentioned lack of space for parking as a major issue.

Through a web search, the study also identified 'green' motorbike manufacturers. The costs of the green bikes, for most part, are less than the bikes being marketed in Karachi today. In addition, their operational costs are 25 per cent of those for petroleum motorbikes. Hybrid motorbikes, which can operate on both petrol and electricity, are also available. Import duty on motorbikes is 65 per cent and other taxes (including the flood relief tax) are 41.5 per cent. This makes motorbikes more than 100 per cent more expensive than what they really cost.

The average commuting costs of the male and female respondents work out to Rs 1,570 per month, for commuting from home to work and back by bus. Meanwhile, the average cost of maintenance and fuel of the motorbike users works out to be Rs 780 per month, including social and business trips, as well as commuting to work and back. The respondents also claim that using a motorbike reduces commuting time to less than 50 per cent as compared to using a bus. Many motorbike users also felt that with adjustment to the seat, a motorbike is suitable for three adults.

The question that arises from the above discussion is whether the use of motorbikes should be promoted as an integral part of the larger mass transit system for the city. This can be done by reducing duties on them, introducing microcredit programmes for their purchase, promoting the use of green motorbikes, creating conditions for women to use scooters, providing physically-segregated motorbike lanes on the main traffic corridors, taking steps to improve safety for motorbike riders, and by accommodating the requirements for motorbike use as an integral part of transport planning, traffic management, infrastructure design, building byelaws, and zoning regulations.

CNG Rickshaw

The Italian-made 4-stroke rickshaw[13] (the predecessor of the CNG rickshaw) was considered a more robust vehicle, with greater engine power and hence seldom accused of slowing down traffic. But these were not environmental-friendly and were less lucrative: they had the capacity of only three people and that too with difficulty. In contrast, a CNG rickshaw can be used for six passengers (with a little modification). One respondent said 'CNG rickshaws are obviously more profitable. A CNG rickshaw owner can earn up to Rs 1,400 (approximately £8.81) a day. In contrast, a KCR rickshaw driver can earn a maximum of Rs 500 (approximately £3.14) per day. It's because of the ever-escalating price of petrol.'[14]

Because of this increased availability of passenger space, CNG rickshaws have been evolved for diverse use. For instance, in low-income localities, CNG rickshaws are hired for marriage ceremonies. It works out cheaper for a family of six, or seven persons. Sometimes three, or four families book a CNG rickshaw each, to attend a relative's marriage together. It's more economical than using a coaster (type of bus) for the same purpose.[15] In 2012, the number of CNG rickshaws reported in Karachi was 60,000.[16] CNG rickshaws have a long life as compared to KCRs, but spare parts are expensive. 'KCR's engine can be completely overhauled with Rs 5,000 (approximately £31.49), while for CNG it takes Rs 10,000 (approximately £62.99) to execute complete overhauling.'[17] The CNG rickshaw driver interviewed for this study was aware of the fact that car drivers are not happy with CNG drivers, but he had a justification for the slow-moving vehicle: 'We also get irritated by them. They honk, push us into speeding unnecessarily, throw tantrums, hurl abuse, and always pass dirty looks. They need to understand that we cannot speed because of the load and also because we cannot apply breaks suddenly; the rickshaw will turn topsy-turvy.' However, the new-generation of CNG rickshaws are better than their predecessors, as they have disc brakes; earlier the rickshaws had washer brakes. The sudden application of breaks, in that case, tore apart the washer.[18]

Peddle Power: Cyclists

Over the years in Karachi, the trend of cycling has succumbed to the ways of a modern city. Consumer aspirations have led to more and more cars and motorcycles on the road instead. In recent years, the development of road infrastructure has remained insensitive to the requirements of cyclists. The lack of maintenance of the existing infrastructure is also a discouraging factor for cyclists. Roads are in bad condition. Potholes are damaging for cycles and cause backaches.

A cyclist, while expressing discontent towards lack of infrastructure, said, 'Because of haphazard traffic and irregular parking, I, to make my way, always crisscross the cycle. We are sick of Qingqis; they don't know how to use the road.'[19]

The popularity of motorcycles due to the easy availability of credit and withdrawal of subsidies for the production of bicycles is cited as one reason for the decline of interest in cycling.[20] The discouraging attitude of police officers is also cited as a reason. According to one group of respondents, 'How can cyclists be a nuisance to other vehicles, or create traffic problems? It could be otherwise. Those police cops just want to extort money from us on the pretext of not having a light on the bicycle, or a bell.'[21] There are no separate cycle lanes to make Karachi a bicycle-friendly city. Neither the long flyovers, nor the traffic signal-free corridors—the new architecture of roads—are helping the culture of cycling. 'We cannot take U-turns and we have to avoid speeding cars. It's also tiring to have to weave in and out of the traffic.'[22]

Infrastructure

Flyovers: For approximately 4,642,196 vehicles,[23] Karachi has a road network of 9,764 km.[24] A complete list of flyovers and underpasses is given in Appendix 4.1. According to the taxi driver interviewed, 'Those (vehicular flyovers) do not help us. Everybody comes from the wrong side and we, to save petrol or CNG, do the same. It is so much in vogue that even at some places the police facilitate that movement...due to ever-increasing number of vehicles on the road those infrastructures will soon run out of space.'[25] However, another respondent thinks otherwise: 'Those underpasses and flyovers are helpful as they reduce the time of commuting over long distances.'[26]

Bus stops: In Karachi, a bus can be stopped anywhere by a commuter although the city has designated bus stops as well. Minibuses usually drop passengers in the middle of the road and at the entry and exit points of flyovers and underpasses. Bus stop culture is almost non-existent. Designated bus stops do not have any names displayed on them. A conductor must shout the name of the bus stop to announce the destination or describe the route. 'No, we are not dropped by the bus drivers on designated bus stops, as they usually drop us on the roads.'[27]

Freeways/signal-free corridors: The respondents blame signal-free corridors for speeding, encouraging drivers to break the law, and discouraging the use of bicycles. These stretches of road have promoted speeding and are a problem for motorcyclists. Due to signal-free fast-track roads, there are few opportunities for motorcyclists to make U-turns and many violate the one-way rule, which proves dangerous. 'This is just to save time and fuel by avoiding distant U-turn areas. I myself violate the rules and move opposite to the one-ways and mainstream traffic. Before the construction of those speedy lanes, that was not the case.'[28] Signal-free corridors are accused of promoting a culture of recklessness in drivers as well. One of the respondents, a police officer, however, thinks that observing traffic discipline is more important. 'It's not a matter of corridors being signal-free or with signals. It is just a matter of observing the discipline of traffic and to pay respect to the law of the land. However, I do believe that there isn't enough capacity on the roads to absorb the ever-increasing volume of vehicles.'[29]

A Note on Pedestrian Bridges

Karachi's pedestrian bridges were installed to enable foot travellers to cross roads safely, in less time and with less effort, particularly at signal-free corridors. Yet Karachi—considered by its citizens to have a population of over 20 million people—has only 113 pedestrian bridges.[30] In addition, pedestrian bridges are difficult for the elderly and incapacitated to use, while the long distances between any two bridges is problematic for many pedestrians (*see* Table 5.2).

S. No	Spot	Distance b/w two points
Table 5.2: The Impossible Gulf of Pedestrian Bridges (Selected Points Only)		
SHAHRAH-E-FAISAL		
1	Nursery to Lal kothi	1 km
2	Lal kothi to Fortune Centre	1 km
3	Fortune Centre to Tip Sultan	700 m
4	Day Inn to Tipu Sultan	1.2 km
5	Awami Markaz to Day Inn	600 m
6	Awami Markaz to Karsaz	800 m
EXPRESS WAY		
1	Qayumabad to Iqra University	1 km
2	Iqra University to Eidgah	1 km
3	Eidgah to Gujjar Chowk	1 km
4	Gujjar Chowk to Shaheed-e-Millat	3 km
Source: Survey by Urban Resource Centre, May 2015		

According to a 'walkability' survey[31] conducted in Karachi in 2009, almost 21 per cent of daily trips are made entirely on foot, and of the nearly 66 per cent of the commuters who use different modes of public transport, a large percentage walk part of their daily commute. Every trip begins and ends with a walking trip, either to the destination, or to another mode of transport.[32] However, open manholes, a lack of footpaths, dilapidated roads, and the unfriendly behaviour of motorcyclists—to name a few factors—contribute to the difficulties faced by pedestrians on a daily basis.

Setting aside debate over the number of pedestrian bridges in the city, it was highlighted in the media that most new overhead pedestrian bridges being built were at places from where people usually did not prefer crossing the road. According to a survey conducted by the author of this chapter, it is important for pedestrian bridges to be near hospitals, colleges, bus stops, and flyovers. It was reported in the press that officials involved in road safety management suggest that the authorities have not bothered to carry out any survey of the roads or the points where the bridges have been proposed. KMC's transport and communications department does not even have the figures to identify how many pedestrians use a particular road in a day, officials say.

Nearly half of the people interviewed do not use the pedestrian bridges at night, as they are considered unsafe due to incidences of snatching and mugging. If they are compelled to use those after dusk, they prefer to do it in groups. Respondents complained about the absence of lights on those bridges, making it difficult to see who is passing next to them. The CEO of an engineering firm believes that people avoid pedestrian bridges because of untidiness and mugging threats, as well as the presence of beggars and homeless people.

Those interviewed mentioned that the bridges are not very well-maintained, and the conditions of the iron sheets are not very satisfactory. Most of the pedestrian bridges are in dilapidated conditions, posing a great danger for pedestrians, forcing them to cross the road from under the bridges. Almost all pedestrian bridges are in shambles. The works and services department of the city government—responsible for the construction of and maintaining these bridges—has held the finance and planning department responsible for not allocating the funds for bridge repair.[33] In March 2012, a portion of a pedestrian bridge in the Maripur locality—a village located west of Karachi—collapsed after a speeding truck hit it (the bridge had collapsed previously as well).[34]

The current design of pedestrian bridges is not suitable for the elderly, or those with physical disabilities, or diseases that make climbing up many flights of stairs challenging. As of now, only one pedestrian bridge in the entire city, located at the Aga Khan University Hospital, has an elevator. The interviewed official of the Karachi Metropolitan Corporation (KMC) mentioned that when ramps were made along a pedestrian bridge at the Natha Khan Flyover, in order to facilitate the physically disabled, commuters began to drive their motorbikes over it and hence it was subsequently blocked by the authorities.

Causes of Traffic Jams

Some respondents said that the increase in traffic volumes is the major cause of congestion and traffic jams. 'The volume of traffic has increased. To the best of my knowledge, a staggering number of 400 vehicles are registered per day at Civic Centre. Now, you multiply it by 300 working days of a year, so an additional 120,000 vehicles per annum are on the roads of Karachi.'[35]

Others mentioned that CNG rickshaws (and Qingqis previously) are also responsible for traffic jams. 'Earlier, the traffic on the roads was less, now it's a hell lot of traffic. Besides the ever-increasing number of cars, Qingqis are also part of problem. They stop anywhere without considering the traffic behind them, make two-to-three parallel lanes, and bikers have to zigzag between them to make their way forward. Minibuses have the same problem: [they] stop anywhere, are driven like airplanes, and never stop at designated bus stops.'[36]

Lending by banks—perceived by many as reckless—has caused an increase in the traffic volume. It is also perceived that the ease of buying personal cars has caused consumers to behave irresponsibly. Traffic volume has increased a lot and it's because of the increase in population and also because of the relative ease of purchasing cars due to bank loans. People are becoming more careless about speeding, as compared to before.[37] However, one respondent, a bank manager, had a different opinion about whether or not bank-lending was reckless: 'I don't think so. These are just because of improper planning for infrastructure and due to the poor maintenance of whatever roads we have. It is not banks that caused the traffic issues of Karachi. It's the mafias that did it and it's the attitude of the public; neither wants to observe the laws…this is the (fault of the) goods-carrier mafia that failed the cargo-carrying services of Pakistan Railways… Earlier, 75 per cent of goods were transported through Pakistan Railways. Transporting goods by rail was much cheaper than trucks, which are a source of traffic jams.'[38]

It was also said that the flow of traffic is severely affected by public rallies and political activism. According to an ambulance driver, 'The rallies, protests, and *dharnas* (sit-ins) are real challenges for us. When every second counts, it takes us considerable time to find our way. Rallies are a bit of an exception, as usually alternative routes are predefined by the authorities, but it increases the time to reach the hospital.'[39] Heavy transport vehicles (HTVs) driving in undesignated lanes also contribute to creating long queues of vehicles behind them and forcing other drivers to change lanes. According to an oil-tanker driver, 'Admittedly, we have our own follies. We drive on the extreme right, which is supposed to be a fast lane and which we shouldn't be doing…as a result, we block the way for ambulances, or other fast-moving vehicles. This practice is more common with newcomers to our profession, who don't know the laws and ethics of driving.'[40]

Parking Problems

One cause for Karachi's traffic jams is the lack of allocated parking spaces in areas with high-density populations. Many drivers park their vehicles horizontally on the road, on elevated pedestrian pathways, besides other parked cars, or on designated bus stops. To tackle these illegal parking practices, in 2014, the KMC created 57 official charged parking sites. The move also aimed to prevent mafia groups from overcharging drivers for parking.[41] The lack of allocated parking spaces for newly built structures is directly correlated with the escalating prices of land.

Some interviewees mentioned that in order to maximize profits, a substantial number of builders circumvent building control regulations: while new building plans include space for vehicular parking, the builders will often sell the space on, or use it to build more dwellings instead. 'Have you ever observed that all those newly constructed shopping malls and housing complexes do not provide enough space for parking? As a result, people have occupied (parked) streets and lanes in the city.'[42] Three new bus terminals were supposed to be built in Karachi, but so far only one has been constructed, The Yousuf Goth Bus Terminal at the Regional Cooperation for Development (RCD) highway. As a result, hundreds of illegal bus terminals have appeared, mostly in District South—in Saddar and near the Karachi Cantonment Railway Station. According to intercity bus terminal manager, 30 per cent of the traffic problems in District South could be resolved by addressing this issue.[43]

An intercity bus service manager states, 'Nowadays, the police have tightened controls, so we park under Saddar Bridge. This gives us only 10 minutes to ask passengers to get onto the bus. We have been asked to abolish the terminal we have in the city. The new terminal at Sabzi Mandi is too far from the city and is not viable for most of our potential passengers. On the other hand, the private terminal at the same place is very expensive and we cannot afford to use it. I think that there should be a terminal at Cantonment Station as well.'[44]

Vendors and service providers also suffer financially from the lack of parking provision. The respondents said that had they been provided with proper parking space, they would have better business prospects. According to one mechanic interviewed, 'Parking is a major problem. We do not have a proper space where we can ask our clients to park their cars. As a result, we park on roads, designated footpaths, and on street corners. If I had properly allocated parking, my business would increase.'[45] The commercial goods carrier also complained of the lack of parking space and the resulting operational impediments. 'It's the congestion on the streets which bothers us. It is difficult to operate on the ever-filled streets of Tariq Road, Liaquatabad, Nazimabad, and the old city areas. We have to wait, as people are not willing to provide us with space. Also, parking is not available in most areas.'[46]

Although KMC has allocated new parking spaces, there is a perceived element of unfairness. According to one interviewee, the designated charged parking space outside government hospitals irritates patients and their relatives.[47] The ambulance driver also complained about the same issue, but in a different context: 'Civil Hospital is the most difficult of the three major hospitals: Abbasi, Jinnah, and Civil. One cannot turn around the ambulance as there isn't enough space to manoeuvre the vehicle and it's because of systematic and sporadic parking, primarily because of para-transport vehicles.'[48] The drivers of water bowsers often park illegally. In the absence of any proper arrangements, they often park close to their dwellings. 'I live in Hijrat Colony, and I park the vehicle nearby to my place. Actually, it's not only me, but other truck drivers also park. So, we pool money for a *chowkidar* (guard), who takes care of all the vehicles that are parked there.'[49]

The issue of illegal parking also affects the rescue and emergency services. Gridlock at main road arteries also results in the loss of lives. In the first two months of 2006, as many as 500 people died in ambulances, on their way to hospital.[50] 'See the road at Golimar and you will see how sanitary shops and the loader pickups and trucks have occupied half of the road.'[51]

The unprecedented number of new schools appearing in otherwise residential blocks means there are not enough parking spaces for those taking children to and from school. There are more than 700 schools in Karachi[52] and the majority of these do not have sufficient parking spaces. 'Schools are also responsible for the traffic jams; very few schools have proper parking. Just visit the Plaza around 1:00 p.m., when school finishes and you will understand why.'[53]

Problems Related to Vehicle Parts

According to a press report, Pakistan suffers annual losses of Rs 10.3 billion (£64.8 million) in tax revenues due to smuggling, counterfeiting, and import duty evasion, due to dishonest declarations and under-invoicing for automobile spare parts. The applicable tax range on the import of vehicle parts varies from 32.5 to 50 per cent. As per estimates for 2012 by the Federal Board of Revenue (FBR), goods worth Rs 170 billion (£1.07 billion) are smuggled through Afghan Transit Trade (ATI) each year.[54] According to a vehicle parts dealer interviewed:

Afghans spoiled the business. They used drug money to finance the business of spare parts. They smuggled items through Torkham border and bulldozed all the legal requirements. On the other hand, we are bound to pay taxes, custom duties, to wait for custom clearances and sometimes have to pay demurrages as well. They (Afghans) have money and they invest enormously in local markets. They sell spare parts much cheaper than us; we are rendered expensive to the end user. Afghans, through their contacts, have developed local networks and we, because of our legal status, are out of that circuit.[55]

Besides illegally imported new spare parts, second-hand used spare parts, popularly known as *kabuli* are also available. Interviewees claimed confidentially that it is common knowledge that spare vehicle parts are often sourced from stolen vehicles. In 2013 alone, 26,352 cases of vehicle theft were reported.[56]

There is also a large trade in 'taxi-cutting' taking place in Manghopir and Katti Pahari (in District West of Karachi). Scrap dealers buy old taxis for Rs 45,000–50,000 (£282–313) each, take out the spare parts and scrap the rest. According to one taxi driver, 'those cab drivers who are running out of the business, sell their taxis to Pathans. The spare parts and anything useful are sold out as *kabuli* and the rest to iron scrappers.'[57] Second-hand parts are also in demand due to a change in working styles of mechanics. He explains to me how the repair business has changed with these developments. 'Earlier, the *ustad* was interested in making repairs. Now the emphasis is more on the replacement of old or damaged parts because both the customer and the mechanic do not have time for meticulous work. Also, after replacing a part, the life of the car increases. People can now order parts from Dubai as well. The availability of spare parts has also forced mechanics to upgrade and diversify their choice of tools, which was not the case earlier.'[58] For instance, 'we now use oil filter spanner instead of chain sprocket to change the oil filter,' he says.[59] Trade in illegal scrapping and importing parts, and the ease of importing, has had a profound impact on the market, the clients, and the mechanics. As per one mechanic, 'I would say that the business of scrapping is very supportive for my business as it makes repair and maintenance affordable and time efficient.'[60] But the availability of spare parts does not always translate into affordability for the end user. Costs are also affected by inflation. One mechanic stated, 'Over the years, spare parts have become costly. For instance, in 2000 the cost of a tyre (for minibuses) was Rs 2,500 (£15.72) and now it is Rs 25,000 (£157). In 1992–93 the cost of a gear box was Rs 3,500 (£22.03) and now it is Rs 75,000 (£472.43).'[61] The consistent devaluation of the Pakistan rupee against the Japanese yen is cited as one of the causes of inflation.[62]

Role of the Police

According to a public opinion poll conducted by Transparency International in 2013, corrupt practices by government officials—especially among the police—are increasing.[63] Many of this study's interviewees (with the exception of the traffic police officer), claimed in confidence that they feel the police department is corrupt to its core. 'It's totally corrupt and is hungry for money. They extort money on one pretext or another.' There are no fixed rates and the cost of bribes is arbitrary. 'It varies as it's a matter of a judgment call by the man on duty. They first ask for a higher amount and after certain negotiations, settle for less.'

According to the interviewees, rates vary from Rs 50 (£0.31) to Rs 2,000 (£12.60). The interviewed police officer admitted that malpractice exists in the police department but differed as to the scale of corruption. He thinks that 'a mere 30 per cent' of police officers take bribes. He was also quick to justify this figure. An ordinary police constable cannot run his kitchen on a meagre amount of Rs 15,000 (£94.44) or Rs 17,000 (£107.04) per month. Have you ever questioned why the motorway police in Punjab do not take bribes? Their salary is one of the main reasons, as the salary of a constable there is Rs 30,000 (£188.89) per month. It's almost double the amount.'[64]

It is not just the traffic police who take bribes. Other police officers refuse to pay small-scale vendors for services.[65] and overlook violations of the law in return for money. 'As per the rules, we are not allowed to enter the city between the two prayer times: *fajar* and *isha*.[66] But you know how the system works here. If we pay a bribe to the policeman, we can enter at any time…the rate varies [and] depends on the policeman and the area. Sindh is the worst in terms of bribery. Here, we have to give [a bribe] to the mobile police and to the traffic police as well.'[67] In addition, according to the respondents, the police also takes advantage of commuters' ignorance of the laws to exploit them. The interviewed group of cyclists revealed that they are often stopped by low-ranking police operators on one pretext or another and the purpose is just to extort money. 'No I don't know about the laws…all I know is that when I was young, I was often stopped by policemen as they thought that me and my other cyclist friends were a nuisance for traffic and particularly for cars…how a cyclist could be a nuisance for other vehicles or create traffic problem?… Those police cops just wanted to extort money from us.'[68]

The response of commuters is to handle police high-handedness tactfully. According to a cargo driver, 'Just pay them Rs 50 and drive away. No need to waste time, as time is precious in this business.'[69] The motorcyclist says he prefers to not stop in front of queues of traffic at signals. Motorcyclists think that police constables are 'too lazy' and scrutinise only riders at the front.[70] A third approach, often used by those who lack the correct legal documentation, is to appear confident by establishing eye contact or staring at police officers. 'We cannot chase them too far as we are shackled by the limitations of our defined jurisdictions,' said the traffic police constable.[71]

Validity of Documents

The prevalence of corruption, practiced by police department officials, has meant that legal documents are often regarded worthless. For instance, vehicle certificates and driving licenses can be illegally obtained. When one respondent asked how he secured his driving licence, he said, 'I got the licence from a motor-training institute by paying Rs 500 (£3.14). It was in 1992.'[72] Even if drivers have all the required documents, due to law and order problems and the general security situation in Karachi, people prefer not to carry their original documents and normally keep a photocopy of their car registration document, computerised national identity cards (CNIC) and driving licence. For example, insurance certificates are commonly saleable items.

Many vehicle owners do not even update vehicle registration documents. According to the motorcyclist interviewed, 'Still it's not in my name. I use just the authority letter to drive it and to be honest with you, I am not driving it anymore. My younger brother, who is employed in a local hospital, is using it and interestingly as per the same authority letter.'[73]

The Motor Vehicle Ordinance of 1965 states that all vehicles require a valid fitness certificate to drive on the roads although usually, only drivers of commercial vehicles are targeted by inspectors. It is common perception that these certificates are obtained by paying a bribe to the vehicle department. The difficulty in getting a certificate through proper channels is cited as a major reason for the malpractice. The official fee for a fitness certificate is Rs 50 (£0.31) for six months, but I give Rs 1,000 (£6.30) to my contact there. If I did not pay [the] bribe, they would take a year to give me the certificate. The office is in Baldia Town (District West of Karachi) and you know that area is not safe. Also, we will waste our petrol and our trips would have an opportunity cost as well. So, it's better to spend Rs 1,000 and just forget about the rest… And now there is another mechanism to it. The personnel come to our place, at the hotel where we all sit, take Rs 1,200 (£7.56) per vehicle and deliver the certificate at our place.'[74] Because of environmental hazards, KCR rickshaws are not allowed to to be driven on the roads, although a limited number do it, as very few fitness certificates are inspected by the authorities. According to one rickshaw mechanic, 'Cylinder rickshaws are illegal now and are not allowed to ply on roads. They don't have fitness certificate as well.'[75]

Health and the Environment

Out of twenty-two megacities in Asia, Karachi has been declared the least environmental friendly because of its poor air quality, inferior transport system, and an inadequate sanitation network.[76] The most common forms of pollutants are sulphur oxides (SOx), nitrogen oxides (NOx), lead (Pb), and carbon monoxide (CO). According to the medical doctor interviewed, many trees have been cut down in Karachi, but new ones are not planted to replace them. 'The lungs of the city are not clean and the air-purifying mechanisms are being compromised. Karachi and Islamabad are the most polluted cities of Pakistan, but for different reasons. Karachi is polluted because of transport.'[77]

These pollutants can be lethal. 'In the presence of exogenous material, the human body can tolerate and perform to a certain level but not after that. It starts reacting in a variety of ways…chest infections, allergies and dermal problems…pulmonary diseases, asthma in children and chronic illnesses like cancers…an eye infection and other viral diseases. Conjunctivitis gets exacerbated in the presence of air pollution. [These] are the outcomes of congestion as caused by traffic…pollution in the air, is the basis of all dermal problems and allergies.' And besides air pollution, the high noise levels caused by the constant honking of horns, ageing engines, KCR rickshaws, pressure horns, ambulance sirens, and police sirens to clear the way for VIPs, is a source of constant stress for drivers, while long hours of driving can also result in physical ailments such as backache and arthritis. High blood pressure is the long-term effect of high noise levels.

There are other psychological repercussions as well. In the short term, behavioural changes can be observed and being intolerant is one of those.[78] Another respondent confirmed this opinion. 'Traffic congestion has also affected attitudes of the drivers of the vehicles. They are more impatient, aggressive, and always remain eager to express road rage through violence. Probably, they are suffering from continuous traffic fatigue.'[79] Though there have been no serious studies conducted on the financial repercussions of environmental degradation due to transport problems, nevertheless, the medical doctor interviewed thinks that these problems can result in economic and productivity losses. 'An asthma patient cannot climb the staircase and a patient suffering from cardiac illness needs to take more rest. Moreover, both have to spend time waiting for doctors/consultants, periodically. So, at one level, productivity declines and on another level, a considerable amount of money is spent on medical care.'[80]

A Brief Note on Women's Problems

Over the years, women's participation in public spheres has increased a great deal, but the design of buses remains unchanged: the space is segregated with two-thirds for male passengers and one-third for women. In the 1981 census, the total population of Karachi Division was reported as 5.4 million with 2.95 million men and 2.45 million women. The 1998 census (the most recent census done in Pakistan) estimated the total population at 9.8 million, with approximately 5.2 million men and 4.5 million women.[81]

The upward shift in marriageable age and an increase in the number of unmarried girls, employment, literacy rates and educational achievements, illustrate the transitional nature of women's issues in Karachi. Surveys show that the desire for job security is slowly replacing the concept of security associated with marriage. Women no longer only aspire to literacy; they also aspire to perform well in the educational field. Nevertheless, the increased participation of women in public spheres is not adequately reflected in the transport sector. 'Yes, we do allow men to sit on women-only seats, as it is not feasible to ply a half-occupied vehicle. But as soon as a woman enters the vehicle, men go to the back seats.'[82]

Table 5.3: Women-only Selected Demographic Indicators (%)		
KARACHI WOMEN	1981	1998
Total married	66.06	59.18
Married	37.42	28.19
Total employed	3.71	3.45
Total literate	48.84	62.88
Educational attainment	20.87	27.7
Divorced	0.23	0.51
Source: FBS various		

These problems are not confined to buses. One respondent confirmed that women travelling in rickshaws (and Qingqis, previously) are always harassed by crossing motorists and motorcyclists. The nature of the harassment varies from constant staring to passing remarks. 'It's a common complaint by women commuters. We can avoid it by having purdah (a covering or veil) in rickshaws as it is practised in Quetta and Peshawar.'[83] However, one female passenger interviewed for this study said that she never experiences these issues. 'I don't have any problems. I never faced sexual or any harassment otherwise, and never got robbed. I think that if women are politically trained and conscious, they can solve such issues very easily.'[84] In addition, from the interviews conducted by the Urban Resource Centre[85] with female passengers, it can be deduced that the availability of public transport to their place of work is the prime determinant for many women's choice of jobs.

Perceptions of Attitudes

Many respondents highlighted issues relating to the perceived irrational attitudes of drivers and the bad manners of younger people and commuters. A lack of observance of laws was also quoted often. Many cited that drivers do not follow rules or respect traffic signals, and that they change driving lanes irregularly. They felt that pedestrians walked on roads and crossed wherever they want to. 'It's because of our attitude. We don't respect laws.'[86]

The use of mobile phones is also cited as a source of trouble on the roads. The ambulance driver interviewed felt that using phones while driving makes drivers careless with regards to emergency vehicles. An ambulance driver states, 'There is an entire new generation of wired youngsters who have headsets plugged in their ears and they don't listen or care less for the hooter of a rushing ambulance…they are insensitive to the emergency situation we deal with.'[87]

A couple of respondents felt that having a formal education does not necessarily corelate with decent driving behaviour. According to one respondent, 'Most traffic problems are caused by educated but disrespectful and intolerant drivers. You can see the educated people in flashy cars using their mobile phones while driving.'[88] The cargo driver interviewed had a similar opinion: 'They (car drivers) are the most intolerant people of all. If by any chance I drive into the extreme left-hand lane, they honk their horns, flash their headlights, and when there is a delay in clearing the lane, they hurl abuse at us.'[89]

Occupying the wrong lane while driving creates difficulties for emergency services operators. 'First of all it is difficult to find a way in traffic as all the lanes are occupied by all. And if by any chance we get our way, we are usually followed by speeding motorcyclists and car drivers. They treat our clearing of the path as an opportunity to drive out of the rush quickly. But they don't understand that we have to constantly change lanes and we often have to apply brakes abruptly. As a result, they often collide with us and cause damage to the ambulance, as well as their own vehicle.'[90]

Besides this, the attitude of police officials is not viewed as helpful by the emergency services: 'They [police constables] are insensitive souls. They tend to ignore the sound of sirens and hooters. They just turn their face and regulate the traffic as usual.'[91] People felt that easy access to loans has also modified the behaviour of drivers, who, they feel, do not value their vehicle assets. According to one mechanic, 'Thirteen years ago, my clientele consisted of more mature people who purchased cars using hard-earned money and hence they valued their asset more. Now…car owners…are less sensitive about their car, human lives and the value of money…I also find people becoming more careless about speeding and driving more rashly, compared to before.'[92]

Security

In a recent statement, Karachi's police chief admitted that despite Operation Karachi,[93] street crime remains unabated. He was of the view that a police force of 30,000 officials is not enough to control street crime in the city.[94] The respondents for this chapter are of the same view and this has an impact on their choice of transport routes and timings—the situation demands extra vigilance daily. 'I take care of timings, change the routes, and try to get myself updated about the evolving scenarios…after dusk I prefer not to go to sensitive areas of Karachi.'[95]

According to data from the Citizens-Police Liaison Committee,[96] 172 police officers were killed in 2013; 122 in 2012; and 53 in 2011. Meanwhile, from 1992 to 2010 around 250 police officers were gunned down in Karachi.[97] 'Over the years, a lot of our comrades were targeted, and the phenomenon remains unabated,'[98] said an officer of the traffic police. '[The] law and order situation [petty crime] is different to the security situation [terrorism] of the city. A lot of times, our passengers are deprived of their respective belongings and valuables. Sometimes it seems to be an insider job, but I cannot say for sure. You need to understand that we cannot check every embarking passenger.'[99]

A couple of respondents mentioned that they have recognised and adapted to the dynamics of working in certain areas of Karachi, including one taxi driver: 'I am up at 8:00 a.m. in the morning and reach the roads, but don't do business until after dusk. I don't go to some parts of Malir, Orangi, Korangi,

Manghopir, New Karachi, and Shershah. Due to the law and order situation of the city, we all go home by evening.'[100]

Road Accidents

Two major causes of accidents are motorcycles and bus/minibuses.[101] Motorcyclists account for 37.7 per cent of accidents in Karachi. In the first seven months of 2015, news reports indicate that 34 accidents claimed 128 lives on the streets of the city, while 117 people were injured.[102]

When discussing these figures, the interviewed police officer was of the opinion that 'Those who do not observe laws are responsible for those accidents.'[103] On the other hand, one car mechanic blamed the rise in new luxury cars on roads for the rise in the number of accidents.[104] For accidents on the highways, a different reason was cited: lack of sleep and fatigue.

According to a bus service manager, 'For the long routes, we usually have two drivers. While one driver drives for eight to nine hours, the other sleeps. Most accidents occur because a single driver is stretched to his limits.'[105]

With the increasing number of women now in workspaces, the trend of employing pick-and-drop services on a fixed monthly payment is also becoming popular. Commuting becomes relatively affordable and hassle-free for women. However, these are time-bound services and drivers are usually hard pressed against the clock. They resort to speeding and irresponsible driving. 'I manage by driving fast, changing lanes, and through honking', said one driver?[106]

Similar views were expressed by an intercity bus service manager, who drafts the bus schedule. 'Time lost because of traffic jams is made up by speeding', he said. 'For instance, during rush hours it takes two hours to drive from Cantonment Station to Sohrab Goth, while in non-rush hours it takes only an hour.'[107]

* * * *

A number of different activities create or influence the transport and traffic scene in Karachi. Almost all of them also influence land-use within the more congested areas of the city. They are closely interconnected, but they are not considered collectively in the official planning process in the city and this is one of the major causes for the failure of most traffic management and engineering projects. Many of the stakeholders (for instance, spare parts manufacturers), do not form part of academic courses on planning, land use, and transport.

Table 5.4: Vehicle Involvement Injury Severity 2008–13						
Type of Vehicle	Fatal 2008	Fatal 2009	Fatal 2010	Fatal 2011	Fatal 2012	Fatal 2013
Motorbike	505	522	492	666	705	642
Mini Van/Coaster	52	81	57	68	42	26
Bus/Minibus / Coach	226	243	253	190	183	157
Truck	134	96	118	89	82	73
Taxi	11	17	16	14	5	8
Bicycle	28	26	39	25	25	13
Car	182	182	163	167	157	160
Water/Oil Tanker	39	36	58	49	36	45
Rickshaw	22	28	42	56	53	40
Dumper	51	62	89	59	49	31
Trailer	72	67	62	75	69	65
Loading Pickup	74	86	73	57	67	45
Others	207	273	157	1	4	6
Animal Cart			7	2	1	1
Push Cart			2	0	53	32
Train			47	27	0	8
Total	1603	1719	1675	1545	1531	1352
Public Transport	311	369	400	328	283	231
Goods Vehicle	370	347	368	329	236	214

Table 5.5: Road Traffic Injury Research & Prevention Centre, Results from 2008 to 2012

DISPOSAL

Disposal	Average	2008 to 2012	%
Minor	24,534	12,2670	75
Serious	6875	34,376	21
Fatal	1208	6040	4
Total	32,617	163,086	100

HOSPITAL-WISE RESULTS

Centre	Average	2008 to 2012	%
JPMC	13,201	66,005	40
LNH	1100	5499	3
AKU	766	3830	2
ASH	9960	49,798	31
CHK	7547	37,954	23
Total	32,604	163,086	100

GENDER-WISE RESULTS

Gender	Average	2008 to 2012	%
Male	28,241	141,204	87
Female	4376	21,882	13
Total	32,617	163,086	100

ROAD USER GROUP

Road User Group	Injury	%	Fatal	%	Total
Rider/Pillion Rider	96517	61	2460	41	98977
Pedestrian	36921	24	2308	38	39229
Passengers	18079	12	758	13	18837
Drivers	4592	3	225	4	4817
Unknown	937	1	289	5	1226
Total	157046	100	6040	100	163086

Table 5.5 (continued)

VEHICLE INVOLVEMENT IN INJURY			
Vehicle Involvement	Average	2008 to 2012	%
Motorbike	25163	125,813	61
Minivan/Coaster	1163	5815	3
Bus/Minibus/Coach	2660	13,298	6
Truck	1024	5121	3
Taxi	467	2336	1
Bicycle	571	2855	1
Car	4739	23,695	12
Water/Oil Tanker	221	1106	1
Rickshaw	2616	13,080	6
Dumper	304	1522	1
Trailer	457	2287	1
Loading Pickup	1451	7256	4
Animal Cart	62	309	0
Push Cart	24	122	0
Train	36	182	0
Total	40959	204,797	100
Public Transport	6906	34,529	17
Goods Vehicle	3156	15,780	8

Box 5.1: Vehicle Hijacking in Karachi

Karachi has become a scoreboard for hijacked cars and motorcycles. It is like watching a cricket match. Every day the score increases, and hapless losers are shunted from pillar to post. All that the relevant authorities do is to start comparing the crime rate in Karachi with those of London and New York. Why do we have to do this? For us to lose a single vehicle is very traumatic. Police statistics in this respect are shady. Most of the time it appears that they are themselves involved. If a report is lodged with the police, and the vehicle is found, the accessories are often found missing. But this is not the end. If the palms of policemen are not greased, to claim your car, you have to face presumptions like the vehicle may have been used for transporting illicit drugs or weapons. It is a sad commentary on the way the metropolis of Karachi has acquired a reputation for it. If the property of an average citizen cannot be safeguarded, what is the function of the guardians of law who have been assigned the sacred duty to protect the citizens? The headline of a *Dawn* report of June 30 says: 41 vehicles taken away (9 cars, 32 motorbikes). If we take the average price of a car at Rs 300,000, it comes to Rs 2,700,000. Thirty-two motorbikes at the average rate of Rs 30,000 each will cost Rs 960,000—the total being Rs 3,660,000. This is just one day's yield. The yearly yield comes to Rs 1,335,900,000 plus the cash and jewelry on person. Even the largest industry in Pakistan has yet to post such a gigantic 'profit'. Who are the beneficiaries of this thriving industry is not difficult to imagine. It is about time something tangible was done by the government to help Karachi rid itself of this menace.

Source: Extract from *Dawn*, 2004.

Box 5.2: Cargo-Driver Diaries

These policemen are always looking to extort money from us. Once, my other cargo-carrier driver was stopped by a traffic constable near Ayesha Bawany Academy at Shahrah-e-Faisal. After scrutinising all the documents, he said that the fitness certificate was not duly stamped, and the truck would be impounded. The driver had an altercation with the police officer and in a much-irritated state of mind he called me up so that I could speak to the police officer. I tried to convince him that it's a mistake by the government official and I would rectify it at the first possible convenience. He insisted on *challan* (receipt for payment) and I said to him, 'Go ahead, but I will ask the driver to park it in such a way that the entire artery of Shahrah-e-Faisal gets blocked.' Since he was out for money he back stepped and the entire episode of half an hour was concluded in a Rs 150 (£0.94) bribe to that constable (…) It's a routine affair (…) Sometimes they ask for documents and sometimes object to side mirrors. They just need money.

Source: Interview with a cargo-carrier driver, 28 August 2015.

Box 5.3: Obtaining Route Permits: A Trick of Technology

Q: How do you make the route permits for Khyber Pakhtunkhwa or Punjab? It must take a lot of your time.

A: I know the trick of making a route permit for every other province from here!

Q: How do you perform this magic?

A: It's technology and contacts. Let me explain. Since I am a resident of Sindh province so a route permit for Sindh is not an issue and that's my primary document. Remember that all other route permits will be based on that primary document. My broker here in Sindh has contacts in all other provinces. So, I take a picture of my Sindh route permit and WhatsApp it (send via mobile phone) to his contact, to let's say in Peshawar. My Sindh agent will call him and before entering Peshawar City, I w¹ll get the route permit for Khyber Pakhtunkhwa, as made by the Peshawar agent. Peshawar police are very strict and if you don't have the permit, they can fine up to Rs 6,000 (£37.79) and could also confiscate the truck.

Source: Interview with a cargo driver, 28 August 2015.

Box 5.4: Besides Road Rage

Yes, they used to bother us a lot and treat us as illiterate and poor. But I want to tell you that I am no illiterate. I have a diploma in *hikmat* (an indigenous method of treating aliments) from Hamdard University. Once I was in an Urdu-speaking dominated neighbourhood in Malir, to drop a consignment of medicines there. The street was narrow and a push-cart vendor selling *haleem* (a stew popular in the Middle East, Central Asia, Pakistan, and India) had blocked the passage. I honked at him to clear the way. The seller waved his hand but made no attempts to move. When I honked for the third time, the *haleem*-seller took out a gun from his wooden money box, ran towards me, and put it to my forehead. I was forced to reverse my truck back onto the main road. But I feel the situation has improved a lot after the Karachi operation.

Source: Interview with a cargo driver, 28 August 2015.

Box 5.5: Theft from a Moving Vehicle

On highways, we feel like *jesey machli paani maen aa jaae* (a fish in a pond). Nobody bothers us except that excise people ask for tax documents which we usually have. We are much more relaxed on highways. But goods are stolen from the containers and that too from the moving vehicle. It usually happens in the night. Big trucks do not have the facility of seeing exactly behind the container. So, the thieves taking advantage of the darkness of night attach a small vehicle to the container so the speed of both the vehicles are synchronised. Then one person unlocks the container and throws the items into the Suzuki pickup. A lot of containers are deprived of their goods by the same method. We now don't fix or weld the container with the chassis (the load-bearing framework of an artificial object) but rotate it 180 degrees through cranes so that the door of the container is blocked with the body of the truck, just behind the driver. That's the only solution as goods worth millions of rupees are involved.

Source: Interview with a cargo driver, 28 August 2015.

6

Actors in the Transport Drama of Karachi

Mansoor Raza

In the previous chapter, we discussed activities that are part of the overall Karachi transport scene. These were derived from interviews of various residents of the city. This chapter consists of case studies of the lives of these denizens, as told by them. They tell us not only of their lives, but also of the nature of Karachi's governance system and their relationship with it, along with their own development. The case studies also give us some insight into the values of Karachi's society and its underbelly. The individuals interviewed come from different ethnicities and remind us of the diversity that is an important part of Karachi's complex mosaic.

Jamil: A Taxi Driver

Jamil hails from Rahim Yar Khan, in Punjab. His father came to Karachi in 1973 looking for work. Jamil was only a year old at that time. His father started working as a mason in North Nazimabad. His maternal uncle, who used to be a mason too, began driving a taxi in 1991–92. He had purchased the car in cash for Rs 75,000. Jamil also started driving a taxi in 1993. He learnt driving from an *ustad* but received his license from a motor-training institute in 1992, by paying Rs 500. He and other people of his village live in a clan-based neighbourhood; they have 30–40 households in North Nazimabad.

Jamil was 20 years old when he started driving a taxi. He did not know his way around town, but he recalls that the biggest advantage in those days was that of functional meters. 'If we didn't know the route, or the distance to the destination, the passengers used to guide us and they paid according to the meter. In fact, they used to leave tips as well,' he remembers.

So why was the use of meters abandoned? 'Meters have disappeared because of the fluctuation in petrol prices and also because the vehicle fitness inspection system fell prey to corruption,' he says. 'It was some 10 to 12 years back when the meter system fell apart. First of all, there were complaints of meter tampering by passengers, which was not far from the truth. Secondly, when meters were charging at Rs 10, or Rs 12 per kilometre, the petrol price was Rs 72/litre. Then, the petrol prices rose to Rs 108 per litre. How could one operate on Rs 10, or Rs 12 per kilometre then? Thirdly, the authorities allowed us to drive taxis without functional meters. Nobody monitored us, so it became acceptable to operate a taxi without meter. Recently, the police have started asking about meters again.' Commenting on the lack of regulation in the traffic department, he says that the mandatory fitness certificate of a vehicle can be acquired by bribing the vehicle department personnel. The official fee for fitness is Rs 50 for six months, but Jamil pays Rs 1,000 to his contact there.

'If I did not pay a bribe, they would take a year to give me the certificate,' he says. 'The office is in Baldia Town (District West of Karachi) and you know that area is not safe. Also, we will waste our petrol and our trips there would have an opportunity cost as well. So, it's better to spend Rs 1,000 and just forget about the rest... And now there is another mechanism to it. The personnel come to our place, at the hotel where we all sit, take Rs 1,200 (£7.53) per vehicle and deliver the certificate to our place.'

He feels the police are equally corrupt and break laws to make some extra cash.

'Go to Sohrab Goth in the morning and you will get to know the reality yourselves. From 5:00 to 8:00/9:00 in the morning, they block all the routes into Karachi and take bribes from all the passengers and taxi drivers coming in from upcountry.' The overall traffic situation is dismal in his opinion. 'The underpasses and overhead bridges do not help us. Everybody is forced to come from the wrong side to save fuel. In some places, even the traffic police facilitate that movement. I also think that the ever-increasing number of vehicles on the road will make these bridges and underpasses run out of space soon.'

I ask him if he knows anything about the 'cutting' business, which he describes in detail. He says that 'taxi-cutting' is rampant in Manghopir and Kati Pahari. Scrap sellers buy old taxis for Rs 45,000 to Rs 50,000, take out the spare parts and scrap the rest. Usually, cab drivers who are leaving the business sell their taxis to these scrap dealers. The spare parts and anything useful, are then sold and the rest goes to iron scrappers. This is done for taxis and old cars. New cars, which are stolen are 'cut' in Shershah. According to Jamil, as soon as a stolen car arrives in these huge, heavily guarded premises in Shershah, they are completely taken apart within 15 minutes. Those separated parts are sold in shops just outside these premises, in the main Shershah market.

Jamil gets up at 8 a.m. and is on the road soon after, but he avoids driving after dusk. 'The law and order situation in the city sends all of us home by evening,' he says. He also avoids going to some parts of Malir, Orangi Town, Korangi, Manghopir, New Karachi, and Shershah areas. The dwindling business has led him to think of selling his taxi and looking for a job as a domestic servant. 'I need Rs 5,000 per month to pay the loan instalment. I purchased the taxi some three years ago, for Rs 250,000. I have paid back almost all the amount, except Rs 30,000, which I need to pay back in six months,' he says. 'There is even less business for taxis these days as people prefer to use the cheaper Qingqis over taxis. This is unfair to us. These Qingqis do not have route permits, or vehicle fitness certificates and the drivers are also usually young and inexperienced.' He regrets coming to Karachi in the wake of diminishing returns. 'Had we not migrated, we would have been better off. We would have our own livestock, our own place and our own people. Here, I pay Rs 7,000 per month (inclusive of utilities) in rent. Business is not good, and I have had to pull my children out of school.'

Khalid: A Mechanic and Panel Beater

Khalid's parents are from Attock, in Punjab. They moved to Karachi looking for better opportunities, but his father remained jobless. His mother worked as a maid in nearby bungalows, in North Nazimabad, to provide for the family. His father died in 1982, when Khalid was only 10 years old. He did his matriculation and joined an *ustad* [teacher] to learn how to mend a car; he used to receive a stipend from the *ustad*. He worked for him for nearly five years and then came to Nazimabad to start working on his own; he got married in 2002.

Khalid's business is not very profitable. He charges Rs 10,000 for a ten-day job of 'denting' (panel beating), at a rate of Rs 1,000 per day. 'Out of that thousand rupees in a day, I have to give some money to the assistants, buy material, and pay the bill for electricity as well,' he says. The electricity tariff is fixed for shops, but the car-painting jobs suffer from the frequent electricity outages as the machinery operates on electric power.

I ask him about any harassment or extortion from either the police, or political parties. 'The police do not pay for labour and material. We have to do their jobs for free,' he tells me. 'The political parties used to force us to pay a sort of protection money in the name of donation. This practice has been discontinued after the Karachi Operation,' he says.

Khalid has observed more congestion on the roads. 'Qingqis are a problem but at the same time it is convenient for the passengers as they can travel cheaply and with the luxury of having a seat as well,' he says. 'We need bigger buses to counter that rush.' In his opinion, speeding luxury cars cause more traffic accidents than any other vehicles.

Since a lot of reconditioned cars are on the road these days, I want to know if the spare parts are easily available. Khalid tells me that it used to be difficult but no more. He cites the availability of spare parts to be a big reason behind the popularity of Suzuki cars. 'Their parts are cheap and readily available in every area of Pakistan. It helps in raising people's standard of living as those who have motorcycles can easily purchase second-hand Suzuki cars.' Finally, Khalid says that the poor remain on the fringes of the transport system in Karachi and he feels that the government must act to improve this situation.

Nimroz: A Rickshaw Mechanic

Nimroz's family was displaced from Torghar, in Khyber Pakhtunkhwa, in 1973, when the Tarbela Dam was constructed. Some members of his clan, including his parents, came to Karachi and settled in Khamosh Colony and Patel Para. Nimroz's father became a rickshaw driver. He wanted his son to study, but Nimroz was more interested in the engineering of rickshaws. *Ustads* were highly respected in his community, therefore, he also wanted to become an *ustad*. It took him seven years to learn the trade, earning a paltry *aath aanas* (50 paisas) daily. After his training was over, he started out from Khamosh Colony on his own. He has been in this trade for the last twenty-five years.

He gives me a detailed description of the kind of rickshaws that are available in Karachi. 'Cylinder rickshaws are outlawed now and are not allowed on roads. They do not have fitness certificates as well. They are two-stroke rickshaws called KCR. Initially, they were imported from Turkey by Khawaja Autos. Then an assembly plant was put up in Kashmore and provided a controlled supply. In contrast, the supply of CNG rickshaws is unregulated and they have flooded the market. The same is true for Qingqis,' he says. 'Do you repair Qingqis as well?' I ask. He says no. 'Qingqis are different. They are just motorcycles with a passenger carrier fitted onto them.'

The situation has changed for rickshaws over the years. 'The vehicle-to-passenger ratio has changed a lot. Earlier, it used to be one rickshaw for every two passengers. Now there are ten rickshaws for one passenger,' he observes. Apparently, rickshaw spare parts are easily available. 'The CNG rickshaws are assembled here so there are no worries about the spare parts. The parts are from China and are also copied here. I am sure you know how our people excel at copying. Spare parts of KCR are available but with greater difficulty.'

I want to know if the two-stroke rickshaws were more profitable than the CNG rickshaws. He denies this right away. 'The CNG rickshaws are obviously more profitable. A CNG rickshaw owner can earn up to Rs 1,400 a day. In contrast, a KCR rickshaw driver can earn a maximum of Rs 500 per day. This difference is due to the ever-rising price of petrol. Two of my three sons are CNG rickshaw drivers. Neither of them wanted to learn to be mechanics, as the occupation no longer has any charm/allure to it.'

I ask him to elaborate on how his business has suffered. 'Our business has decreased. Earlier people used to insist on hiring the services of an *ustad* to fix their vehicles. Now, they look for cheap options. Over the years, rickshaw drivers have picked up some mechanical skills as well. So, they do not go to mechanics for smaller problems and instead fix them on their own. There is no growth in this occupation and it is no longer profitable—people are less quality-conscious now.'

Asif: A Taxi Mechanic

Asif owns an auto workshop in the Paharganj area and is an expert in repairing taxis. He speaks in clear Urdu and a few words in English. 'Where did you pick up English?' I ask in amazement. 'I went to school until class five,' he replies. He belongs to a Pashtun family that migrated from Kala Dhaka to Karachi and settled in Hussain d'Silva Town, in North Nazimabad. Conditions did not enable him to continue with his education, and so his choice of profession was my next point of interest. 'I used to frequent a rickshaw stand near my house when I was a kid,' he says. 'I developed an interest in the mechanics of automobiles and later started working on taxis.'

Asif started work under an *ustad* in 1996; he earned Rs 5 per day and meals. By the time he left that garage four years later, his earnings had risen to Rs 50 a day. 'Why did you leave your *ustad*?' I ask, since the tradition of commitment is strong among the working class. But in Asif's case, it was in fact the *ustad* who moved to Dubai and left Asif to work independently.

He started his own workshop in 2002, in Paharganj and is satisfied with the income it is generating. Now he has an apprentice of his own, whom he pays Rs 30 per day. The rapid evolution of technology does not bother Asif. 'Most taxis are still internal combustion engines, so I don't face any major issues,' he says. 'I have also learnt to repair EFI (electronic fuel injection) engines. I have developed a certain level of expertise on engines and that is why people hire me to repair generators as well. I picked it all up while on the job, with some guidance and trial and error experimentation.'

Along with technology, Asif has also picked up a good sense of the materials and their availability. He feels that the business of scrapping is very supportive for this work as it makes repair and maintenance affordable and time-efficient. Most of the spare parts are available at the famous Shershah market in Karachi. He describes this material as scrap, or second-hand, but of reasonable quality, except for the Chinese goods which he finds to be far inferior. His technical knowledge comes to the fore in this area too. 'Availability of spare parts is not an issue any more with the advancement of technology,' he says. 'One can search on the Internet and order these from Dubai.'

I ask him if he thinks old and dilapidated taxis contribute to pollution and traffic jams in the city. He does not think so. 'In my opinion, only bank managers are responsible for the traffic chaos in Karachi,' he says. 'Taxis and old cars have always been there. These bank managers have extended car loans left, right, and centre just to meet their targets and have increased the traffic volume manifolds. They are just profiteers and salesmen with no sense of moral responsibility. Banks should be blamed for Karachi's traffic woes.' In future, he wants to move back to his native town, Kala Dhaka, which has been carved into a district now. 'I am sure I will be able to do something there. The chaotic pace of city life has become unbearable for me.'

George: A Traffic Police Officer

Traffic officer George's parents were farm labourers in Gujranwala and came to Karachi many years ago in search of a decent livelihood. Karachi attracted them because of the job opportunities available here at the time and with some of their family members initially providing them shelter, they were able to settle down in the metropolis. George, who longed for a government job, was compelled initially to take up as a tailor in Defence Housing Authority (DHA) and later in North Nazimabad. 'I was earning well in that trade, but I wanted to get a government job, which I finally did, in 1994', he says.

When asked if he paid a bribe to get the job, George denies it, but stops short of elaborating on how he did get the job. I inquire if he was properly trained for traffic handling. 'Yes, quite a few times,' he says. 'I received training in 1995 at first. It was a nine-month exhaustive training on my role as traffic officer and the responsibilities associated with it. Actually, a sense of responsibility comes with training depending on your designation. Whenever someone's rank or designation changes, he receives further training for it accordingly.'

I then ask him which area of the city he considers the toughest when it comes to manning traffic. 'Sohrab Goth is the toughest because of heavy traffic and a different type of crowd,' replies George. 'It was here that I was posted first and later at Gulberg. When Gulberg was declared a politically sensitive area, I found it better to get myself transferred back to Sohrab Goth and remained posted there for three years. From there on, it is a story of continuous transfers. I have served in New Karachi, Tariq Road, back in New Karachi, and many other places. In 2005, I was promoted from *hawaldar* [constable] to head constable and again received training at the Police Training Camp at Baldia Colony.'

Is it a coincidence that most of his postings have been closer to his residence in North Nazimabad? 'I prefer to be posted near my house here, in North Nazimabad, to avoid traffic problems,' says George, diplomatically. Endorsing my views that the traffic problems have increased in Karachi, he says it is 'Mainly due to the growing number of vehicles on the roads. This has also exacerbated lawlessness. No one follows the law. Trust me, the majority of drivers here, violate traffic signals.'

However, when reminded that drivers who break the law are often let off the hook by bribe-taking policemen, George appears sympathetic towards the police. 'Seventy per cent of policemen do not take bribes,' he says. 'It is just 30 per cent who bring a bad name to the police force. Having said that, we must also consider the reasons why the police have become notorious. An ordinary police constable cannot run his kitchen on a meagre amount of Rs 15,000 (£94.36) or Rs 17,000 (£106.94) per month.' George argues that better salaries can put an end to the menace of bribery in the police force. 'Have you ever questioned why the motorway police in Punjab do not take bribes?' he asks. 'Their salary is one of the main reasons; the salary of a constable there is Rs 30,000 (£188.85) per month. It's almost double the amount.'

He also cited Qingqis as contributing to traffic congestion in the city, as its drivers constantly violate the one-way rule. I ask him if more signal-free corridors are the answer. 'No,' he says. 'It is not a matter of corridors being signal-free. It is just a matter of observing the discipline of traffic and to respect the law of the land. I believe the roads do not have the capacity to absorb the ever-increasing number of vehicles. Lack of parking space in the city is another issue. Have you ever observed that all these newly constructed shopping malls and housing complexes do not provide enough parking space and as a result, people have occupied streets and lanes in the city for parking their vehicles?'

I ask him how the performance of traffic policemen is monitored. 'My performance is monitored by my seniors which is a part of their duty. It is monitored through training, assessing our performance, we have had drives against tinted glasses, the compulsory use of helmets, and proper number plates. A big indicator is the number of *challans* (receipts for payment) issued during those campaigns. Also, we report to our respective stations on a daily basis.' But despite all this, the number of accidents in the city is at an alarming level, I remind him. 'Those who do not observe the law are responsible for those accidents,' he says. When probed over whether traffic policemen receive any commission, or percentage of the *challans* issued, George denies the existence of any such practice.

I ask him about the challenges traffic police officers face in the line of duty. 'Insecurity,' he says at once. 'Over the years, a lot of our fellow traffic policemen have been targeted by snipers and such violence remains unchecked. Also, we cannot chase a violator beyond our duty point and we feel handicapped because of our defined jurisdictions.'

Jawed: An Intercity Bus Service Manager

Currently in his early 30s, Jawed was born in Rahim Yar Khan. As an adult, he migrated to Lahore to work as a tailor and acquired embroidery skills. In 2008, his maternal uncle, who was employed in the Blue Lines (intercity) Coach Service, brought him to Karachi to work for the company. Jawed was trained on the job and was initially assigned to finding customers for the Blue Line. Later, he became the manager of the booking office.

His company currently has eight coaches and four vans. There are five Blue Line offices in the city and all have a minimum quota for passengers. If a particular office sees a rise in demand, it negotiates with the other offices. These buses travel to Jacobabad, Dera Murad Jamali, and Lahore.

According to Jawed, the fares range from Rs 700 to Rs 2,000. For instance, they charge Rs 700 from Karachi to Thatta, Rs 800 to Jacobabad, Rs 900 to Dera Murad Jamali, and Rs 2,000 to Lahore. But it varies as well. For instance, during Eid holidays, when people want to travel to their villages, the fare from Karachi to Jacobabad rises to Rs 1,300 per passenger, he informs me. The 46-seater buses are almost always full. 'Most of the time, buses and coaches are 95 per cent occupied, except for on holidays,' Jawed tells me.

However, there are no proper bus terminals for these buses. 'We used to park right here in front of this booking office,' says Jawed. 'Nowadays, the police have tightened controls, so we park under Saddar Bridge,' he says. This gives us only 10 minutes to ask passengers to get onto the bus. We have been asked to abolish the *addas* (terminals) we have in the city. The new terminal at Sabzi Mandi is too far away and is not viable for most of our potential passengers. On the other hand, the private terminal at the same place is very expensive and we cannot afford to use it. I think that there should be a terminal at Cantonment Station as well.' He tells me that there is a joint association of intercity bus companies that can make demands like these to the government, but it concerns itself with major issues. For example, the association took up the issue of parking with the High Court recently, he tells me.

I ask how many drivers they employ on each trip, due to the long distances involved. 'For the long routes we usually have two drivers,' he says. While one drives for eight to nine hours, the other sleeps. Most accidents happen because a single driver is stretched to his limits. Usually, the accompanying driver is an apprentice... These apprentices often do not have driving licenses, though the main driver with the responsibility for the vehicle, does have driving a license.'

The drivers are employed on a daily basis. 'For instance, a driver is paid Rs 1,500 to drive to and from Jacobabad, which is a 24-hour duty cycle,' he says. Jawed reports that the bus companies do not have any insurance. Neither the passengers, nor the drivers or vehicles are insured. He feels that this should change: 'It gives us financial protection against accidents and other such mishaps.'

I ask him if these buses are robbed while en route. He says that they are. 'Sometimes, these appear to be insider jobs, but I cannot say for sure. You need to understand that we cannot check every passenger.' Jawed also reports that most often, the police take bribes from them at Al-Asif Square.

I ask him why these buses are notorious for speeding. He says it happens because the driver is trying to make up for time lost waiting in traffic inside the cities. 'During rush hours, the normal one-hour distance from Cantonment Station to Sohrab Goth stretches to two hours,' he says. 'Heavy traffic is not allowed on the Lyari Expressway. We would save a lot of time if it were allowed.'

Jawed speaks of the security threat his business faces in Sindh. 'Many routes are difficult for us because of highwaymen. Dadu–Ranipur is a dangerous route. Similarly, the Sukkur–Shikarpur route is notorious for armed robberies,' he informs me. 'We usually employ Baloch (i.e. local) drivers on the Jacobabad route, and that is the only safety measure we have. We rely on them to know the environment and the people in the area.'

Faisal: A Male Passenger

Faisal is a 25-year-old student at the Federal Urdu University, Karachi. His father migrated from Haripur, Hazara, in Khyber Pakhtunkhwa. He lives in Baldia Town in western Karachi and travels every day to I.I. Chundrigar Road in the south. Faisal has been using public transport for ten years and he mostly uses buses and auto rickshaws (popularly known as autos).

'An auto is good because it is open on two sides and one does not feel suffocated,' he says. 'The old-style Mazda taxis are not airy. Yellow cabs are spacious, but their fares are too high.'

He does not like travelling by minibus very much. 'Riding minibuses is a matter of convenience, though they have the disadvantage of being congested,' he says. 'Besides, this lack of space provides perfect opportunities for sexual harassment. When I was an adolescent, a Pathan had attempted to sexually abuse me...the other disadvantage of a minibus is that the passengers' clothes get dirty and crumpled. The little space forces passengers to lean against each other or the walls and seats of the bus,' he continues. 'The conductors are usually ill-mannered too. They do not know how to talk with elders and they often misbehave with women. They abuse and make fun of transgender people as well.' Still, he concedes that the advantage of travelling by bus is that it offers concessional fares to students.

I ask him how much time he spends on the road in a day. 'On any single day, it is normal to spend two-and-a-half hours on the road just to go to the office and come back home,' he says. 'I spend Rs 38 per day in fares.' The fare has risen sharply over the last decade. He remembers when it used to be less than or around Rs 10.

'To make the situation worse, the fares are increasing but the condition of the buses is deteriorating to the extent that if it rains, water drips from the roofs. The mud gets inside the buses and spoils our clothes.' He agrees that having a motorcycle would be a great advantage. 'It would save time and money and give me a sense of freedom,' he says. 'I would be able to manoeuvre my own way in response, say, to the law and order situation of the city and according to my personal needs.'

Judging by his dislike for travelling by bus, I ask him how he prefers to travel when he is with family. 'I mostly use an auto when I am with family,' he replies. 'Even if the women have to travel without any male escort, I advise them to hire an auto and not take the coach, bus or minibus.'

I want to know if Qingqis are an option for him. 'A dangerous option,' he says. 'Mostly young boys drive Qingqis that have no number plates, or chassis numbers. They do not have permissions or driving licenses. It is not at all safe and these are mostly stolen motorcycles being converted into Qingqis. They remain popular only because they are cheap and ply on routes where buses and minibuses are not operative.'

His recommendations to improve the situation are simple: 'The monopoly of a single ethnic group on the transport system should be broken. Fares need to be reduced because buses run on CNG, but their operators charge fares based on diesel prices. The issuance of vehicle fitness certificates needs to be monitored.'

Naghma: A Female Passenger

Young Naghma is an independent researcher and political activist. She lives in Model Colony, Karachi and has recently graduated from the University of Karachi. She suffers from a fear of driving and travels by auto rickshaw. On average, she spends Rs 2,000 per day on rickshaw fares.

She has been scared of driving ever since she lost her father in a road accident in 2012—one that left her brother critically injured. 'My father and my brother were travelling in a car on the link road that connects Malir Cantonment to the Super Highway and were hit by a speeding car belonging to a feudal lord,' she says. 'I am being treated for this phobia…and am hopeful that I will be able to drive again very soon. A couple of years ago, when I used to drive, I was hit by a motorcyclist.'

When queried about the problems she may be facing as a female while travelling on public transport, Naghma says that exorbitant fares charged by rickshaw drivers during the CNG shutdown days were bothersome. 'They actually charge double the usual fare on such days,' she says. However, Naghma is not wary of travelling late at night. 'I do not have a problem travelling by public transport during the night. I haven't faced any form of harassment, nor have I been robbed. I think if women are more aware of things and are trained to tackle such problems, they can ensure their own safety.'

Another thing she loathes is the misuse of footpaths by motorcyclists which, she says, can make life difficult for pedestrians. While Naghma is comfortable travelling by rickshaw, she does find the Qingqi a bit too dangerous for her liking. However, she does not favour banning Qingqis. 'Many students are suffering because of the ban,' she says. 'I don't understand why the government can't regularise the Qingqis and allow them to operate in a separate lane.' I ask if she finds it difficult to hire a rickshaw since she must search for one every time she wants to go somewhere. Naghma has a simple solution to the problem. 'Actually, there are a few trusted rickshaw drivers who live near my house. I call them by phone, which is convenient, especially in cases of strikes, or some unusual occurrence in the city.'

Finally, I ask her if, as a political worker, she can think of a solution to Karachi's traffic problems. 'Mass transit is the only solution and the revival of Karachi Circular Railway,' she says. 'So many people will benefit from it. Also, roads should be broadened, and the number of buses should be increased. The public transport system should be pro-poor and there shouldn't be any ban on pillion-riding as it proves inconvenient for the underprivileged,' says Naghma.

Muhammad: A Minibus Mechanic and Conductor

Muhammad is originally from Faisalabad, the city was formerly known as Lyallpur. He completed his matriculation in the late 1970s and started working at the Lyallpur Transport Company, which had 80 buses and 14 trucks. Muhammad started as a helper and went on to become a fitter, eventually qualifying as a mechanic. Throughout this period, he slowly acquired theoretical knowledge.

During the Bhutto era, he tried his luck in the Gulf, but was unsuccessful. He finally came to Karachi, in search of better prospects. In 1986, he settled down in New Karachi, where he still lives. He used to earn Rs 600–700 per month when he began working as a mechanic. In three years, his salary had increased to Rs 1,000 per month. He began working as a partner, but soon developed differences with his colleague and turned to a solo career. He has also trained many people who have gone on to work independently.

The first thing I ask him is the reason for the dwindling number of buses and minibuses in Karachi. He is of the view that there are multiple reasons that have brought this situation about. One is that spare parts have become costly over the years. 'For instance, in the year 2000, the cost of a minibus tyre was Rs 2,500, while it costs Rs 25,000 now. In 1992–93, the cost of a gear box was Rs 3,500 which has risen to Rs 75,000 now,' he says.

Secondly, he feels that the fares are on the lower side. 'The distance from New Karachi to Kemari is 35 km and the fare is Rs 17–18,' he says. In Kashmir, the fare for 10 km is Rs 150 and one has to pay extra Rs 50 for baggage. In Faisalabad, Rs 100 is charged for a distance of 35 km.' I ask him to give an estimate of the right fare from New Karachi to Kemari. 'It should be Rs 35 one way, to make the route financially feasible,' he says.

The third reason, according to him, is the rising cost of vehicles. 'In 2003, when a Mazda (minibus) was assembled here, the price was Rs 350,000,' he says. 'The entire operation has been shifted to India and now a vehicle costs Rs 1.4 million. It is difficult to get a zero-meter Mazda these days and the Chinese vehicles, which are available, are not as powerful for carrying loads and do not last long on Karachi roads.' This downward trend affects his business. He tells me that bus owners are increasingly converting their minibuses into contract vehicles. This situation affects the poor the most. 'As many as 450 minibuses used to run on the W-11 route,' he says. 'The number has now come down to 150–70.'

According to Muhammad, 'Earlier, two to three buses used to depart from the terminal every minute and now one bus leaves every two minutes.' He says that the travelling time from New Karachi to Kemari and from Kemari to New Karachi, is an hour-and-a-half. The buses have to wait for two hours at each of the terminals. So, it takes them 3.5 hours to complete one trip. 'Usually, we do two trips in a day,' he says. 'The business becomes profitable in three trips. We do not earn more than Rs 2,000 on a given day. This is our net income. It could be a bit higher if we made three trips in a day.'

I ask him about why people travel on top of buses when it is illegal to do so. There is a fine of Rs 500 for this offence. He explains that many people prefer it as it is very hot inside the bus. 'It is also safer as robbers ignore the people sitting on the top of the bus,' he says. Allowing men to sit on women-only seats is necessary from a financial point of view, according to him. A half-empty vehicle does not make profit. 'But if a woman enters the bus, we make sure the men vacate the seats,' he insists. He feels that the bus drivers' association is a great support in all police-related matters like accidents, or arson attacks. He dismisses the idea that conductors are rude to passengers. 'There are a couple of ignorant people among us who misbehave, but you can find such people anywhere. Tell me about those bikers who appear to be educated but hurl abuse at us.'

Finally, I ask about his experiences with Qingqis. He is quick to condemn them. 'They are a nuisance. Most of the Qingqi drivers are usually very young and inexperienced. They cause all the traffic jams in town and hardly care about the flow of traffic.'

George and Iqbal: CNG Rickshaw Drivers

Both George and Iqbal are in their late 40s to early 50s. Both are Christians and have been driving rickshaws for many years. After sustaining a heart attack earlier this year, George has recently left the occupation, while Iqbal still continues to drive his rickshaw.

During the interview, for the most part, George answered for both of them. When queried about their birthplace and origin, both George and Iqbal have similar stories. Their parents came to Karachi from Gujranwala in search of livelihoods in the early 1970s. They used to be farm workers but were not earning enough to feed the family. It is common wisdom that opportunities in Karachi are better than in any other city of Pakistan.

I ask them if they took up rickshaw driving as a preferred choice. 'No. In the early 80s I was employed in Fateh Ali Chemicals, near Valika Textiles in the SITE area,' says George. 'I had started driving a rickshaw to supplement my income, so it was a part-time occupation.' I ask if he purchased the rickshaw or if it was a rented one. 'Rented,' he says. 'The owner of the rickshaw was a Punjabi and I used to pay him Rs 70 per day. In 1986, I quit my job at Fateh Ali Chemicals and purchased a two-stroke rickshaw for Rs 60,000. By then, I had saved some money and bought that rickshaw for cash, paying the full amount.'

When asked why he left the Fateh Ali Chemicals job, George says he grew tired of the restrictions that come with a salaried job. 'I felt an immense sense of independence in my driving occupation,' he says. 'No boss to report to, no fixed timings to follow, and no pressure of work targets. With driving, I learnt to set my own income targets. For instance, I would tell myself "Mr George, you have earned Rs 800 and now you should go home and spend time with your family". This is the type of independence I enjoy the most. But in the beginning of this year, I suffered a major heart attack and had to give up driving.'

I ask him further if the stress of driving in heavy traffic took its toll on him and caused the heart attack. 'I don't think so, as I have never faced any major problems due to traffic hazards in my long career,' he says. 'I used to carry all my documents with me and my dealing with passengers was actually very good. I think that the heart attack occurred because I was a heavy smoker and consumer of *paan* (betel leaf).'

I ask him how long one could drive a rickshaw for in a single day? 'Considering the condition of the roads, the congestion and the weather, 8–10 hours a day is the maximum time,' he says. 'A young man with exceptional endurance and energy can do it for 12 hours in a go, but not more than that.'

Next I wanted to know when and why the practice of using fare meters ended. George recalls it ending in 2005–6. He believes a lot of things had happened simultaneously in those years: 'The rickshaw drivers tampered with the meters en masse, the CNG prices[1] shot up and the authorities relaxed meter inspections all around the same time.' It has become increasingly difficult to determine the right fare for a journey, he feels. 'The length of the route, the security situation of the city, the time, passenger preferences, and a tacit understanding among rickshaw drivers, are all determinants in asking for the right amount of money. Initially, meters provided some indication of price, but that soon lost its utility.'

George's rickshaw is not legally insured, though he does possess third-party insurance papers to fulfil the requirements of the law. In other words, he is not insured in case of an accident. When I ask him to describe trends in his business, he says that mostly people use rickshaws from the initial days of the month (when they receive their salaries) until the 20th of the month. 'After the 20th, business is mostly nil,' he says. 'The Musharraf era was the best for our business.[2] People had money to spend and hence they were generous in their use of rickshaws… the business went down drastically under Zardari.'[3]

George has a lot of knowledge about the rickshaw-cutting business. He tells me it happens in Kati Pahari, Lyari, Laloo Khet, Bara Board, and Orangi Town. Old and burnt-out rickshaws are usually broken down for spare parts, or *kabuli*. The chassis are claimed by scrap dealers. 'Other stolen vehicles are dismantled in Banaras, Shershah, and near Filmistan at Teen Hatti, within an hour of having been stolen,' he says. 'Spare parts are then sold in Ranchore Lines. All rickshaw mechanics know about it.'

He sees the flyovers as a mixed blessing. 'They are good, but because of faults in their design, traffic is forced to move in from the wrong direction and violate the designated one-ways,' he says. But his biggest problem is the motorcyclists. 'They don't care for traffic laws and are always in a hurry. They do not even have rear-view mirrors. We have to be extra cautious to avoid trouble with them,' George says. 'The police need to be straightened out and everything will be OK then.'

He mentions that CNG rickshaws are also used as a pick-and-drop service, particularly for school children. 'Parents remain comfortable with the arrangement, as it takes less time compared to vans and works out well for us since we receive a fixed monthly amount,' he says.

An Anonymous Vehicle Parts Dealer

The spare-parts dealer is around 30 years old and owns a vehicle-parts shop in Plaza Market, at the Tibet Centre in Karachi. He is cautious and provides limited information. He also refuses to share his name.

I ask him about how he started selling spare parts. He shares a long story that may point towards a possible reason for his reluctance to talk. Reportedly, he was a student at the Pak-Swedish Technical Institute in the Landhi area, where he enrolled after completing his matriculation. All was going well until 1996, when politician and leader of terrorist organisation al-Zulfiqar, Mir Murtaza Bhutto, was suddenly murdered. 'Much political mayhem followed, which scared me from going to the area and so I had to leave my studies,' he recalls. 'I also trained in rehabilitating drug addicts before all this. After leaving my studies, I began to search for a job, to help support my household. It was a long and frustrating search. Finally, an acquaintance set me up with a salesman in Plaza Market, in 2004. My responsibilities included handling of customers and menial work.'

He is disappointed at the current state of affairs. 'Business was at its peak in 2005,' he says. 'The influx of Afghans has spoilt things. They use drug money to finance the business of spare parts. They smuggle items through the Torkham border, flouting all the legal requirements. By contrast, we are bound to pay taxes, custom duties, wait for custom clearances and sometimes have to pay demurrages as well. The Afghans have invested enormously in local markets. They sell spare parts at much cheaper rates than us. We are, in contrast, made to appear expensive for the end user. The Afghans have developed strong local networks. Our legal status keeps us out of that circuit…another reason is that the rupee is constantly getting devalued against the US dollar and the yen.'

Next, I want to know if Shershah market is a competitor to the Plaza Market. He does not think so, because Shershah market also sells new spare parts and at cheaper rates. However, he offers no explanation for this difference. I am curious about the sustainability and survival of the market if the legal spare parts business is not profitable. He quickly provides an alternative: 'It is profitable at the high end—for example, selling spare parts to Toyota and Honda companies is very lucrative.'

Coming to the traffic situation, I ask him about the biggest challenges affecting his business. He immediately comes up with the issue of parking. 'There is no parking space for our clients. They usually have to park their vehicles at considerable distances.' He feels the traffic problems of the city are rooted in our lackadaisical attitude toward laws. Besides, he also holds schools responsible for traffic jams. 'Very few schools have proper parking,' he says. 'Just visit the Plaza around 1:00 p.m. when school finishes and you will understand why.'

Humayun: A Motorcyclist

Humayun's parents were farm labourers in Sheikhupura and came to Karachi in 1972 to look for work. At first, they stayed with a relative in Ranchore Lines and later purchased a small house in the Jubilee area. Luckily, his father found a job in the merchant navy. With the money he made from there, his mother purchased a house in Paharganj, North Nazimabad, in 1978. Humayun was born there, in 1981. He matriculated and later gained a BA degree from Karachi University.

Humayun started riding a motorcycle when he was in class 10. He was forced to start early, as the women in his family needed a male escort for various chores in the absence of his father. 'I used to take my mother grocery shopping and my sisters to school on that bike,' he says. 'It was economical as well. Before I bought a bike, we used rickshaws and taxis, both of which were more expensive.' At that time and age, owning a bike was a sign of prestige among his friends.

'If I remember correctly, petrol was Rs 28/litre at that time,' he says. 'Monthly petrol expenses were Rs 1,000, with Rs 150 per month for maintenance. It was terribly cheap.' Comparatively, he now claims to spend Rs 100 per day on a 27 km route—a complete round trip between home and office, with some errands in between. This trip takes him 40 minutes on weekdays and hardly 20 minutes on a Sunday.

Being underage, he had no legal documents to his name—including a driver's license—for the longest time. He used an authority letter, obtained from the first owner of the bike instead. Seventeen years later, his younger brother is using the same authority letter to ride that motorcycle. I ask him if the police have ever bothered him. He admits to paying bribes: 'The police used to trouble me a lot. I used to get away by giving them Rs 50.' Still, he feels that they are biased against motorcyclists.

This brings us to the traffic problems he faces as a motorcyclist. I want to know the foremost personal issues that he faces in Karachi. His immediate response is in regard to personal safety. 'It is safer to travel in a car when you are with family,' he says. 'A motorcyclist is more at risk of snatching. The snatchers can also observe a motorcyclist easily to know whether he is armed or not. They cannot always tell that about car drivers and hence there is an increased deterrence. Having said that, when I am riding a bike, I can also easily manoeuvre it in narrow streets and spaces with greater ease, unlike with a car. That boosts my confidence.' Still, he is unwilling to allow his children to ride a motorcycle for this reason.

Discussing safety precautions, he recommends being careful about one's timings, frequently changing one's route and staying abreast with the city's law and order situations. 'I prefer to avoid the sensitive areas after dusk,' he adds.

He believes that the biggest problem for a motorcyclist is not having a spare wheel in case of punctures, especially if it occurs while you are travelling with family at night. The ban on pillion riding is another source of inconvenience for motorcyclists. 'I need somebody to accompany me if I am carrying heavy items like a TV set or bulk load of grocery,' he explains.

I ask him how the traffic has changed over seventeen years. He paints a familiar picture: 'The volume of traffic has increased manifold. One problem is the ever-increasing number of cars on the roads; the other is Qingqis. The Qingqis stop anywhere without considering the traffic behind them. They occupy multiple parallel lanes and bikers have to zigzag between them to find their way. Minibuses are the same. They stop everywhere except the designated bus stops and are driven like airplanes.'

In his opinion, the signal-free corridors encourage speeding, which is a problem for motorcyclists. The lack of U-turns forces a lot of motorcyclists to violate the one-way rule. 'They must do this to save time and fuel,' he says. 'I myself violate the one-way rule and ride against the traffic sometimes.' I ask if the traffic constables bother him. He replies, 'In some places, the constables prefer to ignore us because they know that obstructing us will cause a bigger mess... You should ride past them with confidence, staring right into their eyes. This is a psychological trick. They will not bother you then. Another trick is to avoid stopping your bike at the front of traffic signals. Constables want to save time and effort and usually pick on the bikers right in front of them.'

Rear-view mirrors are a hazard, according to him. The mirrors extend outside the vehicle's body and can hit pedestrians and other vehicles, which is especially dangerous when the bike is travelling at high speed. The mirror also gets stolen frequently. Interestingly, rear-view mirrors on motorcycles are considered a sign of backwardness. He says that youngsters generally mock any biker who uses a rear-view mirror, for being old-fashioned.

He dismisses the utility of a mass transit system for himself. 'Over the years, I have become used to having a vehicle on my doorstep,' he says. 'No mass transit can provide that service to me. I don't want to walk.' Finally, Humayun thinks the lack of parking space is a serious issue in Karachi. 'There should be proper parking space every 500 metres,' he says.

Shamoon: A Cyclist

27-year-old Shamoon, a Punjabi Christian, has been a cycling enthusiast for fourteen years. He is called *ustad* (teacher), because he trains new cyclists. He believes cycling is a complete form of exercise. He also owns a car, but finds cycling a healthier and more economical option, especially with the price of petrol rising by the day.

Shamoon cycles to his office daily, in a timespan of 20 minutes and claims to hit a speed of 60 km per hour. I ask him about his biggest challenge. 'The roads are in bad condition,' he says. 'Potholes damage bicycles and give cyclists back problems. Haphazard traffic and irregular parking force us to weave our way forward.'

'I am especially wary of Qingqi drivers who have no idea how to use the road,' he continues. Since similar accusations are made against other cyclists too, I ask Shamoon his opinion on the matter. 'The motorists try to harass the cyclists,' he insists. He admits he has no knowledge of any traffic laws governing cyclists, but he is sure the traffic police are only seeking bribes when they stop cyclists for minor issues, like having a missing bell, or no light.

Shamoon and his group cycle to Punjab once a year, to attend the Mary the Chaste festival. Each cyclist has to show a route permit to the motorway police in the Punjab. To obtain a route permit from the Union Council office, each one of the seventy cyclists pays around Rs 400 in bribes. 'This means we pay Rs 28,000 in bribes every year, to pursue our passion and uphold the tradition,' he says. Shamoon trains new cyclists on the beach every Thursday. However, he feels inflation has made it expensive for cyclists to take care of their diet, while safety gear such as helmets and elbow guards have also become pricey.

Talking about the existing roads and infrastructure, Shamoon reiterates his earlier point about the signal-free corridors and bypasses being dangerous for cyclists. 'We cannot take U-turns and have to avoid speeding cars,' he says. 'It's also tiring to have to weave in and out of the traffic.' He says the number of puncture shops has reduced considerably over time. If a bicycle breaks down, cyclists are forced to make repairs themselves. He also complains about the rising cost of bicycles: 'In 2008, I bought a bike for Rs 6,000 and spent another Rs 8,000 on improvements and decoration. Nowadays, a single bicycle costs at least Rs 12,000.'

Rizwan: Rent-A-Car Driver

Rizwan's parents migrated from India in 1947. He spent his childhood and early youth in Block I of North Nazimabad. His father's cloth business prospered until 2004, when he was forced to close down. That is when Rizwan started his rent-a-car business. He now lives in Korangi.

Since his family business was very different, I ask him why he chose this business. It comes down to his passion for cars. Rizwan bought three cars with the residual money, after his father's business closed down and borrowed four other cars from his friends to assemble a fleet of seven vehicles. From his office at Nagan Chowrangi, he used to rent out a car for Rs 700, or a car and driver for Rs 1,200 per day, in 2004. People hired these cars for family events, such as weddings and picnics and also for religious and other festivals.

Describing his clients, he says they belong to diverse backgrounds. 'But I can tell you who my clients are not,' he says. 'I choose not to lend my cars to youngsters for two simple reasons: they behave like gangsters and drive carelessly.'

I ask Rizwan if he faces any problems, but he says he chooses not to discuss them. 'Things have run very smoothly until now,' according to him. 'It is because I follow two golden principles: ignore and tolerate. You won't believe that I have never been to the police station for the entire span of my business.' I ask if there is a considerable security risk in his line of business. He responds in the affirmative: 'There is and that is why I am very selective in who I lend my cars to, as I don't know the purposes for which they could be used. As a precaution, we ask for the client's original National Identity Card (NIC) and a personal reference. The security situation of the city has adversely impacted this business.'

I ask him to describe the traffic situation in Karachi. He is in favour of the underpasses and flyovers, as they reduce the time of commuting over long distances. However, his main criticism is in regard to people's attitudes. 'Most traffic problems are caused by educated, but disrespectful and intolerant drivers,' he says. 'You can see the educated people in flashy cars, using mobile phones while driving. Clients used to be respectful and honest in their dealings. The new crowd is rough and lacks manners. However, I have observed that more people make way for an ambulance now than in the past. I think awareness has increased in regard to that.' He also feels alarmed by the rising number of cars and other vehicles on the road. 'To the best of my knowledge, a staggering 400 vehicles are registered per day at the Civic Centre', he says. 'It adds up to 120,000 new vehicles per year on the roads of Karachi.'

He feels the traffic police are corrupt and greedy and that CNG rickshaws—and Qingqis, while they lasted—are a big nuisance. 'The drivers of both these vehicles are unaware of laws, they do not have enough engine power and on top of it, they use their pressure horns to bully other drivers,' he laments. 'Also, old and dilapidated vehicles are still on the roads.'

The current state of his business is not encouraging. The company suffered because of his brother's inability to manage the business during Rizwan's brief sojourn in Saudi Arabia. Fortunately, he found a sub-contract to provide a pick-and-drop service to a local media house from I.I. Chundrigar Road, to the Buffer Zone. He says he has reserved two vans for this service. He drives one himself and has hired a driver for the other.

After paying the driver's salary and the maintenance costs of the van, he saves Rs 15,000 per month on the other van, while the company provides petrol. I ask if he still lends cars. 'Yes, I do, but business has gone down since 2006,' he says. 'Inflation has forced people to avoid hiring cars…actually, business has gone down for everyone except the psychiatrists.'

Syed Sohail: A Banker

Syed belongs to the Urdu-speaking migrant community. His father was a government officer and despite financial constraints, he made sure all his children received an education. In the early days of his career at Standard Chartered Bank, Syed provided car loans to customers. He believes that Karachi's traffic problems are not a result of careless lending by the banks, but of poorly planned infrastructure and ill maintenance of roads. 'As a banker, I feel that car loans have actually supported the economy,' he says.

Describing the whole process of screening potential loan customers before lending to them, he tells me that banks discourage lending to owners of buses, minibuses and other public transport vehicles. He says, 'This is necessary because the bus owners generally do not have the required documents and they also usually demonstrate a gangster-like behaviour in their dealings with us. While there is no policy for denying loans to them, I admit that they are not favoured much. The method of verification in their cases is also more stringent.'

Syed explains that loans are not provided to motorcyclists either, though there is no limitation on that. The required documents are a salary certificate, a verified bank statement, and post-dated cheques for the tenure of the instalments, before a legal contract is signed. I ask why they use this process, including charging high interest rates, which seem biased against the poor. He sees it differently. 'We are ready to provide loans for the Qingqis as well,' he says. 'Our only demand is that the papers be genuine and that the motorcycle used for the Qingqi isn't stolen. So, it is not an anti-poor scheme. You have to understand that lending is in the interest of the bank. However, your concern about the interest rates could be valid. Still, compare it with the market rates and consider the fact that we also have to break even, at least, to cover our overhead costs.'

I ask him if banks provide loans to goods carriers as well. Syed says banks do lend to these customers, though reluctantly. 'If you have observed, HinoPak Limited only manufactures the chassis,' he points out. 'The container is installed by the buyer and that creates problems with us and with insurance companies as well. The containers are manufactured locally. We find it difficult to determine the real price and so do the insurance companies for calculating instalments or premiums. This is the [fault of the] goods-carrier mafia that failed the cargo-carrying services of Pakistan Railway… Earlier, 75 per cent of goods were transported through Pakistan Railways. Transporting goods by rail was much cheaper than trucks, which are a source of traffic jams.'

He feels that the banks did their best business between 2004 and 2005, during Musharraf's tenure. 'Interest rates were low, and people applied left, right and centre for loans,' he says. 'It is a rule of thumb that when interest rates are low, people start borrowing from the banks and when interest rates are high, people save more for higher returns.'

Before we conclude, Syed once again insists that it isn't banks that have caused the traffic woes of the city. 'It is the mafias and public together—neither wants to observe the law,' he says.

Rashid: A Car Mechanic

Rashid belongs to an Urdu-speaking family. His parents migrated from India and are currently settled in Sector 5-E, New Karachi. Rashid had a passion for driving that later led to an interest in mechanics. He has five brothers and two sisters, none of whom are in this profession.

Rashid completed his Diploma in Engineering at the Government Polytechnic Institute, SITE, Karachi. After that, he began learning on the job with an *ustad* at Anda Morr, Nagan Chowrangi, on a stipend of Rs 30 per day and meals. He used to work for 8 to 9 hours a day. Rashid was trained in repairing simple engines with plug-points and mechanical fuel-injection systems. In 2006, the market was flooded with EFI cars. That was when he decided to update his knowledge and joined the Honda Company.

'Honda does not have an assembly plant in Pakistan, but they offer repairing services,' he says. 'So, I was trained there and learnt a lot from my seniors. I worked hard and tried to learn as much as possible.' He started working for the company on a salary of Rs 2,800 per month. 'Out of that, I used to spend Rs 800 per month on transport and would bring food from home,' he says. 'At that time, I used to spend 1.5 hours on the road to make the round-trip.'

In 2013, Rashid left the company to start his own workshop. 'In 2013, I was getting a salary of Rs 12,500 and people often told me how blessed I was, and that I shouldn't be taking the risk of letting go of this salary... But I had decided to take the risk and opted for my own set up,' he says. 'I was encouraged by my seniors, who had established their own businesses.' His initial difficulties included looking for a suitable place to rent at a reasonable rate. The monthly rent for his current place is Rs 6,000, with Rs 500 fixed charges for electricity. He did not know anyone in the area, so it was hard to find new customers. 'The initial six months were tough, but with the passage of time, business started picking up,' he says.

Rashid has also hired two apprentices. He pays the older boy Rs 250 per day and the newer one, Rs 50 per. His office hours used to be 8:30 a.m. to 5 p.m. Now, he spends at least 11 hours a day from 10 a.m. to 9 p.m. 'But this is more rewarding and I am satisfied with what I get from here,' he says. Rashid feels his situation would have been far better had there been arrangements for institutionalised and structured learning about the trade. 'I would have been saving time and earning more', he says.

He observes that the volume of traffic has increased a lot. He thinks it might be because of the increasing population, but also because of the relative ease of purchasing cars with bank loans. I ask him if he has felt a change in the attitude of his customers as well. He says he has. 'Thirteen years ago, my clientele consisted of more mature people, who purchased cars using hard earned money and hence they valued their assets more,' he says. 'Now…car owners…are less sensitive about their cars, or about human lives and the value of money… I also find people becoming more careless about speeding and driving more rashly compared to before.' The other traffic problem that bothers him the most are the Qingqis. 'Those are good for the poor, but they are the biggest impediment to smooth driving,' he says. 'They run slowly, occupy extreme right lanes, are always overloaded, and are driven by inexperienced young drivers. You can see how the recent ban on Qingqis has slightly improved the traffic situation. Business for coaches and vans has improved…they profit the most from the ban.'

I ask him what issues affect his business directly. He complains of a lack of parking space. 'We don't have a proper space where we can ask our clients to park their cars,' he says. 'As a result, we park on roads, designated footpaths and on street corners. If I had properly allocated parking, my business would increase.'

I ask him if spare parts are easily available. He says compared to when he started working, they are. 'More Chinese parts are available now,' he tells me. 'Additionally, parts known as *kabuli* are also in abundant supply.' He talks about how the repair business has changed with these developments. 'Earlier, the *ustad* was interested in making repairs,' he says. 'Now, the emphasis is more on the replacement of old, or damaged parts, because both the customer and the mechanic do not have time for meticulous work. It is also because of the fact that after replacing a part, the life of the car increases, and thirdly, people can now order parts from Dubai as well. We also have upgraded tools at our disposal, so we are more comfortable with the variety of spare parts. For instance, we now use an oil filter spanner instead of chain sprocket to change the oil filter.'

His suggestions for ways to improve the traffic problem involve withholding bank loans. 'Also, cars manufactured before 1985 should be taken off the roads,' he says. 'Two-stroke engines, diesel buses, and Qingqis should be banned. But most importantly, the road capacity needs to be increased. Traffic congestion has also affected drivers' attitudes. They are more impatient and aggressive now and develop violent road rage. They are, most likely, suffering from continuous traffic fatigue.'

Sardar: A Cargo Driver

Sardar, a cargo transporter, has experienced many shades of life in the city. He owes a lot to his father, who made him what he is today. He tells me how his grandfather opposed his father's decision to study and which compelled him to migrate to Karachi from Matta, Swat, after the war of 1971. Initially, Sardar's father found accommodation with some other migrants on Tariq Road, but he later shifted to Manzoor Colony and built his own house.

A determined person, who never shirked from hard work, Sardar's father studied in the mornings and drove a taxi in the evenings. Later, he bought a Suzuki cargo-carrier vehicle, in a partnership and saved enough money to buy another one. He worked diligently to market his services to various companies and by 1994, when his business had reached a comfortable level, he bought his first Mazda 3500 truck and began transporting goods upcountry.

I asked Sardar how he became involved in his father's business and what challenges he faces today. 'When my father bought the Suzuki vehicles, he recruited me as a driver,' recalls Sardar. 'As for the challenges, they are many. The congestion bothers us the most, as it is difficult to drive on the bustling streets of Tariq Road, Liaquatabad, Nazimabad and older parts of the city. We have to wait for several minutes, as people are not willing to make space for us on the road. Unavailability of parking space is another problem that we are confronted with on a daily basis.' Another problem is the rule that only trucks with number plates beginning with 'JU' are allowed on the road before late evening, which makes it difficult for cargo carriers to operate. 'In our slang, they are called "*cheh nutta*"—having six bolts.'

Moving to a more sensitive topic, I ask Sardar if his Pashtun descent creates hurdles for him, particularly in different ethnic areas of the city. 'Yes, they used to bother us a lot and treat us as illiterate and poor,' he says. 'But I want to tell you that I am no illiterate. I have a diploma in *hikmat* from the Hamdard University. Once, I was in a largely Urdu-speaking neighbourhood in Malir 15, to deliver a consignment of medicines. The street was narrow and a push-cart vendor, selling *haleem,* had blocked the passage. I honked at him to clear the way. The seller waved his hand but made no attempts to move. When I honked for the third time, the *haleem* seller took out a gun from his wooden money box, ran towards me and put it to my forehead. I was forced to reverse my truck back onto the main road. But I feel the situation has improved a lot after the Karachi Operation.' I ask him if he has a fitness certificate for his vehicle. 'Yes I do, and we purchase it from the relevant department in Baldia Town,' he says. 'By "purchasing" I mean the agent charges some extra amount and it gets delivered to our doorstep.'

Some of the challenges faced by transporters like Sardar, include a hostile police force. 'These policemen are always looking to extort money from us,' he says. 'Once, my cargo-carrier driver was stopped by a traffic constable near Ayesha Bawany Academy, on Shahrah-e-Faisal. After scrutinising all the documents, he said that the fitness certificate was not duly stamped and that the truck would be impounded. The driver had an altercation with the police officer and in a much-irritated state of mind he called me up, so I could speak to the police officer. I tried to convince him that it's a mistake by the government official and I would rectify it at the first possible convenience. He insisted on *challan* (receipt for payment) and I said to him, "Go ahead, but I will ask the driver to park it in such a way that the entire artery of Shahrah-e-Faisal gets blocked". Since he was desperate for money, the entire episode was settled with a bribe of Rs 150 (£0.94) given to that constable... It is a routine affair... Sometimes they ask for documents and sometimes object to side mirrors. They just need money. They can let you go for as little as Rs 50, so why should we waste time in arguing with them? You know that time is precious in this business.'

I tell Sardar that drivers and owners of larger vehicles seem to be in constant conflict with car owners and ask him why he thinks this is so. 'They [car owners] are the most intolerant people of all,' he says. 'If, by any chance, I drive into the extreme left-hand lane, they honk their horns, flash their headlights and when there is a delay in clearing the lane, they hurl abuse at us.'

However, Sardar and his colleagues are most comfortable when driving on highways. 'We feel like *jesey machli paani maen aa jaae* (a fish in a pond),' he says. 'Nobody bothers us, except the excise people, who ask for tax documents which we usually have. We are much more relaxed on highways.'

I ask him if route permits are a problem during intercity or inter-province travel. 'Yes, we are required to have route permits of the relevant provinces to which we are carrying the goods,' he says. 'Since I am a resident of Sindh, a route permit for the province is not an issue and that is my primary document. Remember that all other route permits will be based on that primary document. My broker here in Sindh has contacts in all other provinces. So, I take a picture of my Sindh route permit and WhatsApp it [send via mobile phone] to his contact, to let us stay in Peshawar. My Sindh agent will call him and before entering Peshawar City, I will get the route permit for Khyber Pakhtunkhwa, as made by the agent in Peshawar. Peshawar police are very strict and if you don't have the permit, they can fine up to Rs 6,000 (£37.79) and could also confiscate the truck.'

I then enquire if problems are caused by delays in issuing route permits. 'No, we have alternative arrangements as well,' he says. 'If I don't get the route permit on time, I will stop the truck outside Peshawar and get a fake challan for Rs 200 against my name, by giving Rs 400 to the constable. It looks absolutely original and we manage to get away with it with the authorities. Nobody bothers to verify that fake document.'

I also ask if highway breakdowns are a challenge. 'We usually have two drivers on long routes', he replied. 'One is an "expert", or *ustad* and the other is an apprentice. So, in case of any mishap, one stays with the truck and the other searches for a mechanic. They are usually available at roadside hotels.' In regard to the costs involved in intercity travel, I ask Sardar if a trip to Lahore could be exorbitant. 'Lahore's a five-day trip,' he says. 'The monthly salary of a senior driver is Rs 14,000, so that is a fixed cost. We will spend approximately Rs 3,000 on toll taxes, since Rs 150 is the toll tax for Mazdas and there are around 20 toll plazas (10 each way). While going to Lahore, the diesel costs us Rs 21,000 and Rs 19,000 on the way back to Karachi. The diesel costs on way back is less, because the route to Karachi is mostly downhill, so less diesel is spent. Also, the truck is not loaded on its return and is much lighter. If you include the cost of bribery to policemen, food, lodging, cleaning, shoe polishing etc., it comes to roughly Rs 50,000 for a five-day trip.'

The challenges for truck drivers do not end there. There are also issues like security on highways. 'No security threats, really, but goods are stolen while the trucks are on the move,' he says. 'It usually happens at night. Big trucks do not have the facility of seeing exactly behind the container. So, the thieves taking advantage of the darkness of night attach a small vehicle to the container so the speed of both the vehicles are synchronised. Then one person unlocks the container and throws the items into the Suzuki pickup. A lot of containers are deprived of their goods by the same method. We now don't fix or weld the container with the chassis but rotate it 180 degrees through cranes, so that the door of the container is blocked with the body of the truck, just behind the driver. That's the only solution as goods worth millions of rupees are involved. Also, the highways are in good condition and are often smooth, so there is no threat to the container itself.'

Lastly, the accidents need to be countered as well. 'Accidents happen no matter what you do,' says Sardar. 'Last month, a person was killed after my driver fell asleep near Kathore and hit a car. We tried to settle the matter without involving the police. The deceased person's family live in Tando Adam and he was the only family member earning an income. We gifted a Qingqi rickshaw to his younger brother and provided some additional money for death rituals as well.' According to Sardar, there is no official forum for the large-vehicle drivers to resolve major disputes, but their experience and connections hold them in good stead. 'As we have been in the profession for a long time, we know each other and help each other,' he says. 'My father tried to form an association twice but failed.'

An Anonymous Ambulance Driver

The ambulance driver refuses to share his name. His vehicle is parked near the Qatar Hospital, in Orangi Town, his duty station. He is officially barred from talking to the press about his employers, the Aman Foundation. This is a private organisation providing a paying service to the citizens of Karachi. The ambulances charge Rs 300 to transport a patient to any of the government hospitals in the city. For every ambulance, three teams of three staff members each work in eight-hour shifts on a full day.

The 40-year-old has been driving an ambulance for the last eight years and has been through some gruelling times. The other two staff members of the ambulance are with him when we speak. I begin by asking him to share the challenges he faces daily. His problem is an obvious one. 'First of all, it is difficult to find a way in traffic, as all the lanes are occupied by all,' he says. 'And if by any chance we get our way, we are usually followed by speeding motorcyclists and car drivers. They treat our clearing of the path as an opportunity to drive out of the rush quickly. But they don't understand that we have to constantly change lanes and we often have to apply the brakes abruptly. As a result, they often collide with us and cause damage to the ambulance as well as their own vehicle.'

I ask who gives him the most trouble on the roads. 'The youngsters,' he replies immediately. 'There is an entire generation of wired youngsters who have headsets plugged in their ears and they don't listen or care less for the hooter of a rushing ambulance… They are insensitive to the emergency conditions we deal with.' I ask if the traffic police help in such a situation. 'No, they are also insensitive,' he replies. 'They tend to ignore the sound of the siren and hooter. They just turn their faces away and regulate the traffic as per usual.' He finds that Civil Hospital has the most difficult approach out of the three major hospitals, the other two being Abbasi and Jinnah. Lack of space makes it impossible to turn the ambulance, he says. 'The main reason is haphazard parking, primarily by para-transport vehicles.'

I ask him if the problem is limited to Civil Hospital. He says the problem extends to the entire city: 'You can see it on the main arteries. The newly constructed shopping plazas, high-rises and residential complexes are not too concerned, it seems, about the parking of vehicles. Most of these places do not have any provisions for parking, while the rest provide inadequate space.' He cites the example of the Golimar area, where sanitary material shops and parked vehicles have occupied almost half of the main road.

He experiences other unusual problems too. I want to know about how he deals with the patients' relatives during emergencies. 'At times, the relatives exhort us for speeding,' he says. 'I understand their position and their sentiments. Our staff includes doctors as well. The Aman Foundation provides the only ambulances that supply patients with a transpiration service and medical care while they are being transported to the hospital. So, the staff try to convince the relatives that the patient is getting the best possible first aid. Sometimes relatives help in assisting us in clearing a path amidst the traffic.'

Gunshot victims, however, are a different story. 'It has happened quite a few times that the relatives of gunshot victims put pistols to my head to force me to hurry.' One would think these episodes were the most difficult times for him. But setting aside personal fears and threats, he thinks the real difficulties lie in the obstructions he has to face during political rallies, protests and sit-ins. 'These are the real challenges for us,' he says. 'It takes us considerable time to find our way through such disturbances, when every second counts towards someone's life.' He makes a distinction for planned political rallies, as the authorities usually prescribe alternate routes for these, though an alternate route often takes longer.

His other problem is not related to traffic issues. He reports that when an ambulance brings a dead body to the hospital emergency room, the medico-legal officer at that particular hospital often tries to implicate or involve the staff in the police report. 'We do not want to be involved in legal matters,' he says. The solution to Karachi's traffic problems is simple, in his opinion: 'I think that a separate lane must be allocated for ambulances. I also think that traffic policemen on motorcycles should provide an escort to ambulances passing through their respective areas.'

Mohammad Saeed: A CNG-Rickshaw Driver

Mohammad Saeed's father used to work in Quetta as a police officer; he brought his family to Karachi when Mohammad was four years old. They settled in Baldia Town, near Qatar Hospital, where he still lives. Mohammad used to drive a three-seater and then briefly switched a six-seater, but soon returned to the former. I ask him why. 'I did it because of the ban on the Qingqis,' he says. 'If the administration does not want these, why did they allow them to be manufactured in the first place? The assemblers and the marketers should be apprehended, as should those police officers who allow Qingqis on the road.' I ask him if that means Qingqis are more profitable than CNG rickshaws. He says that rickshaws make a profit in the initial days of the month, when working class passengers still have money from their salaries to spend. 'Qingqi is profitable all year round because of being cheaper,' he adds. 'For instance, it can take you from here to the Board Office, for Rs 20 only.'

His main clientele are lower-income groups who pool money and travel in groups. The CNG rickshaw benefits the poor more, he feels. In the absence of meters, the fare is determined by mutual consent, though he feels that people are often unfair when setting a price for his service. 'They think in terms of distances, kilometres, and the cost of CNG,' he says. 'They do not bother to consider the expenses of a rickshaw's maintenance and the driver's need to feed his family. There is an extra Rs 200 per day to be paid as extortion money too.'

The CNG rickshaws are accused of causing traffic jams by moving slowly. Mohammad agrees. The weak chassis forces the drivers to go slowly and avoid the potholes. The rickshaws are always loaded to capacity with the weight of the CNG cylinder as well. 'As the CNG stations are not allowed to work all week, so the drivers keep the cylinders full in order to avoid wastage of time and long queues at the CNG stations,' he points out. Mohammad tells me that if the rickshaw is rented, the driver has to pay Rs 300 per day to the owner. Another Rs 200 per day is spent on maintenance. Buying the CNG for the day is also the responsibility of the driver. After all the expenses, his net income comes to around Rs 500 in a day. 'You know it is difficult to run a household on that meagre amount,' he says.

Mohammad feels much safer in Karachi now in the wake of the Karachi Operation. But there are still plenty of unsafe places in town. 'In some areas like Kati Pahari, we have to climb up the slope and the rickshaw is forced to slow down; even a person on foot can rob us there. I usually avoid going to Pak Colony, old Golimar and some areas of New Karachi.'

I observe that most car drivers do not like rickshaw drivers. He replies that the feeling is mutual. 'They irritate us too,' he says. 'They honk unnecessarily and push us to speed up, throw tantrums, shout abuse, and give us dirty looks. They need to understand that we cannot speed because of the load and also because of the fact that the rickshaw will overturn if we are forced to brake suddenly while going at a high speed.'

He adds, however, that the new generation of CNG rickshaws are better than their predecessors, as they have disc brakes, while the earlier rickshaws had washer brakes. The sudden application of brakes in those rickshaws used to tear the washers apart, he recalls. He feels that the KCR rickshaws were better than the CNG ones in this respect. 'Keeping aside the issue of environmental degradation, the two-stroke combustion engine of KCR had power, so those rickshaws could be driven fast,' he explains. However, the capacity issues made those less lucrative. 'A CNG rickshaw can be used for seating up to six passengers and it can be hired for events like wedding ceremonies as well. It is cheaper for a family of six or seven persons. Sometimes, three or four families book three to four CNG rickshaws to go to a wedding together. It is more economical than hiring a coaster for the same purpose,' he adds. 'A CNG rickshaw has a longer life as compared to the KCR but its spare parts are more expensive. A KCR's engine can be completely overhauled for Rs 5,000, while it takes Rs 10,000 to completely overhaul a CNG engine,' he adds.

Mohammad agrees that women face harassment from other commuters in CNG rickshaws and suggests installing curtains in rickshaws like the ones in Quetta and Peshawar.

Saeed: An Oil-Tanker Driver

Saeed is an Afridi Pashtun and hails from Darra Adam Khan. He migrated to Karachi about twenty-five years ago. Saeed drives a ten-wheeler oil tanker that has a carrying capacity of 50,000 litres. His trips are mostly between Karachi and Peshawar, but he can go to other cities as well. He has been in this business for a decade. Saeed started driving trucks as he was fascinated by big buses and long-distance travel since childhood. 'The huge body of the bus, the speed, the sound system, and the design fascinated me,' he says. 'I also wanted to see Karachi, as I had heard a lot about it. I used to travel with the elders of my area on tankers, going from our area to Karachi. With time, I learnt the routes and locations of various areas, including Karachi.'

He found Karachi to be full of opportunities but feels that Darra's culture is far more developed and superior. I ask him if he is involved in the Afghan transit trade, as it was supposed to be more lucrative. 'No. I must admit that the Afghan transit trade is far more profitable than our business, but the Taliban kill people and we are scared,' he says. According to him, a loaded truck from Karachi takes 40 hours on average to reach Peshawar, while an empty one takes 30 hours. The trucks are usually loaded from Karachi to Peshawar, so it takes longer. The tankers often return empty to Karachi.

I ask what items he carries on his return trip. 'Sometimes we pick up molasses from sugar industries or cooking oil, to take to Karachi.' When he confirms that he carries cooking oil and industrial oil in the same tanker, he hardly notices my surprise. 'We just rinse the container and use it for transporting molasses or cooking oil,' he says.

I turn the conversation to the main challenges he faces on the streets of Karachi. 'Two main problems bother us,' he says. 'Firstly, bikers and Qingqis are a big nuisance. They overtake us narrowly and often from the wrong side. These drivers have no idea that we cannot apply brakes abruptly as it would overturn the truck. Secondly, the volume of traffic is much higher in Karachi and for that matter, in other big cities of Pakistan. That drives us crazy.'

Other people complain about tanker drivers as well, I remind him. He admits his fault. 'We often drive on the extreme right which is supposed to be the fast lane, and we obstruct the way for ambulances or other fast-moving vehicles,' he says. 'Still, this practice is more common in new drivers who have no knowledge of the laws and ethics of driving.' Then he adds, 'The weather is also a big problem. In hot weather, the truck heats up like a furnace. We cannot afford to use air conditioning as it will raise our fuel consumption to the extent of making it unaffordable.'

The tankers are legally banned from entering the city during the day, but you can often find oil tankers on the streets at any time. 'You know how the system works here,' Saeed says. 'Officially, we are only allowed in the city between the two prayer times: *isha* and *fajar*. But if we bribe the policemen, we can enter any time.' I ask how much he pays in bribe usually. 'Between Rs 200 and Rs 2,000,' he says, adding that it depended on the police officer and area. He is very conscious about documents and carries every original paper on his trips up-country; even then, he claims to pay an approximate amount of Rs 5,000 per trip.

'Sindh is the worst in terms of bribery,' he laments. 'Here, we have to bribe the police mobile vans and the traffic police as well.' Sharing his experience of bribery in all provinces, he declares Khyber Pakhtunkhwa to be the least corrupt. 'I feel Khyber Pakhtunkhwa is much better than the Punjab and Sindh. These days, the police in Khyber Pakhtunkhwa are much more professional and honest. It has become difficult to even obtain a license in Khyber Pakhtunkhwa as they test you properly now. According to my experience, Sindh is the worst of all three provinces.'

Things have changed over the years, in his opinion. Trips are becoming less frequent. 'Earlier, we used to wait for hardly two days to receive an order but (now) it takes eight to ten days for a job to arrive,' he says. The laying of pipelines to transport crude and refined oil is the main reason behind this shrinking business. 'If the pipeline network is extended to other parts of the country, we would become redundant,' he says. In conclusion, I ask him if he wants to share anything else. He asks that taxes be reduced. 'Just because of taxes, a single tyre costs Rs 50,000 to Rs 80,000 and a single tyre lasts no more than six months.'

Zaeem: A Water-Tanker Driver

Zaeem is from Kohat, Khyber Pakhtunkhwa and has been delivering water from tankers in Karachi for the last ten years. He is a friend of Saeed and sat with us when I interviewed Saeed. He lives in Hijrat and parks his tanker close to his home, where a group of drivers have pooled money and hired a watchman to guard the parked vehicles.

He tells me that old and discarded oil tankers are re-used as bowsers, each costing Rs 1.8 to Rs 2 million. He takes water from a hydrant located in Garden East and from another one at Recksor. His tanker has a total capacity of 2,000 litres. The price of the water varies from area to area. Sweet water is expensive as compared to slightly brackish water. For a bowser of 1,000 litres, the price of sweet water varies from Rs 3,000 to Rs 5,000. I ask him if driving a 2,000-litre tanker is difficult in Karachi. He says, 'It is difficult when the tanker is fully loaded. I am especially bothered by motorcyclists. They have no idea how difficult and dangerous it is to apply brakes to a fully loaded vehicle.'

But tanker drivers are accused of rash driving as well, I insist. He agrees: 'When my tanker is empty, I do drive at speed on my way to the hydrant or home.' In order to avoid traffic, most tanker drivers prefer to supply water at night between 9 p.m. and 10 a.m. 'After that I go to sleep,' he says.

Zaeem feels that the traffic volume has increased a lot compared to previous years. Haphazard construction has narrowed the streets and contributed to tanker drivers' difficulties. They are also not allowed to use underpasses. He feels that areas like Defence Housing Authority, PECHS Society, and Gulistan-e-Jauhar are easy to drive in, as their streets are wider and well-planned, compared to the colonies. He tells me to ask the authorities to broaden the roads.

The hydrants pay money to the Karachi Water and Sewerage Board. The tanker drivers bribe the police. The rate varies between Rs 200 and Rs 500. 'The Seth[4] always accompanies me in a tanker,' he says, adding that Seth also provides him the money which he has to pay as a bribe. Zaeem feels that the business has decreased over the years because a lot of houses have dug wells or have boreholes. It is possible, he believes, that the business of supplying water through tankers may come to an end in the next ten years or so.

Sajjad: A Medical Doctor

Sajjad is a member of the Pakistan Medical Association (PMA) and is Pashtun by descent. He specialises in public health. Being a self-made man from a modest background, Sajjad comprehends the challenges confronting Karachiites. His father served as a clerk in the Karachi Port Trust (KPT). It was his mother who despite being illiterate was the driving force behind Sajjad and his sisters acquiring a higher education. Sajjad, who also practices privately besides being a PMA member, is perturbed by the alarming rate of increase in pollution in Karachi, which he says endangers lives.

He makes a direct connection between traffic pollution and health problems. 'The vehicle fitness certificate is a saleable commodity,' he says. 'All public transport is unfit to be on the roads and causes pollution, leading to illnesses like pulmonary disease, asthma in children and cancer.'

He finds Karachi and Islamabad to be the most polluted cities of Pakistan, but for different reasons. Karachi is polluted by transport emissions and Islamabad by the pollen grains that produce allergies. He says that trees are being ruthlessly chopped down and new ones are not being planted. 'The lungs of the city are not clean and the air-purifying mechanisms are being compromised,' he says. These pollutants can be lethal. 'In the presence of exogenous material, the human body can tolerate and perform to a certain level, but not after that. It starts reacting in a variety of ways.'

I ask him if he knows that CNG-rickshaws were better than their predecessors—the Italian made 4-stroke rickshaws. He says that theoretically, the CNG rickshaws are much better than the 4-stroke ones, but only if they are maintained properly. 'And that unfortunately is not the case, so they are adding to pollution,' he insists. He says that the issue of poorly maintained vehicles is not limited to rickshaws. 'The rising price of petrol and state policy has pushed cars to switch to CNG, which is supposed to be environmental-friendly. However, the cars are also not maintained properly and emit fumes which are full of contaminants.' But people live on M.A. Jinnah Road despite the pollution and congestion, I interject. 'It is all about planning,' he says.

'After a day's hard work, people want peace and quiet. But circumstances force them to live here only because they know that schools are close by and work is not far away. So, they prefer to sleep less comfortably, inhale toxins, just to spend less time on the roads and less money on commuting.'

To combat problems like these, he suggests, 'You must plan sub-cities like Bahria Town, whose management has announced a bus service from Bahria Town to the central business district.' He believes traffic is causing a large impact on people's health and behaviour. 'High blood pressure is a long-term effect of high noise levels. Other psychological events occur as well. In the short term, behavioural changes can be observed and being intolerant is one of those. Air pollution also results in eye infections and other viral diseases. It worsens conjunctivitis. Air pollution is at the base of all dermatological problems and allergies.'

He thinks that these problems can result in economic and productivity losses. 'An asthma patient cannot climb the staircase and a patient suffering from cardiac illness needs to take more rest,' he says. 'Moreover, both have to spend time waiting for doctors/consultants, periodically. So, at one level productivity declines and on another level, a considerable amount of money is spent on medical care.'

Is it harmful sitting in a vehicle or driving for long hours, I ask, in view of the prolonged traffic jams in the area. He replies, 'Backache and body aches are common complaints in people these days and that is why the most frequently sold medicines are pain killers. In males, sitting for long hours also reduces their sperm count. Arthritis can also set in. Besides that, psychological effects include drivers becoming intolerant and violent.' In terms of noise pollution, motorcycles, and Qingqis make a lot of noise but both are very popular. Sajjad believes this is because of convenience. 'If the state cannot provide the people with mass transit, they are going to create their own solutions.'

He is critical of the role of banks in causing traffic congestion on the roads. 'They have provided loans without any vision, any checks and balances, and without any coordination with the planning and other similar departments,' he laments. 'In fact, banks have seized the opportunity created by the social change in Pakistani society—the rise of an urban middle class that aspires to a better-quality of life.' He also holds builders and property developers responsible, especially for the parking troubles in Karachi. 'The Sindh Building Control Authority asks for allocation of parking spaces as a condition for approving new building plans. The builders include these in the plans, but they do not care, in reality. After receiving their certificate, they alter the structure and make more money by selling the parking areas as "godowns", or for building additional residences.'

A 2006–7 UNICEF study, of which I was a part, concluded that the traffic constables who stand on duty over the course of three to four years in congested spots, fall prey to chest infections, allergies, and dermatological problems. Their output declines and they seek either early retirement, or a post in an office environment. The role of the PMA is limited to organising awareness walks and issuing statements against the timber mafia and other actors, who are responsible for environmental degradation. 'I am not sure if this is a solution,' he says. 'People cannot escape the follies of the system but at least they should be aware of where they are heading.'

Kamran: An Environmentalist

Kamran believes he has an analytical mind and that his sound education background serves him well in his current job as an urban specialist (environment) at the International Union for Conservation of Nature. After graduating from NED University of Engineering and Technology, Karachi, in 2011, Kamran studied for his master's degree in the United Kingdom and taught there before returning to Pakistan.

I ask him about the complex transport system of Karachi. 'Well, it's a vast subject and let us start by saying that there is no mass transit system in Pakistan and in Karachi, that can replace the exorbitant number of vehicles, so that's one reason of pollution in the air,' he says. 'Secondly, the ownership of a car or even a motorcycle is a part of socially upward mobility and is a status symbol, hence the glut. There are other factors as well. After the ban on Qingqis some two months ago, people had little choice but to purchase their own bikes and that's why you suddenly see an increased traffic density on the roads. The motorcycles have occupied and engaged all the roads today. Earlier, Qingqis actually supported the dilapidated bus system in Karachi and the masses were frequently using it for shorter distances in particular.'

Kamran insists that public transport in the informal sector has become expensive, comparing the cost of motorcycle with that of bus travel. 'The market today is flooded with Chinese bikes and you can now own a motorcycle by paying Rs 1,500 as a down payment and Rs 1,000 per month in instalments,' he. 'This is less than the monthly expense incurred on bus travel, which comes to a minimum of Rs 1,300, assuming there are twenty-six working days and Rs 50 for each round trip from the working-class areas to the central business district and back. Also, the buses are neither sufficient in number to cater to the commuting public, nor are they in good condition and therefore the ill-maintained engines, because they are overloaded, consume more fuel, and have more emissions which creates problems and cost a packet.'

Finally, Kamran makes a valid point when he says that although women in Pakistan are increasingly participating in public spheres, the designs of buses are still the same: there is more space for men, but far less for women, which discourages them from opting for public transport. I ask him if this scenario adds considerably to the growing pollution in Karachi. 'Yes, and besides pollution, it's a burden on the economy as well. If we had a mass transit system, it would take 20 per cent of the vehicles off the road, it will be a great contribution towards the national exchequer.'

Keeping in view Kamran's expertise as an urban environmental specialist, my next query is about the effect of pollution on built structures. 'Karachi, like every other city, has spatial limitations,' he says. 'How many flyovers can one build? How many underpasses can one make? You cannot widen the roads further. The human population is bound to grow and thus the population of vehicles will as well; all the more reason that we should focus on a mass transit system. Pavements, footpaths, and roundabouts are compromised, just to maximise whatever spaces are available for vehicles.'

In light of his reply, my next question to Kamran is about the effects pollution has on human health, especially in a city like Karachi. 'The mode of conveyance and the difficulties in travelling, do affect human health,' he says. 'It results in a loss of productivity as increasing fatigue results in transported-related worries. Commuting is like breathing as it is an everyday activity.'

Finally, I ask him whether the elite—those who own a car each, or more—are really bothered about having a mass transit system. 'If they are not, they soon will be,' he says. 'The same elite will be a big proponent of mass transit very soon because they need open spaces to run their luxury cars and SUVs. For me, the core issue is how to plan and coordinate amongst various urban institutions to improve the existing transport system.'

* * * *

As the formal planning sector asserts itself, informal activities that are part of the Karachi transport world will come under stress, since many of them are in violation of existing rules and regulations. As a result, costs of repair and maintenance of vehicles will rise and a large number of 'encroachments' will be removed. It is necessary for planners to integrate this world of informality sympathetically in the future transport vision for the city.

7

Women's Transport Issues

URC and Anadil Iftekhar

In-depth and open-ended interviews with fifteen women were arranged by the Urban Resource Centre, Karachi, for this chapter. The interviewees were from various walks of life and all used public transport for commuting. The gist of their interviews is given in the sections below; excerpts of the interviews are provided after this summary. The interviewees consist of domestic help workers (maids, cleaners); caretakers at schools and offices; white-collar workers at banks and other corporate sector entities; school teachers; students at high schools and universities; and professionals. It is believed that the ratio of working women has increased due to unemployment and inflation. The number of women enrolling at educational institutions has also increased.

A very small and congested portion in front of the bus has been allocated for women. It is because of this that they have to wait for a long time before a bus with vacant seats arrives at their stop. The situation for men is different; they stand by the gates of the bus and sit on the roof as well—women do not do this. Male passengers and/or male bus conductors standing by the gates make it difficult for women to get on and off the bus. Often times, buses do not stop for women who are accompanied by their children or are carrying luggage.

In order to save money, many women opt to take lifts in open Suzukis and sometimes, in containers (*see* Box 7.1 for a case study done by the URC that elaborates on this). These are congested and uncomfortable modes of transport and the state of the roads only worsens the experience; women complain of getting injured and their clothes being damaged. The likelihood of an accident also increases when women and children travel together on motorcycles.

Most interviewees claimed to have experienced some sort of sexual harassment. Men in cars and on motorbikes stop and offer lifts while they are waiting at bus stops. This turns into pestering. Men enter the women's compartment of the bus and refuse to leave when asked to do so. Rickshaw drivers constantly stare at female passengers through their rear-view mirrors while driving. Women complain of men staring a lot. This continues to occur while women walk either to or from their bus stops. Women drivers are also followed, taunted, and verbally abused by men driving cars or motorcycles. Apart from the acts of harassment themselves, women also feel an intense paranoia every day before, during, and after their journeys. Every woman tries to avoid the seat by the partitioning metal bar as men poke their fingers through it.

Many women say that it is due to prevalent harassment that they choose to travel in a veil but that still does not completely prevent harassment.

However, it does help them feel more secure.[1] It is common for women to wear the *hijab* or cover their heads while travelling and to remove them once they are in their workplace.[2] Many interviewees feel insecure while travelling and face some form of sexual harassment. As such, they prefer to take a Qingqi, which is open and visible, or a crowded and uncomfortable bus, rather than a taxi which has locked doors. However, when they travel in groups, they feel secure.[3] It has also been observed that if male university students are in a bus, harassment does not take place.[4] There are also women who claim that they have never been subjected to any kind of harassment.[5]

The interviewees reported that travelling to and from work, caused exhaustion and stress due to high levels of pollution, discomfort, and the many hours spent in commute. This puts them in a bad mood and makes them incapable of doing any other work after returning home.[6] During pregnancy (and by implication in various other difficult circumstances), it is impossible to use the public transport buses.[7]

A number of women also claim that they walk long distances to save on bus fare. To save money, some prefer to take one crowded and uncomfortable bus trip rather than spend more money taking two buses that may not be as crowded and involve shorter routes. For comfort, they also get together to share a Qingqi. This makes the Qingqi as affordable as a bus. However, it is difficult to make such an arrangement, since destinations and timings vary, even though one may live in the same neighbourhood.[8] The highest earning interviewee claims her income is Rs 25,000 and she spends Rs 4,000 on commuting.[9] Due to the unreliability of transport, especially when there are demonstrations in the city and on non-CNG days, it is common to arrive late at work. In such cases, the interviewees get scolded by their bosses and in some cases, there are heavy deductions from their salaries.[10]

The location of a workplace is a determining factor. Usually, one looks for a job in one's own neighbourhood, even if it involves relatively low pay. One of the interviewees also changed her profession and another turned down a good job offer, because of transport-related discomfort.[11] However, many interviewees feel that (motorised) rickshaws and Qingqis have made life easier and more comfortable, provided you can afford them, or share them with a group.[12] But there are other problems here too. Karachi's fast, signal-free roads make it difficult for a pedestrian to cross a thoroughfare other than by pedestrian bridges, which tend to be few and far between. As a result, where it used to take 5 minutes to cross a road, now locating and using a pedestrian bridge can take over 15 minutes. People have made alternative arrangements, like cutting the barrier in the middle of the road to squeeze through or to jump over. Women find this difficult to do.[13]

Another common complaint is that the conductor of the bus often does not return the change of a Rs 20 note when the fare is Rs 17.[14] In one case, the interviewee has sleepless nights thinking of the haggling she will have to do with the bus conductor the next morning, so as to retrieve the extra money.[15] There are other issues too that surface in these interviews. One is the presence of pickpockets, who skilfully rob passengers of their belongings. The other relates to the gas cylinder, which, as already noted, is normally placed behind the driver in the women's compartment. Women consider it to be a live bomb, waiting to explode. The government agencies are aware of this issue. They have taken note and issued orders to where and how the cylinders must be placed, and those who do not place the cylinders as per the government's directions, will have their bus routes cancelled and in addition, a heavy fine will be imposed on them. Nevertheless, the cylinders stay put where they are.[16] Women also have issues related to over-speeding, unrequested stops, being asked to get off the bus into a new bus, or to fend for themselves.

More recently, a great deal of emphasis on women's transport issues is being placed in the planning process in Karachi. The Asian Development Bank has held extensive discussions with women's groups and with Aurat Foundation, for the planning of its Red Line BRT. Women have voiced the concerns mentioned above at the meetings they held with the Asian Development Bank consultants. It is hoped that their concerns will be addressed in the design of the project.

Interviews with Women on Women's Transport Issues[17]

Saima Ismail Shah (age 33)

Saima lives with her sisters in Kharadar; both her parents passed away when she was twelve years old. She lives in an extremely congested locality that experiences daily traffic jams. By profession, she is a freelance graphic designer and is currently enrolled in a course at the Arts Council Institute of Arts and Crafts. She has been working for the past ten years. Buses have always been her only mode of transportation. Her work requires her to travel distances that are too expensive to be covered by rickshaws. There was a time when she rode W-11 all the way from the main road to Karimabad. Located in Karimabad is the famous Memon Markaz, a vocational centre for women, where Saima has taken many courses, including those involving computer training.

Her commuting issues are far worse than those of others, due to the long distances she has to travel. 'I hate it when men enter the lady's section,' she says. 'And when the ladies get up on the bus, the gents refuse to vacate the seats!' When the bus is bursting at its seams with people, many passengers have to resort to standing at the door, and sometimes when the bus screeches to a halt, many passengers fall over.

Saima has often been asked to get off the bus halfway before her destination, when the bus breaks down. The bus engine often fails, or a tyre bursts, or sometimes there is no specific reason. The passengers are loaded onto another bus and the fare is adjusted, but sometimes they have to fend for themselves.

The bus journey, with its unsolicited stops, often results in Saima turning up late for her appointments. When she was studying different courses at different universities, being late resulted in missing out on content of the course, receiving reprimands from the teachers and general disapproval. For her office jobs, it resulted in monetary loss. At the advertising agency she worked for, Rs 250 were routinely deducted from her salary for arriving late. She has worked in various firms on a one-year or two-year contract.

Eventually, she decided to become a freelancer, as the daily commuting was killing her. Now, she has to go to the office either once a week, or every ten days. While commuting, she had to carry heavy material, such as a drawing board, sheets etc. for her work. These things take up space and are cumbersome to carry on buses. 'There is not a single day when men or other women don't harass me,' she says. The seat by the partitioning metal bar is forbidden as men constantly poke their fingers through the grill. If the women reprimand them, men act as if they are unaware of the accusation being hurled at them. She gets depressed and talks about theft instead.

'Last week, my sister, along with two other women, were robbed by armed women in the bus,' she says. 'Her money and CNIC were both in the purse.' While the lady thieves were busy in the women's section, the men's section was being robbed by male thieves. Saima firmly believes that theft will continue unabated.

While she prefers not to reveal her salary, she does say that bus rides may be the cheapest option available, but they too aren't very economical. Her range of fare is from Rs 10–17, for huge buses like 4K and Rs 20–25 for coaches, even if only a single bus is taken. But if a single bus doesn't take her to her route, then changing the bus can make one way of the journey as high as Rs 40–45. Even within the parameters of Saddar, a ride takes at least 30 minutes, while the trip to Karimabad can take up to 90 minutes. In addition, too much time is lost in walking and crossing roads. At Shahrah-e-Faisal, she has to walk a long distance to reach the pedestrian bridge, which she then has to cross to reach the other side of the road. If she can cross the road, it will take only 5 minutes, but taking the pedestrian bridge increases the time to 15 minutes.

At the end of the day, when she gets back home, she is in a bad mood and feels sick. Saima doesn't like to work when she gets back home, but she has accepted that things aren't going to change.

Bushra

Unlike the other passengers, Bushra, a bachelor's student at Jinnah University for Women, has no complaints with regards to commuting. Her house is located in sector 5-C-4, North Karachi and Jinnah University is approximately 14 km away, near the Board Office in North Nazimabad. Her daily fare is Rs 40. During the days of CNG closure, she pays an extra Rs 10. Her life was made much easier with the introduction of the Qingqi in the locality. Previously, she had to take a bus, but it was too taxing. All the girls from the university take a bus and it tends to get extremely crowded. Her commuting time is approximately 30 minutes.

Apart from the luxury of the direct route of the Qingqi, Bushra also has the advantage of being surrounded by an army of students of Jinnah University, both in the morning and evening, at her bus stop. So, crossing the road in the morning isn't a problem, as the sheer volume of girls forces the traffic to be responsive to their presence at the Board Office signal.

Similarly, in the afternoon, a number of girls walk with Bushra to the signal, so she has been spared the sexual harassment, although she says that men do stare and make the girls feel uncomfortable. If the city's situation worsens and the Qingqis disappear from the roads, then some three or four girls living close to her house would hire a rickshaw and divide the fare between them. On being asked the choice of her university, Bushra replies that she didn't even consider any other option because Jinnah was so convenient. 'Karachi University isn't that far, but I heard cases where the point service was a misery for the girls; so Jinnah it was,' she says.

Other than her university commute, Bushra hardly goes out on her own. With family, she has to resort to whatever mode of transport they may choose. Since she does not travel far and wide, Karachi transport is not that much of a hassle for her.

Rimsha (age 15)

A student of The Citizens Foundation (TCF) School, in Gulshan-e-Zia, Orangi Town, Rimsha had to move from her grandmother's house to her parents' place because of the inconvenience of bus rides. She was more comfortable living in her maternal grandmother's house in Gulshan-e-Bihar, where her aunt would also help her with studies. The journey time from her grandmother's house was approximately 15 to 20 minutes, but in the morning, catching a bus was quite an ordeal due to the lack of vehicles. More than often, Rimsha, along with her other friends, would have to walk for up to 30 minutes. She is not sure of the distance, but it could be around 8 km, according to her, and since there is no footpath or pavement, it is often a painful experience.

The zooming bikes and buses that tend to drive recklessly have made Rimsha and her friends extremely cautious. The locality in which her school is located, is extremely under-developed. Her school has a radius of 2 km of unpaved road. In fact, the topography is slightly rugged, with a mole nearby. At home time, Rimsha has to wait for at least half an hour for the bus and when it finally arrives, a sea of students climb onto it, making it extremely crowded and congested. Rimsha often has to stand at the edge of the door. In such situations, the fear of falling out of the bus is ever present.

The bus fare is Rs 2 per ride. All TCF students pay this amount. Sometimes, however, the bus driver refuses to stop his vehicle for students, on the pretext that other passengers would pay the normal fare, which is higher than the student fare. As Rimsha travelled on the bus with lots of other girls, the group companionship saved them from sexual harassment. 'No one ever bothered me because there were too many of us,' she says.

As if crowded buses weren't enough of a discomfort, the drivers are often under the influence of drugs and drive rashly. The way the bus swerves on a straight road, there is always the possibility that an accident may occur. At times, the buses start racing with each other on the roads, endangering the lives of all those on board.

'I was fed up of the daily ordeal, so I decided to move in with my parents, who live very close to my school,' she says. She misses her grandmother's house but can save a lot of time living in her parents' home. She has more time to study, do household chores and carry out her embroidery work, which is a huge cottage-based industry in Orangi Town. While Rimsha was lucky to have an option of moving closer to school, her friends continue to suffer from commuting woes every day.

Shahnaz Anjum (age 27)

People say life gets harder for women after they get married. For Shahnaz this is true, especially when it comes to commuting. Prior to getting married, she lived in Nagan Chowrangi, from where a Qingqi ride of Rs 20 took her to the school in North Nazimabad, where she works as a librarian. Her new home is in Hussainabad. This area is almost 4–5 km from her school, but there is no direct Qingqi ride. The bus, with its cylinder and congestion, does not appeal to Shahnaz. Taxis, with their jammed doors are not inviting either, therefore rickshaws are her only option.

But rickshaws offer no fairy tale rides. She is charged Rs 80 each way, which means Rs 160 a day. And on days of CNG closure, she is charged up to Rs 120. Her monthly cost of commuting falls between Rs 3,600 to Rs 3,800. And so, almost Rs 4,000 of her monthly income of Rs 25,000, goes towards commuting such a short distance.

She could take two Qingqis and walk to cut her costs. However, the problem is that she is pregnant and the pollution and heat make her nauseous. Shahnaz leaves home at 7:20 a.m., to arrive at work by 7.45 a.m. She gets home by 4 p.m. or 4:15 p.m. Her travel time also depends on the availability of the rickshaw and the mood of the driver. Every day is an uphill struggle for Shahnaz, as she always has to negotiate the fare. She often has a tense night's sleep as she anticipates the bargaining process for the next morning. 'It is not just about bargaining. Even if the fare is decided to be Rs 80, on reaching my destination, I give the driver a Rs 100 note. The driver keeps the extra Rs 20 saying he has no change. When the fare is set at Rs 120, I give him Rs 100 and 50 notes. He doesn't bother returning my thirty rupees,' laments Shahnaz. She struggles to carry change but is not always successful.

On days of CNG closure, drivers act as if they are doing her a favour or giving to charity. 'Give me Rs 120, or go to hell,' they remark insolently. While the rickshaw is the best option available, it is still a pain. There are too many mirrors where drivers can observe all parts of women's body. Then there is the problem of reckless driving. Slowing the rickshaw at speed breakers would avoid the vehicle from tumbling over. The nasty bumps that occur make Shahnaz sure that one day her rickshaw will topple over. Speeding rickshaws often collide into other speeding vehicles, even motorcycles.

In addition, choosing a rickshaw is not very different from shopping for clothes, according to her. Apart from the fare, the driver's mood and temper, she also has to make sure it is cylinder-free. Many rickshaws carry LPG cylinders, or unchecked CNG cylinders that have been termed as walking time bombs. Sometimes, she is lucky to find a cylinder-free rickshaw, or the old-fashioned 2-stroke rickshaws that make too much noise. But putting up with the heat, bumps, and noise is now becoming too painful for Shahnaz.

As her pregnancy progresses, she is fearful of continuing her job. And much more worrisome is the fact that once the baby arrives, she doesn't know how she will manage. She will have to carry the baby in the rickshaw because there is no one to take care of it at home. And the school doesn't have day care. On reaching home, she has to also prepare food for her husband and herself. She skips lunch because she is so tired and exhausted. Sometimes, hunger wins and causes her to resort to unhealthy packet noodles. She might even have to leave her job for a while at least, until the baby is old enough to be left with an aunt or uncle. This is a matter of grave concern, as she needs to work in order to run her house.

Sanjeeda (age 35)

Sanjeeda's day begins early, shortly after *fajr* prayers. She often does her morning chores while having breakfast, or else the early Shama Coach would depart without her. She has to reach the bus stop of Korangi No. 2.5 by 6 a.m., as the coach leaves at 6:05 a.m. If that coach is missed, Sanjeeda is doomed. The next Shama Coach leaves after 7:30 a.m., but this is the time that she has to reach her workplace. On days of CNG closure, she often runs late and gets reprimanded by her managers.

Sanjeeda works as a maid in a school in North Nazimabad Block B. She commutes a daily distance of 18 km. The Shama Coach drops her at the Karimabad stop, from where she walks approximately 2 km. Sometimes, when she is running late, or when the heat is unbearable, she would take a Qingqi ride for Rs 10. Her routine bus fare is Rs 40 each way.

The bus route takes 90 minutes. 'I sleep en route—what else can one do on the congested bus ride anyway?' she says. Sanjeeda leaves the school at 4 p.m. and arrives home by around 5:45 p.m. or 6 p.m.

The bus nap is not just a way to kill time, it is essential to recharge this mother of three children, who on reaching home, has to run household errands. Her eldest child, a 15-year-old daughter, helps her with the housework. Her husband has set up a food stall near their home.

Why did she choose to work in North Nazimabad if she resides in Korangi?

'I was working for a private school in Baloch Colony. The madame of the school got transferred to its North Nazimabad branch, taking me with her. After working for almost a decade in the area, I came across a vacancy at another school's new branch,' she says. She applied and got the job.

Life was already hard on her and the bus rides only add to her stress. She is tortured mentally and often physically on these rides. The seat by the metal bar, which segregates the male and female compartments, is one where every female sits as the last resort. The simple reason being that it is the hotspot for sexual harassment. Men sitting behind are often accused of poking fingers to touch the woman's body.

Sanjeeda narrates a similar ordeal that occurred in 2000. Forced to sit on the hotspot seat because all others were occupied, she took her usual nap. In her slumber, she felt something touching her hip and back. She woke up and realised that the man behind her was harassing her. She lashed out at him.

Apart from sexual harassment, timings and congestion, the bus ride has also become a haven for thieves. 'There are two types of thieves,' she says. 'One is armed men and the second is groups of unarmed women pickpockets draped in *chadors*, or *burkas*.'

The armed male dacoits snatch stuff from men but refrain from touching the female passengers in Sanjeeda's experience. They point their guns at women and ask them to hand over their belongings. Thefts often take place near Purani Sabzi Mandi and Hasan Square. The second group takes maximum advantage of the rush and congestion and swiftly swipes valuable items like wallets, money, and phones. 'It was, I guess 2012, when I was carrying a Rs 1,000 note in my wallet, which was in a shopping bag,' she recalls. 'I was standing, but when a seat was vacated nearby, I offered it to another lady. That lady stole my money.' As the heat intensifies in the months of May, June, and July, Sanjeeda's bus rides grow increasingly suffocating; but she can't leave this job, as the supply of labour for school janitors has increased. She earns Rs 8,000, without which she cannot run her house.

Christine (age 31)

New to the world of commuting, Christine is a resident of Essa Nagri, located opposite the Civic Centre. Her husband is a mechanic and they have three children.

Christine currently works at a private school in Gulshan Block 7. She has been working for six months now. Before this school, Christine worked at another school at Maskan Chowrangi for two years but left because her new employer offered more money. She also had the option of working for a school at Johar Mor but didn't avail the opportunity as no single bus took her to that location from Essa Nagri, despite the driving distance of 10–15 minutes. Therefore, she chose her job on the basis of available transport. She had to change two buses and that tended to get exhausting and time-consuming. Her children were of a young age and she wanted to make sure that she spent time with them, so, she quit the job. Currently, she leaves her children in the care of two other families that reside in the same house.

Christine took a gap and re-joined the workforce in 2011 as school maid. Her work timings are 7:30 a.m. to 3:45 p.m. She leaves her house at 6:15 a.m., so that she can reach her bus stop by 6:30 a.m. The buses are usually empty in the morning, so Christine can sit comfortably. She reaches her destination stop by 7 a.m. She walks a further 2 km to reach the school, which is located deep in the web of alleys that cut through a residential area. The school connects to Ispahani Road, but Christine gets off at main Gulshan Road, which runs from Gulshan Chowrangi to Maskan Chowrangi. She leaves the school at 4 p.m. and walks for 10 to 15 minutes, to reach the bus stop. On the way back, the bus is often full, to the extent that she has to hang onto the door. She gets home by 5 p.m.

Since she has only been commuting for a few years, she has not faced any experience of sexual harassment, or theft. 'Maybe because a lot of university boys are on the bus and they don't do anything to me,' says Christine. The only thing that bothers her, other than the long walks, is that the bus conductor doesn't return the change. Her fare usually varies from Rs 15–17. She hands a Rs 20 note but has to ask the conductor to return Rs 5, or Rs 3. Often, the conductor says he doesn't have the full change and returns only Rs 2, or so.

On days of the public transport shutdown, she would use the Qingqi or, more than often, take a rickshaw with other maids from her school, as well as maids from neighbouring schools, whose shift ended at the same time as her's.

She really looks forward to the time when the school will provide her with transport.

Sughra (age 48)

Sughra lives in Essa Nagri. She is married, but her husband lives with his other wife. She has four children, two of whom are married and live separately. Out of the remaining two, one daughter works at a beauty parlour. The son lives in Punjab with her mother—away from the city, as he suffers from asthma. Sughra also used to live in Punjab, but she moved to Karachi some fifteen years ago.

Sughra works at a private school in Gulshan Block 7, which earns her a salary of Rs 7,500 a month. She also works at a house located within the Karachi University premises. 'I have been working for them for a really long time', she says. She earns Rs 2,000 from her second job. Her daily fare adds up to Rs 50 and at times far higher than this, depending on whether she takes a bus—or when she used to take a Qingqi—and this also depends on how much she walks.

She leaves her house early in the morning, walking for 10–15 minutes up to the main road in front of the Civic Centre. From there, she goes to the school in Block 7. Again, she has to walk almost 2 km. She leaves her school at around 4 p.m. and goes to the house where she works as a maid. She often opts to walk the distance between her two employers, to save on fare. She finishes her chores by 6:30 p.m. Finally, after a long and exhausting day, she gets home between 7:30 p.m. and 8 p.m.

'The second job is tiring, but I need to save money for my son's treatment,' she says. With Rs 50, or more spent every day as fare, her monthly budget for commuting amounts to at least Rs 1,500. Rs 4,000 of her total earnings goes towards the house rent. This leaves her with roughly Rs 4,000 to run her house, buy groceries, and pay for her son's medical expenses.

Even though the distance she travels is not far, commuting takes up much of her precious time, owing to the slow movement of public transport and the time it takes to cross roads. And that is not all. At times, the bus conductor refuses to return the change. More than often, the bus arrives late, causing Sughra to reach her destination late. 'I get scolded a lot for being late, but it isn't my fault,' she says. In fact, she had been fired from a few houses where she worked as a maid, due to her lack of punctuality. She hasn't faced any sexual harassment. As far as theft is concerned, she is safe because she doesn't carry a large amount of money on her.

Tina (age 26)

Tina works at the customer service department of a renowned bank at I.I. Chundrigar Road. She lives in North Karachi, which is far from the main city. After graduating, she received job offers from different companies, but had to turn many of these down because she was unable to arrange for transport. 'I don't want to spend half my day on the roads,' she says, referring to some of the lucrative job offers she received in the localities of Clifton and Defence. She doesn't want to disclose her salary.

Tina got married recently and is continuing with her job. But each day is an ordeal for her. It takes her 1 hour and 40 minutes to reach her office in the morning and nearly 2 hours to return home in the evening. Tina mostly uses the bus, but sometimes has to opt for the rickshaw, depending on her stamina. She finds the bus rides a great misery, but owing to the lower fare compared to rickshaws, she tends rely on these.

Tina claims that more than often, she wastes time waiting for the bus. And the buses are so loaded with passengers that she has to stand for the entire length of the journey. What bothers her the most is that there are males in the female compartment, both in the morning and evening. Even though the male compartment has more seats and many sit on the rooftop, men still continue to enter the ladies' section; passengers end up fighting for a seat. As staring is a national hobby, men ogle from the back at the women in the front, no matter how well-covered the woman is, she claims. And if that wasn't enough, the over-speeding of the bus is another concern. Even though it is commonly assumed that bus drivers stop the vehicles for women, Tina says that it always depends on the bus driver's mood.

Besides the incidents inside the bus, many events at the bus stop also irritate her. 'It is common for desperate men to stop their cars and bikes in front of the female passengers and offer them rides.' Since those males are complete strangers, Tina feels insecure and annoyed.

Moreover, Tina is extremely tired and feels low on reaching home. She is unable to participate in any household activities with energy. She sincerely hopes that the harassment decreases so that girls like her can feel safe.

MS (age 31)

MS is an employee at a private company on I.I. Chundrigar Road. She joined the company in 2005. She lived in Gulshan Block 1. MS relied on the public buses back then to commute all the way to I.I. Chundrigar Road. She commuted on the buses for two-and-a-half years after which she got married and resigned. However, a year later, in 2009, she re-joined the same office.

Back in 2006, an incident occurred that shook MS. She used to take the U or U-4 from Gulshan Block 1 to Urdu Science College, from where she boarded another bus. At her first stop, a 35-year-old man started harassing her. His timings matched with her's, so she would cross paths with him daily. One day, she felt the man coughing behind her. At first, she thought it was her imagination. But the coughing persisted on a daily basis. The man would either stand behind her at the stop or sit behind the metal railing in the bus. MS started avoiding sitting on the seat by the metal railing. This ordeal continued for a month, until finally she stopped getting on the bus if she saw that that man board it. 'I wasted my time waiting for another bus, but I had to do something,' says MS. Sometimes she would leave work early. After a while, the man disappeared.

MS suffered the usual issues of time and exhaustion while commuting on the bus. She now uses only rickshaws, as she has lost her stamina and patience for the bus. She has a little daughter and still lives in Gulshan, in an apartment block on Rashid Minhas road. A rickshaw ride costs her Rs 250–300 and takes up to 45 minutes. 'Harassment is prevalent in rickshaws as well,' she says.

The driver touches your hands while taking the money and keeps staring through the mirrors. Passengers on bikes and cars also peep in the rickshaws if they see a woman sitting inside.

Her office provides her with transport in the morning and evening. MS can't take advantage of the facility in the morning, because she has to look after her daughter until her mother comes home. She then drops the baby off at her mother's house. In the evening, she uses mostly office transport, or her husband picks her up on his bike. She has tried her best to find decent jobs in her area, where the timings can be flexible enough for her to look after her daughter, but she has been unsuccessful in this thus far. She loses a significant portion of her income on commuting.

MJ

MJ is a resident of Agra Taj Colony, in Lyari and is in her early thirties. She studied at Karachi University. It was quite a hassle for her to commute every day, but this was some ten years ago, when the traffic and violence were not as bad as they are today. And so, she didn't have much difficulty.

After graduating, MJ worked for a private company in the city's commercial hub, I.I. Chundrigar Road. Initially, she came on public coaches. After a few years, she moved to another private firm, also on I.I. Chundrigar Road. She has been with this company for the past many years. Although the distance between her house and workplace is not much, she gets disturbed by the constant violence in Lyari. Often, the streets become a no-go area, or are blocked. But she has learned to survive.

In fact, just six months back, her office agreed to provide her with transport, both in the morning and evening. Life has become very comfortable since then. However, before this luxury, MJ used to come on her own in the morning. Someone in her family dropped her, or she used public transport.

On her way back, she got the office van to drop her off. 'I have been using the drop service for the past two years', she says.

Once, back in 2005, MJ was sitting in the bus, on the seat by the door, in the woman's compartment. Mobile phones had just become popular and MJ had bought herself a new one. She had slightly taken out the phone from her purse to check the message she received. A man came into the ladies' section and hung by the door. MJ thought he was the conductor. Unfortunately, he wasn't. As MJ's grip on her purse loosened, the man snatched her purse, jumped out of the bus, and in 2 minutes disappeared onto the streets of Karachi. It was a big loss, as it contained money and documents.

MJ used to sit in such fear and insecurity, like many other girls in Karachi. She was paranoid that someone would harass her. However, since the provision of office transport, her miseries have lessened. She is single and has many family members living in her house, so she doesn't have many domestic responsibilities.

Anonymous (age 24)

TR has a master's degree in economics from a renowned local university. She resides in Rizvia society, Nazimabad. She earns around Rs 40,000 per month, working at a research organisation situated on Tariq Road.

TR has commuted on buses all her life. She has to walk up to the main road of Nazimabad No. 1 and then use the underground crossing to reach the other side of the road. The underground crossing is necessary, as the main road is barricaded and being a girl, she can't jump over the fence, or squeeze through. However, she has been crossing it since childhood, so now it seems like routine.

The buses are always overcrowded, and she stands for most of her ride. She does get stared at, but that is not frequent. Nevertheless, she still feels uneasy in the bus and stays alert. 'I can't think of using the public transport after 7 p.m.,' she says. If office work holds her back, then she calls her father to pick her up.

Like most young girls, TR has also suffered from sexual harassment, even though she dons the *abaya*. More than on the bus, it is at the bus stops where the men ogle and try to intimidate girls, in TR's experience. However, once a bus conductor tried to touch her in a very subtle manner.

She spends Rs 50 per day if she travels on the bus, but the rickshaw cost goes up to Rs 200. Sometimes, TR takes the bus or the rickshaw, while at other times her father also picks her up. Because she earns a decent salary, she can afford the rickshaw rides. She is single and doesn't have many responsibilities at home. Her mood is good when she reaches home, but on the days when the bus is overcrowded, she gets exhausted and just wants to rest.

Zara (age 23)

Zara is single and lives in Garden West, near Fawara Chowk, with her mother, niece, and nephew. She spent her life commuting on public transport. She did her BCom from Commerce College, PIB, in 2012. She went to Kharadar for tuition.

While going to college was not regular as per the trend, Zara often went to the coaching centre at Kharadar, which took 30 minutes and a fare of Rs 15 each way. If she went to her college, she went from the coaching centre. The bus took 15 minutes and cost Rs 10.

Zara never travelled alone. She had a group of friends with her at all times. They always took precautions. They never sat on the seat by the metal bar, which segregates the ladies' section. Zara has been lucky to not have ever been robbed, but her friends have lost their mobiles to thugs and women pickpockets. In 2011, a group of women boarded the bus and very quietly stole her friends' mobile phones. The girls realised it much later. Zara was spared, because she was sitting on the front corner seat.

'Once, a scary incident happened near Lea Market, in 2012, four armed young boys entered the bus and looted everyone in the men's section,' shares Zara. 'I nearly fainted at the sight of the gun, but for some reason they didn't approach the ladies' section,' she continues. Zara tells me that while the looting took place, the driver had increased the volume of the song so that the sound of the robbers screaming, and threatening passengers would not be audible to anyone outside the bus, providing a smooth escape for the criminals.

After graduating, Zara taught at a school 10 minutes away from her house. She also enrolled in a master's programme at a university in North Nazimabad. While going to school in the morning was not inconvenient, commuting all the way to North Nazimabad in the evening was exhausting. She usually does household chores in the morning and departs for the university at 5 p.m. Her class is from 6 p.m. to 9 p.m. She used to take a Qingqi that drives on a direct route from her house to her university. Her fare each way was Rs 30.

When her class finishes at 9 p.m., she leaves with two friends who live in her neighbourhood. They cross the pedestrian bridge and hail a Qingqi on the other side of the road. 'People stare at me suspiciously as if I am a prostitute,' says Zara.

She doesn't usually wear a veil, but travelling alone daily forces her to do so, though she takes it off once she gets to the university. Zara is hopeful that once her master's degree is complete, she will have the relief of not needing to travel in the evenings and find a day job.

Zaib-un-Nisa (age 30)

Zaib-un-Nisa is a resident of New Karachi, sector 5-D and a mother of three. Her eldest child is 13 years old. Her husband died three years ago, after which she moved in with her mother and brother. Initially, she took up stitching, as she didn't want to leave her children unattended. Unfortunately, she didn't receive enough orders and for the ones she did get, women in her locality were paying less. Therefore, she decided to join a school as a maid and was hired by a school in Gulshan.

Zaib commutes via Masood Coach, as it takes her directly to her destined bus stop. Although buses start their early morning journey from New Karachi and Surjani Town, more than often, Zaib finds the bus overcrowded. She still boards it, even if there is no seat available. 'I will rather stand and take one bus than sit and take two buses,' she says. Sometimes the Masood coach doesn't even have space to stand, so she takes the F-18. But it drops her at another stop, from where she catches another bus. Using two buses costs her double the amount. Her charge for one way of the journey is Rs 17, but the conductor doesn't bother to return her change of Rs 3. When she takes the F-18, she pays Rs 20 and then Rs 10–15 for the second bus ride. Her fare goes up to Rs 60 if she takes two buses.

In the morning, she has to walk a short distance that takes up to 10 minutes. The bus journey itself takes approximately one hour. In the morning, she reaches the bus stop by 6:30 p.m., as buses coming after that time are packed. She leaves her school by 4:30 p.m. to 5 p.m. and reaches home by 6 p.m. She does take part in household chores, but her mother helps her a lot in looking after her three children.

Once, Zaib was carrying Rs 500 in her purse, but by the time she got home, her purse was missing. 'It was in my shopping bag; how can someone take it without me noticing it?' she wonders.

Recently, she sprained an ankle while boarding the bus. The vehicle had started to move as she tried getting on, causing her to lose her grip. Zaib hopes that the school provides her with transport, or some sort of facility, so that she could save money and enjoy some comfort while on the road.

Fatima (age 30)

Fatima is a bathroom cleaner at a hotel on Shahrah-e-Faisal. She started working there only fifteen days prior to the interview. She worked at the Kidney Centre for two years and Saylani Welfare for eighteen months prior to that. Her current job will bring her Rs 10,000 a month. Her husband has been diagnosed with diabetes, which has rendered him unemployed.

Fatima is only middle-pass and got married when she was 14 years old. She has six children, three of whom study at formal educational institutes, while the rest receive tuition in the neighbourhood.

Fatima doesn't like travelling on buses, because she needs to save every penny she earns. She walks every day to and from work to save on the transport cost. She lives in an area called Bizerta Lines, which is close enough, but her journey on foot takes 30 minutes.

'Sometimes my feet hurt, but I still walk because I want to save the ten rupees that the Qingqi, or bus costs,' says Fatima. Her sister lives in Malir, but she doesn't go to meet her that often because she can't afford to spend so much money on transport.

However, it is her eldest daughter's journey that drains money from the family budget. The 17-year-old is studying at an intermediate college in Zamzama. She is dropped off at Cantt station in the morning by her father, from where she takes a bus to Zamzama and then walks to her college. On the way back, however, she often has to wait for the bus for quite some time or walk further. In both cases, car drivers slow their vehicle around her, making her very uncomfortable. 'We give her Rs 100 every day, of which around Rs 50–60 is spent on commuting,' says Fatima. 'She needs the rest of the money for stationery and a canteen lunch'.

She is determined to educate her daughter so that she can work at a bank. Her daughter has already taken a computer course and will be enrolling on an English language course, which will increase her chances of becoming a receptionist, or computer operator at a bank. For this reason, Fatima will continue to walk and not take public transport.

Sehrish

Sehrish is considered to be privileged as, unlike the vast majority, she has the luxury of possessing her own car. She has been driving for the past seven years. Before that, she used school vans and rickshaws. Her father has always been stationed out of Karachi for work. She lives with her mother and is the only child.

Sehrish is a teacher at a school and resides near Millennium Mall, in Gulshan Iqbal. 'The reason why I learned to drive is because once I was walking due to the unavailability of rickshaws to the shop with my mother; when we were near Johar Mor, a drunkard in a Prado started chasing us, shouting profanities. It was a very scary episode,' she says.

The fuel and maintenance of the car doesn't leave her pinched for cash, she nevertheless faces the same hardships as many other female commuters.

In 2012, a motorcyclist took a wrong U-turn and came in front of her car. She had to pull her hand brake. The motorcyclist, instead of apologising, came out to her car, pulled out the car keys from her ignition, and started abusing her. She had to scream for help. Luckily, a policeman came and dealt with the motorcyclist.

She isn't spared the sexual harassment either. 'I was dressed up with a lot of makeup at around dusk, when two boys on a motorcycle deliberately manoeuvred their bike next to my car window.'

'Look at her,' one of them said to the other. The other boy turned to look at her and showed her his middle finger. They both zoomed away, but Sehrish was upset. She picked up her pace with that of the motorcycle and swirled her car in front of the bike. The bikers took a sharp turn to avoid collision but ended up hitting the boundary wall of the flyover.

Recently, a white corolla also chased her. She used her driving skills and took a sharp turn, leaving the driver with his car rammed into the boundary wall of another flyover. 'It is easy to manipulate the drivers on a flyover due to blind spots,' she says proudly.

Apart from sexual harassment, she had the bitter experience of dealing with the police, who penalised her for a car sticker marked '2013'. This despite the fact that she had the registration and slip of tax registration for the year 2014. This incident happened near Time Medico.

In March 2014, as she was leaving her university in Gulshan Block 13, at 9:30 p.m., she realised that the battery of her car was missing. It was very frustrating. She had to call her mother, who came in a taxi, with a mechanic. The mechanic towed the car with a rope, while Sehrish returned home with her mother. She had to purchase a new battery. 'As a girl, it was scary to stand alone at night, when everyone around me could see that my car battery was missing and I was helpless,' she says.

While she doesn't have to worry about wasting time commuting, negotiating over fares and the worry of transport availability, she nevertheless faces gender-related problems.

* * * *

The history of the transport sector shows that sound recommendations can very easily be developed, but their implementation requires rules, regulations and procedures, and training for those who manage the system. To create a female-friendly transport system, it will be necessary to train transported-related staff to behave properly with women and help them feel secure and safe from harassment. Changing attitudes is often a difficult and lengthy process that needs monitoring, modification (over time) and nurturing.

Box 7.1: A Bus Route for Women Domestic Workers

In March 2012, the URC Social Organiser noticed that groups of women at bus stops or crossroads stop vehicles to get a lift as a group. The vehicles they usually stop are trucks and/or vans carrying cargo. He observed this for some time and then gave a group of six women a lift in the URC Suzuki van. Discussions followed. After these initial discussions, further discussions with women at the crossroads were initiated. And a number of findings emerged.

The women were domestic workers and consisted of various ethnicities. However, members of a group belonged to the same ethnicity and came from the same area. The URC focused on the group belonging to the Baloch community who live in Macha Goth, Yousuf Goth, and Saeedabad, all in North Karachi. Contacts in these settlements led to the discovery that between 1,500 to 2,000 women move every day from these low-income settlements in the north of the city to the middle and elite areas of the city in the south, to work as domestic workers. On their way from their homes to work (a 25 km journey), they take public transport which costs them Rs 35 to Rs 40. For the journey, they have to change buses. If they did not have to change buses, the cost would be Rs 16 to Rs 20 one-way.

To save costs, they try and get a lift on the way back. Thus, they save about 8 to 10 per cent of their income. The journey from their home to their places of work can be anything between 90 to 120 minutes and they have to be punctual which is not required on their way back.

Discussions with the women showed that their transport costs would be halved if they did not have to change buses and travel time would also be reduced. Understanding this, the URC approached the general secretary and coordinator of the Sindh Pakistan Peoples Party (PPP) (which is the government in Sindh) in August 2013 and discussed as to what could be done to provide transport for these women. It was suggested that a new route should be developed from the settlements to the areas where these women worked. The URC identified such a route and made it pass through locations that would be lucrative for the operators.

With the PPP coordinator a visit was made to the RTA secretary's office and the decision to issue a route permit for the URC identified route, was agreed upon. On 10 February 2014, the route permit was issued in the name of the URC. Since then, URC has been trying to get the transporters to ply ten buses (the minimum required under law) on this route. However, the transporters say that given the low fares, they are not willing to invest in this venture. The URC, currently, is looking for alternatives.

Source: Urban Resource Centre, Karachi

8

Recommendations

Arif Hasan

This chapter attempts to draw some conclusions and suggests broad recommendations based on the findings in the preceding chapters. Perhaps the most important conclusion that can be reached is the fact that there is a clear link between the nature of governance, the technology used for transport, affordability, housing, land use, access to livelihoods (especially for women), health, family well-being and the quality transport. In short, transport must be viewed as an integral part of a larger city-planning exercise.

Institutional arrangements for government transport programmes for Karachi are related to the structure of governance at the time at which the programme was proposed and implemented. Since governance structures have changed from time to time, transport programmes have suffered due to a lack of continuity. The transporters, government officials, and public all agree that Karachi needs large buses that can provide a comfortable means of commuting. However, the purchase and operation of these buses is costly, and the service cannot be made affordable to the public without the provision of a subsidy.

Government programmes have failed in their objectives for several reasons. Without a subsidy, these programmes operated at a loss and were unsustainable. One instance where the government did promise such subsidies, it did not deliver the same. There were also maintenance issues, such as the use of substandard spare parts, which adversely affected the performance of the vehicles. There were also the pilferage of funds and a loss of vehicles due to riots and political violence. So as to keep transport affordable to the public, the government did not permit the private sector to raise its fares in proportion to the rising cost of fuel. As a result, the formally and informally-financed private sector was unwilling to invest in conventional transport modes such as minibuses. The result has been a decline in the number of buses and the quality of the service.

The courts have added to the transport crisis by ordering all public transport vehicles to convert to CNG. This order was issued without a proper understanding of the availability of CNG, or of the government's plans regarding energy-related issues. The various governments in Pakistan (after the order was issued) did not challenge the courts' decision.

There are institutional issues as well. The various government departments dealing with transport in the city are not coordinated. As is evident from the interviews (*see* Appendix 3.2) with government officials, they have differences in opinion. In addition, police corruption is rampant and as a result, public transport vehicles operate without roadworthy tests and certificates. Unregistered public transport vehicles operate on the roads and the drivers who pay a monthly bribe to the police can violate traffic rules and regulations, causing traffic jams and inconvenience to commuters.

The free transport policy of 1971 was a step in the right direction, given the problems the city faced at that time. However, the fact that individuals, or groups who wished to operate a vehicle had to purchase it on hire, or at high rates of interest, led to the creation of a group of moneylenders controlling the informally financed transport system. The fact that these financiers belong to a particular ethnic group and favoured it over other groups, resulted in the introduction of ethnic politics in the transport sector in the city. If the government had financed these vehicles through bank loans, the situation would have been very different, and the menace that Karachiites refer to as the 'transport mafia' would have been very different in nature.

Government programmes have not been able to compete with the informally financed private sector for a number of reasons and have suffered as a result. The service provided by this sector has meant considerably cheaper minibuses, low paid and overworked drivers and conductors, and almost no administrative overheads, or paperwork. However, this sector understands the city and its commuters, and the ability to identify lucrative routes, promote its own interests in dealing with the police, and through the power of its associations, negotiate effectively with government agencies. The sector has managed to provide cheap (albeit uncomfortable) transport, which the government has not.

This immense knowledge of the informally financed sector has not been made use of effectively in government plans. The sector is confident that it can operate large buses successfully, if it is provided with loans from banks for the purchase of buses at normal rates of interest. Its vehicles are provided with protection by insurance companies; and if police corruption can be contained. One of the reasons given by the transporters for police corruption is low pay.

The railway option, which has consisted of expanding the KCR and more recently, of rehabilitating it, has not been successful. This is because the proposals have been far too expensive, and the federal government has been unwilling to provide sovereign guarantees to the bidders, or to loan-providing governments and agencies.

There has also been an unresolved disagreement between the various state actors, over whether to develop and expand the railway network, or opt for a BRT system. It seemed that the JICA Plan had resolved these issues. However, problems related to resettlement of populations living along the railway track have created considerable controversy within government departments. Moreover, recently, the project has been categorised as being part of CPEC, while the JICA plan has been shelved. It is important to note that proposals by Pakistan Railways and its ex-chief engineer, for developing a far cheaper system, comparatively, built and operated by the railways, have never been pursued by successive governments from 1989 to date. This can be attributed to the desire of politicians for grand projects that are considered 'modern'.

Karachi's traffic problems are increasing due to the large number of vehicles that are added to its roads every year. Congestion is also increasing due to the conversion of various roads from residential, to high density commercial land use and encroachments by hawkers and informal businesses on corridors used by public transport. These encroachments serve the needs of the lower and lower-middle income commuting public. There is also poor traffic management because of the limited number of police officers on traffic-related duty. Wardens were introduced by the city government to help the police in traffic management, and this seemed to be a good and effective idea. However, as explained earlier, they were removed as a result of Karachi's ethnic-based politics and its turf-related conflicts.

The market response to the shrinking of buses has been extremely innovative. The emergence of the Qingqi, the cost-effectiveness of its design, the manner in which it used to operate (before it was banned) with informally created terminals, stands, routes, timekeeping and the continuous modifications to its operations and design (on the basis of the changing context in the city), was a tribute to its entrepreneurship and an understanding of the politics of the transport sector. The emergence of motorbikes and their rapidly increasing numbers is also a market response that has brought immense relief to the families that own them. However, both modes are considered unsafe and have led to congestion and poor traffic management in the city.

The impact of the transport crisis on people's lives is enormous. Travelling in environmentally-degraded conditions for long hours results in physical and mental health problems. This affects family and social life and limits peoples' choice of livelihoods (especially in the case of women), since they wish to work in areas that they can easily access through the existing transport system. Increasingly, transport availability and quality is also determining where they would prefer to live. The market has responded to this issue by informally densifying those *katchi abadis* that are nearer to the city, or its main work areas.

The fundamental issue in dealing with the transport crisis in Karachi is related to governance. It has been noticed that an elected local government (2001–7) was more effective in accessing funds from the federal and provincial governments for development purposes than the earlier bureaucratic system, which has now been reintroduced. Decentralisation, as practiced between 2001 and 2007, has problems because of Sindh's relationship to its capital city, which is predominantly Urdu-speaking, whereas the province, as a whole, is predominantly Sindhi-speaking. A system is required that empowers the city and at the same time protects the interests of the Sindhi-speakers in accessing and controlling Karachi's enormous assets. Such an arrangement would also help the province deal more effectively with the federal government in Islamabad.

There are a number of issues that need to be resolved if the situation in Karachi is to be improved. At the conception level, the current vision for the city, based on which planning is being carried out, is that Karachi will be a 'world class city'. It is recommended that the vision should be changed to Karachi becoming a 'pedestrian and commuter-friendly city'. This would help in promoting the interests of the majority (who are public transport users). CDGK's role in designing, implementing and managing the development of transport should be enhanced. Some form of elected system should be reintroduced that satisfies the needs of the city and at the same time satisfies all political parties. This will establish the city's ownership of the transport sector and give the CDGK additional powers to negotiate at the federal level.

At present, there is a lack of coordination between the different traffic and transport-related agencies, because of which some of their programmes are ineffective and court orders cannot be implemented. A higher-level organisation that brings these agencies together needs to be created. At the same time a thorough reform of the police force must be conducted. This has often been suggested—and sometimes planned—but never implemented. Meanwhile, the ad hoc densification of the city is resulting in congestion and environmental degradation, making the development of an effective and comfortable transport system difficult. It is suggested that the Master Plan Group of Offices (MPGO) be revived and strengthened, so as to prepare a densification plan that takes transport (among other things) into consideration. For such an exercise to become possible, the Sindh Building Control Authority (SBCA) will have to be made subservient to the MPGO.

The mass transit master plan should be implemented incrementally, as proposed. However, the government will have to provide the required subsidies to bridge the gap between the revenue generated and actual costs. These subsidies can be derived from a small transport tax on petroleum products, an increase in road tax on private vehicles of over 1300-cc and a sliding vehicle insurance surcharge (putting the burden on luxury vehicles). Additionally, to solve the housing–transport link, land at the intersections of the KCR and the major arteries of the city, should be developed as low-income housing. This will help in reducing travel time and costs and at the same time make the KCR and the proposed BRTs economically feasible. In addition, it can also subsidise KCR development and operation and its maintenance costs.

Maintenance processes should see to it that mistakes made in the past should not be repeated. It should be guaranteed that budgets for maintenance are available and that there is no compromise on the quality of spare parts that are used for the rehabilitation of vehicles. Part of the transport master plan consists of BRTs on the major corridors of movement in Karachi. However, most of the city will not benefit from the plan. The private sector (existing at present and planned for in the future) should be supported by developing routes that the JICA plan will not serve, or those routes that link areas currently left out of the route, to the BRT corridors. To make this possible, a comprehensive transport plan for the city is required and one that will need to be periodically upgraded. Moreover, to support the private sector, bank loans for purchase and/or rehabilitation of buses should be provided and insurance companies should be encouraged to insure their vehicles. Proper locations for their depots and terminals should be a part of the above-mentioned larger plan.

A decision needs to be taken on whether the purchase of motorbikes should be promoted, or restricted. If they are to be promoted, then duties and taxes on them should be reduced, or removed. If they are curtailed, taxes should be increased. However, it would be unfair to make them more expensive when Karachi has a badly functioning transport system. Motorbikes already need infrastructure, such as dedicated lanes, proper parking facilities and safety measures; these have been proposed but never implemented.

Similarly, a reduction in the increasing number of cars is necessary. It is recommended that the import of second-hand Japanese cars should be banned and extra tax on cars should be imposed as a deterrent to the purchase of cars. This would be difficult because of the political power of the automobile and banking sectors that give loans for car purchases, opposing such a move. However, this move should be initiated.

It has to be understood that hawkers and informal businesses are an integral part of the commuting scene. Space should be provided for them at all bus stops, inter-and intra-city terminals, and railway stations. The locations where they are operating at present need to be re-planned to accommodate them in a manner whereby they do not adversely affect the existing and proposed transport systems. A number of studies of certain locations have been made with a view to accommodate the hawkers. In addition, a media campaign that promotes a culture of respect for traffic rules and regulations, especially related to the issue of double car parking, should be launched. This should also be made a part of the primary and secondary school curriculum. However, this can only be successful if car parking space is guaranteed. Here, once again, the role of a revived and powerful MPGO is required.

The above recommendations cannot all be implemented in one go. It is proposed that this transformation take place over a fifteen-year period. The process and timeline can only be successfully managed if the existing private sector—consisting of minibuses and rickshaws—is made an integral part of the planning and implementation process.

Stakeholder Perceptions

The majority of the stakeholders' perceptions about the transport issues of Karachi are valid. Nonetheless, individual perceptions need to be analysed and connected and attempts to create a larger picture from the individual anecdotes, presented in Chapter 5, need to be made.

The exponential increase in Karachi's population, the change in its demographic indicators, the spatial spread of housing and the geographical concentration of livelihoods opportunities, demand a response from the formal transport sector. The majority of working class and lower-middle class commuters rely on buses and minibuses for their daily commute, which are relatively cheaper compared to other modes of transport. However, bus services in the public sector are insufficient and informal sector buses and minibuses are not financially viable for these operators. The rising costs of spare parts and maintenance are two main impediments for making those feasible. The institutional failure of Karachi's authorities to maintain the road infrastructure also contributes to the cost of vehicle maintenance.

The continuing devaluation of the Pakistani rupee against relevant foreign currencies is also a barrier to the upkeep of the public transport, both in the formal and informal sectors. When travelling on public transport is problematic, the desire to own a vehicle appears natural. However, many feel that the banks' uncoordinated lending for the purpose of purchasing cars has taken its toll on pavements, footpaths, and roundabouts. In the fiscal year 2013–14, Pakistan imported cars worth $145 million.[1] A considerable number of these ended up in Karachi. Besides that, the local manufacturing of cars for the same fiscal year, increased by 1.85 per cent.[2] The culture of walking has succumbed to car culture. A desire for upward social mobility means that those who are not able to afford a car, resort to motorcycles.

Karachi's local market is flooded with economical Chinese motorcycles that can be obtained for a small down payment of Rs 1,500 (£9.45), with easy-to-repay instalments of Rs 1,000 (£6.30) per month.[3] Because of ever-increasing demands, local assembly of vehicles is also thriving. 'Import of completely knocked-down kits and semi-knocked-down kits (CKDs/SKDs) for assembly of overall bikes rose by 22 per cent to $64 million in July-March 2014–15 from $52.5 million in same period last fiscal year.'[4]

In the absence of convenient and sufficient pedestrian bridges, the signal-free corridors and speedways have become an issue for pedestrians, who have no other option but to cross those high-speed roads at dangerous spots. The shrinking roundabouts further add to their problems. The transport landscape is characterised by an absence of a mass transit system, institutional indifference towards improving conditions for pedestrians, the biased attitude of law enforcers against preferred modes of travel used by low-income groups such as rickshaws and previously, Qingqis.

The promotion of high-speed traffic corridors in development and planning, and the high rates of interest charged on loans by banks, create the impression that transport policy has an anti-poor bias. The informal sector had responded to consumer demands for cheaper travel, by introducing Qingqis. Economically viable and convenient for low-income groups, these vehicles have increased levels of traffic congestion. Even a cursory glance at the roads of Karachi shows that after the recently imposed ban on Qingqis, the number of motorcycles on roads is increasing. The emissions from poorly maintained vehicles, congestion and longer travelling hours, not only result in financial losses, they also have a negative impact on health and attitudes.

A conservative estimate shows that due to congestion on the roads, Rs 250 billion (£1.574 billion) is spent annually on fuel on just one of the main arteries of Karachi, Shahrah-e-Faisal. If estimates are made for the whole of Karachi, the amount could be as much as Rs 400 million (£2.52 million) per annum.[5]

Hypertension and road rage are outcomes of the congestion. There have been no serious studies on road rage in Karachi, however, increasing incidents and daily observations suggest that patterns are emerging. The recent incident, in which a famous national cricketer was shot at in Karachi, is just one of many.[6]

Mass transit seems to be the only viable option for reducing congestion on the roads. A rail-based system could cater for 5–6 per cent of the commuting public. Delhi's railway caters for 4.8 per cent and Bangkok's 3 per cent. But rail-based transit is expensive. Bus rapid transit (BRT) is comparatively cheap but cannot operate without subsidies. The 20 km BRT track from Shahdara to Gajju Matta in Lahore, charges Rs 20 (£0.12) per person only because it receives a large annual subsidy of Rs 1 billion (£6.305 million) from the provincial government. If that amount were to be withdrawn, the fare for the same distance would cost Rs 80 (£0.50) per person and be unaffordable for many. For this reason, in the absence of a publicly subsidised mass transit transport system, the informal transport sector will remain essential to the poorer members of Karachi's society.[7]

In the absence of a mass transit system, city planners must answer two questions: will they facilitate the use of motorcycles institutionally, or curtail them and compromise the social realities of Karachi's masses? If the answer is in favour of motorcycles, how will that decision be institutionalised?

The Motorbike Issue

The surveys carried out by the authors establish that motorbikes will increase faster and by a greater number than what has been estimated by the study for the Karachi Transportation Improvement Project (KTIP).[8] This is because apart from the initial cost of purchasing a motorbike, it is far cheaper than other modes of transport. Its average monthly maintenance cost is Rs 784 (between Rs 250–1,000) as opposed to the average bus commuting cost of Rs 1,570 (Rs 1,248–3,000). An important factor in these estimates is that the motorbike maintenance cost covers a number of other trips, including family outings, while the bus costs are only for the journey from home, to work and back. In addition, according to the respondents, commuting using a motorbike reduces travel time by at least 50 per cent as compared to commuting by bus.

It must also be understood that a rail-based mass transit system and an improved bus system, as envisaged by the KTIP, will take well over a decade to complete. Phase 1 of the Karachi Circular Railway will be completed in four years, after work on it has begun. On its completion, it will serve no more than 0.75 of the trips generated in the city. On completion of Phase 2, it will serve 2.25 trips generated. The project will cost $1.52 billion. The long time taken to complete this project and the fact that is small-scale, will be an incentive for the purchase of motorbikes.

In addition, cost of rail and improved transport systems will be much higher than today. Similar systems have been put in place in Bangkok, Delhi, Manila, and Kuala Lumpur. Bangkok's light rail caters to 3 per cent of the commuting public and its average fare one way is 25 Baht (Rs 65). The Delhi Metro's average cost of a one-way journey is Rs 19 (PKR 38). A day travel card is Rs 100 (PKR 200) and a three-day travel card is Rs 250 (PKR 500).

Kuala Lumpur's costs are even higher. It is unrealistic to expect that the improved Karachi transport travel costs will be any less. This will make public transport even more expensive as compared to commuting by motorbike and this will be an added incentive to purchase one.

As it is, attractive loan packages already exist for the purchase of motorbikes. Repayment at Rs 1,200 per month is considered reasonable by most prospective purchasers. This in spite of the fact that there is a 90 per cent duty on motorbikes. Motorbikes will also increase if women start riding them. It is more than likely that this will happen, as surveys establish that younger women wish to ride motorbikes and only 5 out of 68 respondents (7.35 per cent) felt that riding a motorbike was against their religion, as opposed to 40 per cent of men who thought that religious culture did not permit women to ride a motorbike.

Also, studies on family structures and behaviour patterns in Karachi show an increasing independence for women, which is supported by their parents, who are culturally very different from the older generation. As a result of the fading away of the joint family system, there has been a major change in social values and gender relations.[9] The authors and female NGO activists feel that the time has come to promote women riding motorbikes.

It has recently observed that a few women have already started using motorbikes in Karachi and Lahore. It has been repeatedly observed that women in urban Pakistan do not straddle the motorbike seat. As such, the introduction of the 'scooty' would make it easier for them to adopt riding motorbikes. However, Lahore Police women have been given motorbikes (not scooties) and they are using them and there has been no objection regarding their use from them, or the public.

The number of motorbikes per thousand population is increasingly creating air and noise pollution, congestion, and an increase in fatal road accidents and injuries. Today, 39.2 per cent (7.418 million) of Karachi's population of 18.93 million, is economically active. This means that there is one motorbike for 7.4 economically active persons (or 57 motorbikes for every 1,000 of Karachi's population)[10] and if two persons travel on a motorbike, then 2 million people use this facility. If even 25 per cent of economically active women ride motorbikes, this will increase the number of motorbikes by about 10 per cent.

It is also estimated that in 2030, the economically active population of Karachi will be 43.3 per cent (13.698 million) of the total population of 31.698 million. The number of motorbikes in 2030 is estimated at 3.642 million or 115.3 motorbikes per 1,000 population. This means that there will be one motorbike for 3.76 economically active male persons. These figures do not take into consideration women riding motorbikes.

Meanwhile, findings of the web search make a good case for the promotion of 'green' motorbikes and scooters, as their cost is the same as that of normal petrol operated motorbikes, while the operation cost is lower than that of petrol motorbikes, at Rs 1 per km as opposed to Rs 2 per km for similar cc petrol motorbikes. Given Karachi's electricity outages, the hybrid motorbike (which is being manufactured in Pakistan), is suitable since it can run on both petrol and electricity. It should be noted that the fuel costs for electrical power are approximately 25 per cent of the cost of gasoline power.

Based on the above discussion, the authors feel that since the motorbike option is cheap and convenient for users, it should be made an integral part of transport planning, traffic management, and infrastructure design. This can be done by reducing duties on motorbikes and related spare parts, to make them affordable to a greater number of people and by introducing micro-credit programmes for the purchase of motorbikes.

Women have already started using motorbikes and steps must be taken by civil society and the media to promote and advertise it, as there is no reason why women should not benefit from a commuting facility already enjoyed by men.

The government and motorbike manufacturers and importers must promote the use of 'green' motorbikes, which have already started operating in Karachi. The print and especially the electronic media can be effectively used for it. In addition, as green motorbikes increase, battery-charging facilities must be incorporated at every petrol pump and at relevant commercial and business centre and a system for the safe disposal of used batteries should also be developed.

For the sake of traffic discipline, a physically segregated lane must be provided for motorbikes on all the major arteries of Karachi. Luckily, most of the arteries are wide enough to accommodate such a lane. Also, building byelaws and zoning regulations of the city should be made to accommodate the needs of motorbike owners and markets in relation to designs of flyovers, underpasses, expressways, housing projects, and parking spaces. Architecture, planning, engineering professional, and academic institutions can play an important role to help develop byelaws and zoning regulation, and in designing the relevant infrastructure.

Options should be available to the motorbike purchaser for the type of seat he/she wishes to have in their vehicle. The seat size can be increased to accommodate three adults. It has been observed that people are already doing this by themselves. Most accidents involving motorbikes take place because of the absence of rear-view mirrors. Motorbike riders complain that they get stolen. A product that cannot be stolen needs to be designed and marketed to save lives and injuries. Product designers and manufacturers could look into the problem and come up with a solution.

Pedestrian Bridges

Karachi's corridors and arteries are marked, though insufficiently, with pedestrian bridges. They are installed with the aim of facilitating foot travellers to cross roads safely, in less time and with less effort than at signal-free corridors. After going through whatever news items are available and by conducting a quick survey with forty-eight people in the city, it can be safely assumed that all the above-mentioned objectives remain unfulfilled due to lack of proper planning on the part of the city administration.

For one, the placement of the pedestrian bridges is at far off distances and the potential users find it cumbersome to get to them. Then they are not convenient for access, because one has to climb a staircase at least 18 feet high, which is difficult for the elderly, pregnant women, and labourers carrying weight.

One of the reasons for speeding on principal corridors is because much of them are now signal-free. The lack of pedestrian bridges forces people to cross the roads from the point of convenience. This results in pedestrian-related accidents in the city. In addition, the non-maintenance of pedestrian bridges also makes them dangerous for use and as a result, people shy away from them. However, the most adverse aspect of it is that the placement of pedestrian bridges is dictated more by the income earned from advertisements on them, as compared to pedestrian-related considerations.

Taking into consideration the above, it is necessary to understand the key reasons for the underutilisation of an otherwise important component of pedestrian infrastructure. What is required is a comprehensive spatial survey that defines the functional integration of human and space needs. The findings of the recommended survey should decide the appropriate locations for pedestrian bridges. In addition, decisions regarding pedestrian bridges should be taken in the larger interests of the working class, differently-abled and elderly population of society. Preference should be given to hospitals, educational institutions and signal-free corridors.

* * * *

In the conclusions and the future directions mentioned in this chapter, the authors have tried to generalise rather than be specific. This is because a lot of flexibility in the application of principles and conclusions is required, since contexts, even within a single neighbourhood, can vary. It is in light of this reality that the final chapter must be understood.

Notes

1 | KARACHI: THE CHANGING URBAN LANDSCAPE

1. Pakistan Bureau of Statistics, 'District-wise Census Results', 2017.
2. Both the Urdu and Sindhi speaking populations of Karachi consider the census population figures as understated.
3. MPGO, Karachi Strategic Development Plan 2020, CDGK, 2006.
4. Government of Pakistan, Census Report 1998.
5. MPGO, Karachi Strategic Development Plan 2020, CDGK, 2006.
6. Transport and Communication Department, Karachi Metropolitan Corporation, February 2014.
7. A Qingqi is a 70cc motorcycle which is converted to a vehicle carrying six persons. Recently, due to its popularity and demand, nine-seater Qingqis have also been added to the transport sector in Karachi. Transport experts (interview no. A-07 Shamsuddin Abro [Director of Karachi Public Transport Society]) do not consider it to be reliable or durable.
8. Transport and Communication Department, Karachi Metropolitan Corporation, February 2014.
9. CDGK, Geography and Demography, City District Government, Karachi, 2010.
10. Correspondent, 'Presence of Aliens: "Law enforcers have no idea how many illegal immigrants roam the city",' *The Express Tribune*, 5 January 2015.
11. Government of Pakistan Census Figures.
12. Ibid.
13. MPGO and CDGK (August 2007), The Karachi Strategic Development Plan 2020. *See*: https://www.scribd.com/doc/6788059/Karachi-Master-Plan-2020.
14. Arif Hasan, 'Karachi's Changing Demography & Its Planning-Related Repercussions', *The Express Tribune*, 7 February 2014. *See*: https://tribune.com.pk/story/668864/karachi-changing-demography-its-planning-related-repercussions.
15. Arif Hasan, 'Urban Land Reform.' *Dawn*, 15 July 2015. *See*: https://www.dawn.com/news/1194490.
16. S.H. Steinberg, ed. *The Statesman's Yearbook 1959* (London: Macmillan & Co., 1959).
17. Geography and Demography, City District Government (CDG), Karachi, 2010.
18. MPGO and CDGK (August 2007), The Karachi Strategic Development Plan 2020.
19. Urban Resource Centre, data collected from Transport and Communication Department, Karachi Metropolitan Corporation, 2014.
20. One respondent interviewed mentioned the number as 400. *See* Chapter 6, interview of Rizwan, a rent-a-car driver.
21. 'Only Mass Transit System can end Karachi's Traffic Woes,' *Pakistan Today*, 14 August 2014.
22. Interview with Engr. Nadeem Ahmed Khan, former director of the Sindh Building Control Authority (SBCA), July 2018.

2 | Transport Sector in Karachi: Post-Independence History

1. Appendix 3.5, interview with Irshad Bukhari (President, Karachi Transport Ittehad).
2. City District Government of Karachi website. Accessed on 22 August 2010.
3. Appendix 3.5, interview with Irshad Bukhari (President, Karachi Transport Ittehad).
4. Government of Pakistan Census Report, 1941; Government of Pakistan, Census Report, 1951.
5. Arif Hasan, *Housing for the Poor: Failure of Formal Sector Struggles*, City Press, Karachi, 2000.
6. Aquila Ismail, *Transport: URC Karachi Series*, City Press, Karachi, 2002.
7. Ibid.
8. Appendix 3.5, interview with Shamsuddin Abro (Director, Karachi Public Transport Society) and Mohammad Athar (Director, Transport & Communication, KMC).
9. Ibid., interview with Shamsuddin Abro (Director, Karachi Public Transport Society).
10. Shehri website.
11. Appendix 3.5, interview with Mohammad Athar (Director, Transport & Communication, KMC).
12. Author's observation.
13. Appendix 3.5, interview with Irshad Bukhari (President, Karachi Transport Ittehad); Mohammad Athar (Director, Transport & Communication, KMC); and Shamsuddin Abro (Director, Karachi Public Transport Society).
14. Ibid., interview with Ghazanfar Ali Qadri (Secretary, Regional Transport Authority).
15. Karachi Mass Transit Cell, 'Private-Public Partnership based Environmental Friendly Public Transport System for Karachi,' February 2006, prepared by the of the City Government for the Karachi Strategic Development Plan 2020.
16. Ibid.
17. Regional Transport Authority (2010), Government of Sindh, February 2014.
18. URC Karachi, 'Bus Routes Karachi', 2010. *See:* http://urckarachi.org/wp-content/uploads/2020/07/Bus-Routes-Karachi.pdf.
19. Mahim Maher, 'Timekeeping and transport: The Minute Men of Karachi,' *The Express Tribune*.
20. Environment Management Consultants, *Revival of Karachi Circular Railway*, prepared for the Karachi Urban Transport Corporation, 2009.
21. Appendix 3.5, interview with Shamsuddin Abro (Director, Karachi Public Transport Society).
22. Arif Hasan, *Housing for the Poor: Failure of Formal Sector Struggles*, City Press, Karachi, 2000.
23. Author's unpublished interview with engineer Mohsin Rizvi who was in-charge of the project.
24. 'Mass Transit Study 1990: Final Report on the Evaluation of Alternatives', prepared by the Karachi Development Authority and Maunsell Consultants Limited, London and Parsons Brinckerhoff International Incorporated, New York and Llyassons and Associates, Karachi, 1990.
25. CFMT, 'Karachi Mass Transit Programme: Citizens' Concerns and Possible Alternatives,' URC, 1994.
26. KMTC, 'Private-Public Partnership based Environmental Friendly Public Transport System for Karachi,' February 2006.
27. S.M.H. Rizvi, 'Revitalisation of the Karachi Circular Railway as part of the Karachi Mass Transit Programme', unpublished paper, 1995.

28. Ibid.
29. Argued by Abul Kalam at a 2002 meeting at the NED University.
30. 'KCR Project to be Ready by 2017', *The News*, 9 April 2012.
31. Arif Hasan, Noman Ahmed, Mansoor Raza, Asiya Sadiq, Saeed ud Din Ahmed, and Moizza B. Sarwar, 'Land Ownership, Control and Contestation in Karachi and Implications for Low Income Housing', Urbanization and Emerging Population Issues, Working Paper 10, IIED, UK.
32. Imtiaz Ali, 'Project Cost Rises by Rs 100 Billion in Three Years', *The News*, Karachi, 6 July 2012.
33. All prices given are from the year 2015.
34. Appendix 3.5, interview with Shabbir Sulemanjee (Chairman, All Pakistan CNG Association).
35. Ibid.
36. Newspaper reports.
37. Appendix 3.5, interview with Mohammad Athar (Director, Transport & Communication, KMC).
38. Ibid., interview with Shabbir Sulemanjee (Chairman of All Pakistan CNG Association).
39. Ibid.
40. Ibid.
41. Transport and Communication Department, KMC, February 2014.
42. Worked out from the statistics of the Excise and Taxation Department, Government of Sindh, June 2018.
43. DIG Traffic, Khurram Gulzar in news report, *Express Tribune*, Karachi, 1 November 2011
44. '80pc of rickshaw drivers not qualified to give you a ride,' *The News International*, Karachi, 23 April 2012.
45. W. Bhatti, 'Vehicular Emissions yet to be Controlled', *The News*, Karachi, 17 January 2010.
46. Appendix 3.5, interview with Dr Qazi Mujahid Ali.
47. KMTC, 'Private-Public Partnership based Environmental Friendly Public Transport System for Karachi,' February 2006.
48. Arif Hasan, Asiya Sadiq Polak, and Christophe Polak, *The Hawkers of Saddar Bazaar: A Plan for the Revitalization of Saddar Bazaar Karachi Through Traffic Rerouting of Its Hawkers*, Ushba Publishing International, Karachi, 2008.
49. 'Traffic Woes: Little Being Done to Ease Gridlock on Saddar Streets,' *The Express Tribune*, 27 May 2013.
50. Orangi Pilot Project-Research and Training Institute (OPP-RTI); website: www.oppinstitutions.org.
51. 'Traffic Woes: Little Being Done to Ease Gridlock on Saddar Streets,' *The Express Tribune*, 27 May 2013.
52. Appendix 3.5, interviews with Mohammad Athar (Director, Transport & Communication, KMC) and Fazal Karim Khattri (DG, Mass Transit).
53. Bhagwandas, 'Karachi: Fares Register Steep Rise in 18 Months,' *Dawn*, 9 November 2009.
54. Ibid.
55. Arif Hasan, 'Karachi's Changing Demography & Its Planning-Related Repercussions,' *The Express Tribune*, 7 February 2014.
56. http://www.roadsafetypakistan.pk/.
57. Mahim Maher, 'Devastating New Law Empowers Private Association of Developers,' Shehri Newsletter, July–September 2014.

58. Arif Hasan, 'Karachi's Densification,' *Dawn*, 27 April 2014.
59. Appendix 3.5, interview with Mohammad Athar (Director, Transport & Communication, KMC).
60. Ibid.
61. Transport and Communication Department, KMC, February 2014.
62. Zahid Farooq, unpublished research notes, March 2014.
63. Irfan Aligi, '2-stroke rickshaw owners regret changing engines,' *Dawn*, 29 April 2008.
64. Appendix 3.5, interview with Hafiz-ul-Haq Hassan Zai (President, Karachi Taxi & Motor Rickshaw Yellow Cab Owners' Association).
65. PPI, 'Karachi: ANP Assails Ban on Faulty Rickshaws,' *Dawn*, 4 September 2007. *See*: https://www.dawn.com/news/264390/karachi-anp-assails-ban-on-faulty-rickshaws.

3 | RESPONDING TO THE TRANSPORT CRISIS IN KARACHI

1. Fifty-three men and twenty-seven women were interviewed at bus stops which serve low-income areas. Rest of the seventy interviews were carried out in factories and with college students
2. Appendix 3.5, interview with Akbar Khan and Syed Khattri (President and Finance Secretary, All Karachi Qingqis & Rickshaw Association).
3. Ibid.
4. Appendix 3.5, interview with Shamsuddin Abro (Director, Karachi Public Transport Society).
5. Correspondent, 'Off the Roads: Qingqis Banned Across City,' *The Express Tribune*, 10 October 2013. *See*: https://tribune.com.pk/story/615792/off-the-roads-qingqis-banned-across-city/.
6. Jamal Khurshid, 'Qingqi Rickshaws with Permits Free to Ply but not on the Main Roads,' *The News International*, 12 October 2013.
7. Ibid.
8. Sidra Arshad, 'Chingchi Rickshaws Better Transport Then Buses & Coaches in Karachi,' Awami Politics, 31 October 2013.
9. Zahid Farooq, unpublished research notes, March 2014.
10. Arif Hasan and Mansoor Raza, 'Motorbike Mass Transit,' unpublished report prepared for IIED UK, June 2009.
11. Ibid.
12. Zahid Farooq, unpublished research notes, March 2014.
13. 'Environment-friendly e-bike comes to Pakistan,' *Dawn*, 12 November 2014. *See*: https://www.dawn.com/news/1143984.
14. These arrangements are well-known to most Karachiites.
15. Appendix 3.5, interview with Irshad Bukhari (President, Karachi Transport Ittehad).
16. KMTC, 'Private-Public Partnership based Environmental Friendly Public Transport System for Karachi,' February 2006.
17. Ibid.
18. Appendix 3.5, interviews with Irshad Bukhari (President, Karachi Transport Ittehad) and Mehmood Afridi (President, Muslim Minibus).
19. Ibid.
20. Ibid.
21. Interview with Irshad Bukhari (President, Karachi Transport Ittehad).
22. Zahid Farooq, unpublished research notes, March 2014.

23. https://paycheck.in/labour-law-india/compensation/travel-reimbursement/commuting-time-and-travel-reimbursement.

24. Appendix 3.5, interview with Mohammad Athar (Director of Transport & Communication, KMC).

25. Ibid., interviews with Mohammad Athar (Director, Transport & Communication, KMC) and Ghazanfar Ali Qadri (Secretary, Regional Transport Authority).

26. Ibid., interview with Iftekhar Hussain (Addl. District Officer, Transport & Communication, KMC).

27. Ibid., interview with Shams-ud-Din Abro (Director, Karachi Public Transport Society).

28. Ibid., interview with Mohammad Athar (Director, Transport & Communication, KMC).

29. Ibid., interview with Ghazanfar Ali Qadri (Secretary, Regional Transport Authority).

30. Ibid.

31. Appendix 3.5, interviews with Iftekhar Hussain (Addl. District Officer, Transport & Communication, KMC) and Shamsuddin Abro (Director, Karachi Public Transport Society).

32. Ibid., interview with Fazal Karim Khattri (DG, Mass Transit).

33. Ibid., interviews with Mohammad Athar (Director, Transport & Communication, KMC) and Fazal Karim Khattri.

34. Chapter 6, interview, Section 3.16.

35. Ibid., interview of Mohammed Saeed, a CNG rickshaw driver.

36. Appendix 3.5, interview with Arif Hanif (DIG, Traffic Police, Garden Road).

37. Ibid., interview with Mohammad Athar (Director, Transport & Communication, KMC).

38. Ibid., interview with Fazal Karim Khattri (DG, Mass Transit).

39. Ibid., interview with Ghazanfar Ali Qadri (Secretary, Regional Transport Authority).

40. Ibid., interview with Fazal Karim Khattri (DG, Mass Transit).

41. Ibid., interview with Ghazanfar Ali Qadri (Secretary, Regional Transport Authority).

42. Ibid., interview with Shams-ud-Din Abro (Director, Karachi Public Transport Society).

43. Ibid., interview with Tahir Ahmad Khan (Secretary, Transport).

45. Mahim Maher, 'Public Transport: Race to build Karachi's BRT Gets Too Many Green Signals,' *The Express Tribune*, 20 March 2015; Bhagwandas, 'Sindh Government to Fund Red Line After ADB Backs Out of the Project,' *Dawn*, 21 March 2015.

46. Japan International Cooperation Agency (JICA), Karachi Mass Transit JICA Masterplan 2020 Summary, September 2014.

4 | THE RIDE HAILING CULTURE: THE WIDENING GAP BETWEEN THE HAVES AND THE HAVE NOTS

1. Haamiz Ahmed, 'Rozee's Survey Reveals the Ride Hailing Preferences of Pakistanis,' ProPakistani, 10 June 2017.

2. 'Katchi Abadis House Half of Karachi's Population,' *The News International*, 15 November 2013.

3. Rich Fitzgerald, Trevor Brown, and Molly Turner, *The Future of Work: The Rise of the Gig Economy*, National Association of Counties, Washington, DC, 2020.

4. Arif Pervaiz, 'Assessing Walkability in Karachi,' *The News International*, 17 September 2009.

5. Ibid.

5 | EXPLORING KARACHI'S TRANSPORT SYSTEM PROBLEMS: DIVERSE PERSPECTIVES OF STAKEHOLDERS

1. Baber K. Khan, 'Traffic jams in Karachi result in losses worth of millions each day,' Pakwheels.com, 30 January 2014. *See*: https://www.pakwheels.com/blog/traffic-jams-karachi-result-losses-worth-millions-day/.

2. Exponent Engineers Consulting Engineers and Project Managers (December 2005), Person Trip Study of Karachi City, Japan International Cooperation Agency (JICA).

3. MPGO and CDGK (August 2007), The Karachi Strategic Development Plan 2020.

4. Chapter 6, interview of Faisal, a male passenger.

5. Ibid., interview of Mohammad, a minibus mechanic and conductor.

6. PKR150 equal to approximately £1.00 (0.935 GBP).

7. Chapter 6, interview of Mohammad, a minibus mechanic and conductor.

8. Ibid.

9. Minibuses in Karachi are popularly called 'Mazdas'.

10. Chapter 6, interview of Mohammad, a minibus mechanic and conductor.

11. Ibid.

12. Arif Hasan and Mansoor Raza, 'Motorbike Mass Transit,' unpublished report prepared for IIED UK, June 2009.

13. Karachi Circular Railway (KCR) rickshaws are two-stroke engine rickshaws which use petrol instead of CNG as fuel.

14. Chapter 6, interview of Nimroz, a rickshaw mechanic.

15. Ibid., interview of Mohammed Saeed, a CNG-rickshaw driver.

16. '80pc of rickshaw drivers not qualified to give you a ride,' *The News International*, Karachi, 23 April 2012.

17. Ibid.

18. Ibid.

19. Chapter 6, interview of Shamoon, a cyclist.

20. Jam Sajjad Hussain, 'Bicycle Pedals Down Memory Lane in Pakistan,' *The Nation*, 20 April 2011. *See*: http://nation. com.pk/lahore/20-Apr-2011/Bicycle-pedals-downmemory-lane-in-Pakistan.

21. Ibid.

22. Ibid.

23. Total number of vehicles registered in Karachi up to June 2018, Excise and Taxation Department, Government of Sindh.

24. MPGO and CDGK (August 2007), The Karachi Strategic Development Plan 2020.

25. Chapter 6, interview of Jamil, a taxi driver.

26. Ibid., interview of Rizwan, a rent-a-car driver.

27. Ibid., interview of Faisal, a male passenger.

28. Ibid., interview of Humayun, a motorcyclist.

29. Chapter 6, interview of George, a traffic police officer.

30. Mansoor Raza, 'The Pedestrian Bridges of Karachi,' Urban Resource Centre, Working Papers Series No.1/15, October 2015.

31. Arif Pervaiz, 'Assessing Walkability in Karachi,' *The News International*, 17 September 2009.

32. Ibid.

33. 'Karachi: Pedestrian Bridges in a Shambles,' *Dawn*, 28 July 2003. Retrieved from: https://www.dawn.com/news/132307.

34. 'Karachi: Part of Pedestrian Bridge Collapses in Maripur,' Samaa Digital, 12 March 2012. Retrieved from: https://www.samaa.tv/news/2012/03/karachi-part-of-pedestrian-bridge-collapses-in-maripur/.

35. Chapter 6, interview of Rizwan, a rent-a-car driver.

36. Ibid., interview of Humayun, a motorcyclist.

37. Ibid., interview of Rashid, a car mechanic.

38. Ibid., interview of Syed Sohail, a banker.

39. Ibid., interview of an anonymous ambulance driver.

40. Ibid., interview of Saeed, an oil tanker driver.

41. '57 Charged Parking Spots Notified by KMC,' *The News International*, 18 July 2014. *See*: https://www.thenews.com.pk/archive/print/514832-57-charged-parking-spots-notified-by-kmc.

42. Chapter 6, interview of George, a traffic police officer.

43. Agence France-Presse, 'Illegal Bus Terminals Thrive in Karachi,' *Geo News*, 3 June 2013. *See*: https://www.geo.tv/latest/59892-illegal-bus-terminals-thrive-in-karachi.

44. Chapter 6, interview of Jawed, an inter-city bus service manager.

45. Ibid., interview of Rashid, a car mechanic.

46. Ibid., interview of Sardar, a cargo driver.

47. 'Charged-Parking System at Hospitals Irks Patients,' *Dental News*, 1 September 2015. *See*: https://www.dentalnewspk.com/charged-parking-system-at-hospitals-irks-patients/.

48. Chapter 6, interview of an anonymous ambulance driver.

49. Ibid., interview of Zaeem, a water tanker driver.

50. 'Karachi: Traffic Jams Take 500 Lives in 2 Months,' *Dawn*, 9 April 2006. *See*: https://www.dawn.com/news/186956/karachi-traffic-jams-take-500-lives-in-2-months.

51. Chapter 6, interview of an anonymous ambulance driver.

52. 'Schools in Karachi: Private and Government School List,' ILM.com.pk, 20 October 2015. *See*: http://ilm.com. pk/directories/schools-directories/schools-in-karachilist.

53. Chapter 6, interview of an anonymous vehicle parts dealer.

54. 'Auto Parts Smuggling Causes Rs 10bn Loss to Exchequer,' *The News International*, 8 April 2012. *See*: https://www.thenews.com.pk/archive/print/355337-%E2%80%98auto-parts-smuggling-causes-rs10bn-loss-to-exchequer%E2%80%99.

55. Chapter 6, interview of an anonymous vehicle parts dealer.

56. Gibran Ashraf and Faraz Khan, 'Karachi 2013: The Deadliest Year of All,' *The Express Tribune*, 6 January 2014. *See*: http://tribune.com.pk/story/653889/karachi-2013-thedeadliest-year-of-all/.

57. Chapter 6, interview of Jamil, a taxi driver.

58. Ibid., interview of Rashid, a car mechanic.

59. Ibid., interview of Rashid, a car mechanic.

60. Ibid., interview of Asif, a taxi mechanic.

61. Ibid., interview of Mohammad, a minibus mechanic and conductor.

62. Ibid., interview of an anonymous vehicle parts dealer.

63. 'Land Services, Police Most Corrupt in Pakistan: Transparency International,' *The Express Tribune*, 9 July 2013. *See*: http://tribune.com.pk/story/574577/land-servicespolice-most-corrupt-in-pakistan-transparencyinternational/.

64. Chapter 6, interview of George, a traffic police officer.

65. Ibid., interview of Khalid, a mechanic and panel beater.

66. In Islam, *fajr* (morning) is usually associated with morning prayers and *isha* (night) is usually associated with evening prayers.

67. Chapter 6, interview of Saeed, an oil tanker driver.
68. Ibid., interview of Shamoon, a cyclist.
69. Ibid., interview of Sardar, a cargo driver.
70. Ibid., interview of Humayun, a motorcyclist.
71. Ibid., interview of George, a traffic police officer.
72. Ibid., interview of Jamil, a taxi driver.
73. Ibid., interview of Humayun, a motorcyclist.
74. Ibid., interview of Jamil, a taxi driver.
75. Ibid., interview of Nimroz, a rickshaw mechanic.
76. A. Zia, 'Karachi Least Environment Friendly City in Asia: Report,' *The News*, 15 February 2011.
77. Chapter 6, interview of Sajjad, a medical doctor.
78. Ibid.
79. Chapter 6, interview of Rashid, a car mechanic.
80. Ibid., interview of Sajjad, a medical doctor.
81. Government of Pakistan, Census Report, 1998.
82. Chapter 6, interview of Mohammad, a minibus mechanic and conductor.
83. Ibid., interview of Mohammed Saeed, a CNG-rickshaw driver.
84. Ibid., interview of Naghma, a female passenger.
85. Anadil Iftekhar, *Women Transport Issue and Problems: Interviews from Women in Karachi*, URC. Unpublished. December 2013.
86. Chapter 6, interview of an anonymous vehicle parts dealer.
87. Ibid., interview of an anonymous ambulance driver.
88. Ibid., interview of Rizwan, a rent-a-car driver.
89. Ibid., interview of Sardar, a cargo driver.
90. Ibid., interview of an anonymous ambulance driver.
91. Ibid.
92. Ibid., interview of Rashid, a car mechanic.
93. The Karachi Operation started on 5 September 2013, after a meeting of the Federal Cabinet on 2 September 2013. The objective of the Operation was to curb the sectarian and ethnic killings in Karachi. The other factors that propelled an ever-worsening law and order situation were turf wars, illegal land occupation and fights between various religious and political parties.
94. 'No Decline in Street Crime Despite Operation: Karachi Police Chief,' *Dawn*, 22 August 2015. *See*: www. dawn.com/news/1202003; Federal Bureau of Statistics, Census Reports, various.
95. Chapter 6, interview of Humayun, a motorcyclist.
96. 'Not a Good Year to be a Cop: 172 Policemen Killed in 2013,' *The Express Tribune*, 1 January 2014. *See*: http:// tribune.com.pk/story/653067/not-a-good-year-to-be-acop-172-policemen-killed-in-2013.
97. Ibid.
98. Chapter 6, interview of George, a traffic police officer.
99. Chapter 6, interview of Jawed, an intercity bus service manager.
100. Ibid., interview of Jamil, a taxi driver.
101. Data collected by URC Road Traffic Injury Research and Prevention Centre, Rasheed Juma Institute, Karachi.
102. The newspapers include *The Express Tribune* and *Daily Times*. Websites of media channels were also searched, including SAMAA TV and ARY News.

103. Chapter 6, interview of George, a traffic police officer.
104. Ibid., interview of Khalid, a mechanic and panel beater.
105. Ibid., interview of Jawed, an intercity bus service manager.
106. Ibid., interview of Rizwan, a rent-a-car driver.
107. Ibid., interview of Jawed, an intercity bus service manager.

6 | ACTORS IN THE TRANSPORT DRAMA OF KARACHI

1. CNG was selling for Rs 18/kg in 2005 and the price later increased exponentially.
2. Pervez Musharraf, President of Pakistan 2001–8.
3. Asif Ali Zardari, President of Pakistan, 2008–13.
4. Businessman. Here, the owner of the organization.

7 | WOMEN'S TRANSPORT ISSUES

1. Interview: TR.
2. Author's observation.
3. Interviews: Shahnaz Anjum, M.J., Xara, and Zaib-un-Nisa.
4. Interviews: Saima Ismail Shah, Bushra, Shahnaz Anjum, Tina, and Fatima.
5. Interviews: Bushra and Sughra.
6. Interviews: Sanjeeda, Sughra, Tina, and TR.
7. Interview: Shahnaz Anjum.
8. Interviews: Bushra, Sughra, and Zaib-un-Nisa.
9. Interview: TR.
10. Interviews: Saima Ismail Shah and Sughra.
11. Interviews: Christine, Tina, M.S., and Zaib-un-Nisa.
12. Interviews: Bushra, Christine, and TR.
13. Interviews: Saima Ismail Shah and TR.
14. Interviews: Christine, Sughra, and Zaib-un-Nisa.
15. Interview: Shahnaz Anjum.
16. Appendix 3.5, interview with Ghazanfar Ali Qadri (Secretary, Regional Transport Authority).
17. These interviews were conducted by Anadil Iftekhar between December 2013 and May 2014.

8 | RECOMMENDATIONS

1. Hassan Hayat Khan (director), *Aik Naya Safar* (A New Journey), a documentary about sustainable transport in Pakistan, a joint production of PTV Home and IUCN, 2014. *See*: https://www.dailymotion.com/video/x283im1.
2. Ibid.
3. Chapter 6, interview of Kamran, an environmentalist.
4. Muhammed Hanif Memon, 'Made in Pakistan—Yamaha Win's Race in Good Looking New Model,' *AutoMark Magazine*, June 2015. *See*: https://www.automark.pk/made-in-pakistan-yamaha-wins-race-in-good-looking-new-model.
5. Hassan Hayat Khan (director), *Aik Naya Safar* (A New Journey).

6. Faraz Khan, 'Suspect Involved in Road Rage Shooting at Wasim Akram "arrested",' *The Express Tribune*, 7 August 2015. *See*: https://tribune.com.pk/story/934147/suspect-involved-in-road-rage-shooting-on-wasim-akram-arrested.

7. 'Lahore Metro—Unsustainable?' *The Nation*, 11 March 2019. *See*: https://nation.com.pk/11-Mar-2019/lahore-metro-unsustainable.

8. JICA and CDGK Karachi Mass Transit Cell, 'Study for the Karachi Transportation Improvement Project: Progress Report–2,' 2 February 2011.

9. Arif Hasan, 'Demographic Change and Its Socio-Economic Repercussions: The Case of Karachi, Pakistan,' *International Development Planning Review*, Vol. 31, Issue 3 (2009), pp. 229–234.

10. JICA and CDGK Karachi Mass Transit Cell, 'Study for the Karachi Transportation Improvement Project: Progress Report–2,' 2 February 2011.

Appendices

Appendix 3.1: Literature Consulted

Aquila Ismail, *Transport (URC Karachi Series)*, City Press, Karachi 2002.

Arif Hasan and Mansoor Raza, *Motorcycle Mass Transit*, IIED funded unpublished report, 2011.

Arif Hasan, et al., *Karachi Master Plan: Report of the Evaluation Mission for the UNDP*, Islamabad, July 1991.

Arif Hasan, *Understanding Karachi*, City Press, Karachi, 2000.

Detailed study on a *Private-Public Partnership based Environmental Friendly Public Transport System for Karachi*, prepared by the Karachi Mass Transit Cell of the City Government for the Karachi Strategic Development Plan-2020, February 2006.

Government of Pakistan Census reports.

JICA Study Team, *Karachi Transport Improvement Project: Preliminary discussions on future population framework and concept of urban growth*, PowerPoint presentation, 16 October 2010.

JICA, *Feasibility Study on the Electrification of Karachi Suburban Railway and Preliminary Feasibility Study Report on Mass Transit System*, Government of Pakistan, March 1997.

Karachi City Transport Shortages, Causes, Accidents and Suggestions; prepared by the Karachi Bus Owners' Association at the request of the Transport Minister, Government of Sindh; 1993.

Karachi Development Authority, *Environmental Impact Assessment of Corridor-1*, Government of Sindh, 1994.

M. Sohail and the URC Karachi, *Urban Public Transport and Sustainable Livelihood for the Poor: A Case Study of Karachi, Pakistan*, WEDC, Loughborough University, UK, 2000.

Mass Transit Study 1990: Final Report on the Evaluation of Alternatives; prepared by the Karachi Development Authority and Maunsell Consultants Limited, London and Parsons Brinckerhoff International Incorporated, New York and Llyassons and Associates, Karachi, 1990.

Ministry of Communication, *Feasibility Study for the Introduction of Rapid Transit System as a part of An Integrated Mass Transportation Plan for Karachi and Lahore*, Government of Pakistan, December 1975.

Minoru Shibuya, *Karachi Transportation Improvement Project (Progress Report-2 Presentation to the Technical Committee)*, 2 February 2011.

Mir Shabbar Ali, Waheed-ud-Din, Muhammad Imran, *Urban Transport Policy for Karachi and other Pakistani Cities*, Joint Research Project University of Mississippi, US-Aid and NED University, Karachi.

MPGO, *Karachi Development Plan 2000*, KDA, 1989.

MPGO, *Karachi Master Plan 1975-85*, KDA, 1973.

MPGO, *Karachi Strategic Development Plan 2020*, CDGK, 2007.

Person Trip Study of Karachi City, prepared by Exponent Engineers/Japan International Corporation Agency (JICA) for the CDGK, December 2005.

Railcop, *Proposal for Upgrade of the Karachi Circular Railway*, Railway Constructions (Pakistan) Limited, Islamabad, 1996.

Report of the Committee on Proposed Metropolitan Transport Authority by the Transport Commission Working Group which was looking into the shortages of transport and making recommendations included improved bus designs, prevention of road accidents, public transport discipline, mass transit fares and acts, rules and regulations relevant to them, 1982.

Report on the Transport Sector: Karachi Strategic Development Plan-2020, prepared by the Master Plan Group of Offices, City District Government Karachi (CDGK), February 2007.

Revival of Karachi Circular Railway, prepared for the Karachi Urban Transport Corporation by Environmental Management Consultants, 2009.

URC compiled transport related press clipping and articles, 2009 to 2014.

Websites
www.arifhasan.org
www.kmc.gos.pk
www.shehri.org
www.urckarachi.org

Acts
Karachi Metropolitan Transport Authority Act, 1998
Karachi Transport Commission's Report, May 1982
The Karachi Division Traffic Engineering Act, 1985

Selected Important Press Clippings (2007–2013)

1.	Transporters reject ban on rickshaws	Pakistan Press International; AAJ News Archives	17 September 2007
2.	2-stroke rickshaw owners regret changing engines	Irfan Aligi; Daily Dawn	29 April 2008
3.	Delays push KCR project cost up to $1.58 bn	Asadullah, The News-13	2 July 2009
4.	CDGK to construct six more fly-overs on Sharea Faisal	The News-20	2 July 2009
5.	Opposition leaders slam carbon surcharge	Dawn-15	3 July 2009
6.	85,000 road mishaps in city in 2.5 years	DailyTimes-B1	8 July 2009
7.	Cop arrested for selling fake licences	Gibran Ashraf, The News-14	12 July 2009
8.	Hapless commuters suffer torrid time	Fawad Ali Shah, Daily-Times-B1	15 July 2009

9.	Naval officers making Sharea Faisal prone to accidents	Shahid Husain, The News-13	21 July 2009
10.	The beginning of a transport revolution?	The News-13	28 July 2009
11.	Oil import bill shrinks by 17 per cent	Mubarak Zeb Khan, Dawn-1	26 July 2009
12.	Man dies after falling off bus roof	The News-14	29 July 2009
13.	1,600 CNG buses on Karachi roads soon	The News-13	11 August 2009
14.	Transport fares register steep rise in 18 months	Bhagwandas, Dawn-13	9 November 2009
15.	VVIP movement, Boulton Market reconstruction lead to massive gridlocks	The News-13	5 January 2010
16.	Vehicular emissions yet to be controlled	M. Waqar Bhatti, The News-20	17 January 2010
17.	Non-operative bus routes cause hardship for public	Gibran Ashraf, The News-20	31 January 2010
18.	Notices issued in petition against CDGK flyovers	Tahir Siddiqui, Dawn-13	17 March 2010
19.	The Karachi tramway of yesteryear	Owais Mughal, The News-39 Kolachi	4 April 2010
20.	CDGK given one week to submit SFC-IV EIA report	M. Waqar Bhatti, The News-13	9 April 2010
21.	The W-11 legend	Naimat Haider, The News-39 Kolachi	20 June 2010
22.	New tax incentive for CNG bus operators proposed	Dawn-15	30 June 2010
23.	Traffic nightmare on city roads	Dawn-15	7 September 2011
24.	JICA expert gives presentation on Bus Rapid Transit System	The News-13	12 October 2011
25.	Karachi Circular Railway victims still awaiting legal cover	Imtiaz Ali, The News-13	10 November 2011
26.	Pak Suzuki posts 73% growth, sales up by 17% in 9MCY11	Daily Times-B2	23 November 2011
27.	Plight of women in public buses	Riaz Ahmed, Karachi, Dawn-6	6 April 2012
28.	80pc of CNG rickshaw drivers not qualified to give you a ride	Qadeer Tanoli, The News-13	23 April 2012

29.	Auto-rickshaw fare meters: a thing of the past	Qadeer Tanoli, The News-13	26 April 2012
30.	Bus mechanics struggling to make ends meet	Qadeer Tanoli, The News 16	11 June 2012
31.	CNG crisis	The News 07	12 June 2012
32.	KCR project to be ready by 2017	The News-15	9 April 2012
33.	Less people died on Karachi's roads last year, annual report shows	The Express Tribune13	11 May 2012
34.	MQM opposes assessment of fly-overs, bridges	The News-13	27 April 2012
35.	Registration, licences for truck stands	Dawn-17	26 February 2012
36.	Transport safety: CNG cylinders killed more people than US drones: Report	Aroosa Shaukat, Tribune-3	10 April 2012
37.	With new projects in mind, transport dept seeks Rs4.3b	The Express Tribune-15	4 June 2012
38.	Project cost rises by Rs100bn in three years	Imtiaz Ali, The News-20	6 July 2012
39.	Circular railway: 'Japanese govt will cover 93% cost of KCR'	Saad Hasan, The Express Tribune-14	12 July 2012
40.	SHC moved against ban on import of CNG kits	Jamal Khurshid, The News-14	29 August 2012
41.	A better public transport sector can boost city's economy	The News-14	10 September 2012
42.	Traffic nightmares may come true	The News-20	16 October 2012
43.	Roads of Karachi to be cleaned up by checking 3,000 vehicles every month	The Express Tribune-13	2 November 2012
44.	Rationalisation of bus fares in the city overdue	The News-14	4 November 2012
45.	In an explosive city, a different kind of bomb roams the streets	Sohail Khattak, The Express Tribune-15	14 December 2012
46.	Transporters to go on strike against new 'sky-high' traffic fines	The Express Tribune-13	29 March 2013
47.	Traffic woes: Little being done to ease gridlock on Saddar streets	The Express Tribune-14	28 May 2013

Appendix 3.2: List of Interviewees

A. **Interviews with Government Officials. Interviewers Rizwan-ul-Haq and Zahid Farooq**

A-01. MUHAMMAD ATHAR (Director, Transport & Communication); KMC, Office, 8th Floor, Civic Centre; Ph: 021-99230655; 29 January 2014.

A-02. ARIF HANIF (DIG Traffic Police, Garden Road); 31 January 2014.

A-03. FAZAL KARIM KHATRI (DG Mass Transit); Office, 6th floor Civic Centre; 4 February 2014.

A-04. GHAZANFAR ALI QADRI (Secretary Regional Transport Authority); Office, 3rd Floor Civic Centre; 12 February 2014.

A-05. TAHIR AHMED KHAN (Secretary Transport) Office, 3rd Floor Tughlaq House, Sindh Secretariat; 17 February 2014.

A-06. SYED IFTEKHAR HUSSAIN (Addl. District Officer Transport & Communication, KMC).

A-07. SHAMSUDDIN ABRO (Director, Karachi Public Transport Society); 17 October 2014.

B. **Interviews with Transporters. Interviewers Rizwan-ul-Haq, Zahid Farooq, and Mansoor Raza**

B-01. IRSHAD BUKHARI (President, Karachi Transport Ittehad); KTI Office, Akbar Road, Saddar, Karachi, 0333-2149965; 20 12 2013.

B-02. SHABBIR H. SULEMANJEE (Chairman, All Pakistan CNG Association); Office, 5th Floor, Business Centre, Shahrah-e-Faisal, 0321-9288350; 15 January 2014.

B-03. MEHMOOD AFRIDI and TAWAB KHAN (President, Muslim Minibus & Vice President), 021-32737822 & 0333-2232190; 20 January 2014.

B-04. Akbar Khan and Syed Khattri (President and Finance Secretary, All Karachi Qingqis & Rickshaw Association), 0321-8992782 and 0300-2624937; 07.02.2014.

B-05. HAFIZ-UL-HAQ HASSAN ZAI (President, Karachi Taxi & Motor Rickshaw, Yellow Cab Owners' Association); Office, Patel Para; 0300-2416676 & 0321-9209637; 10 February 2014.

C. **Interviews with the Public. Interviewer Rizwan-ul-Haq**

D-01. AMJAD ALI, Khuda-ki-Basti, April 2014.

D-02. JAWED SULTAN, Khuda-ki-Basti, April 2014.

D-03. NADEEM BAKHSH, Khuda-ki-Basti, April 2014.

D-04. MUHAMMAD YASEEN, Khuda-ki-Basti, April 2014.

D-05. BASHEER, Khuda-ki-Basti, April 2014.

D-06. DR QAZI MUJAHID ALI, Surjani Town, 26 March 2014.

Appendix 3.3: Questionnaires and Analysis

(English translation of Urdu questionnaire)

Interview with the transport passengers

1. **Name:** _____

2. **Contact No.:** _____

3. **Home Address:** _____

_____

4. **Office Address:** _____

_____

5. **What kind of transport do you use to travel to work?**

    i. Bus   ii. Coach   iii. Mini Bus   iv. Qingchi

    v. Rickshaw   vi. Taxi   vii. Contract Bus

    viii. Others: _____

6. **Duration of one way travel:**

    _____ Total: _____

    Duration of wait at the bus stop: _____

7. **Fare of one way travel:**

    _____ Total: _____

    Note: If the fare is being paid monthly kindly mention the details.

8. **Problems faced during travelling:**

    i. Long waiting for the transportation   ii. The duration of the travel is long

    iii. Have to change two buses/vehicles   iv. Have to change three buses/vehicles

    v. Others: _____

9. **Is the environment of the vehicles/buses proper?**

    i. Yes   ii. No

    If no, what are the problems present?

    i. They are over-crowded   ii. They are too noisy   iii. Improper seats

    iv. Broken windows   v. Others: _____

10. Is it difficult to travel in the buses/vehicles while standing?

   i. Yes   ii. No

Details: _____

11. The conditions of the buses/vehicles:

   i. Good   ii. Bad   iii. Satisfactory

Details: _____

12. Is the route number of the buses/minibuses clearly mentioned on them?

   i. Yes   ii. No   iii. Don't Know

13. If the route number is not mentioned on the vehicle, what problems do you have to face?

   i. Have to confirm it from the people or the bus conductor

   ii. Identification of the vehicle becomes difficult

   iii. Have to run after the vehicle   iv. No difficulty

   v. Others: _____

14. How do you usually travel?

   i. I find a seat ii. Stand   iii. On the roof iv. Have to sit on the engine

   v. By hanging on to the door vi. Others: _____

15. What is the attitude of the drivers and the conductors?

   i. Satisfactory   ii. Good   iii. Bad   iv. Worse

Details: _____

16. The speed of the bus/vehicles:

   i. Satisfactory   ii. Slow   iii. Fast   iv. Very Fast

17. Does the bus/vehicle stop at the bus/vehicle stop?

   i. Always   ii. Sometimes   iii. Never

Details: _____

18. When climbing up or down the bus/vehicle, are children, women and senior citizens taken care of?

   i. Always   ii. Sometimes   iii. ever   iv. Don't know

19. Do the passengers get hurt when climbing up or down the bus?

   i. Often   ii. Sometimes   iii. Never   iv. Don't know

20. Are women harassed in the buses/vehicles?

   i. Never   ii. Sometimes   iii. Often   iv. Don't know

21. **Are passengers asked to get down from the bus in the middle of the road?**

    i. Sometimes ii. Often   iii. Never

    Reasons: _____

    _____

22. **Do the drivers change the routes by themselves?**

    i. Sometimes ii. Often   iii. Never

    Reasons: _____

    _____

23. **Is it difficult to catch a ride on a strike day?**

    i. Yes   ii. No   iii. Sometimes

24. **How do you travel on a strike day?**

    i. Skip work   ii. Suzuki/Van   iii. Rickshaw/Taxi   iv. Hitch a ride

    v. By walk   vi. Qingchi   vii. Contract Bus

    viii. Others: _____

25. **Is it easy to find a bus/vehicle at night?**

    i. Yes   ii. No   iii. Sometimes   iv. Don't know

    Details: _____

26. **In case of a CNG strike, it is difficult to find a bus/vehicle.**

    i. Yes   ii. No   iii. Sometimes   iv. Don't know

27. **If there is no bus/vehicle available, how do you travel?**

    Details: _____

28. **During travel the condition of the clothes/shoes is also affected.**

    i. Often   ii. Sometimes   iii. Never

    Details: _____

29. **Are you satisfied with the steps which the government is taking to improve the situation of transport?**

    i. Yes   ii. No   iii. Don't know

    Details: _____

30. **Should the number of seats for women be increased?**

    i. Yes   ii. No   iii. Don't know

31. **Is there a need for separate transport for women?**

    i. Yes   ii. No   iii. Don't know

    Reasons: _____

32. **Do you think it is safe for women to travel at night?**

    i.   Yes   ii. No   iii. Don't know

    Details: _____

33. **Do the drivers increase or decrease the speed by themselves?**

    i.   Yes   ii. No   iii. Don't know

34. **Are the buses stopped at the stands appearing in the middle of the routes?**

    i.   Yes   ii. No   iii. Don't know

    Duration of the stop: _____

35. **In your opinion, are the CNG/LPG cylinders properly fitted in the vehicles?**

    i.   Yes   ii. No   iii. Don't know

    Your opinion: _____

36. **Passenger vehicles have proper foot rests?**

    i.   Yes   ii. No   iii. Don't know

    If not, reason: _____

37. **Is the rate of the rent uniform throughout?**

    i.   Yes   ii. No   iii. Don't know

38. **Do you prefer music while travelling?**

    i.   Yes   ii. No

    Details: _____

39. **Are you satisfied with the performance of the traffic police?**

    i.   Yes   ii. No   iii. To an extent only

    Details: _____

40. **Do you have to face theft/robbery during travelling?**

    i.   Never   ii. Once   iii. More than one time

    Details: _____

41. **Does a good transport system contribute to a better employment?**

    i.   Yes   ii. No   iii. Don't know

    Details: _____

42. **In your opinion is Qingchi a beneficial ride?**

    i.   Yes   ii. No   iii. Don't know

43. **In your opinion is a motorbike a better option than public transport?**

    i.   Yes   ii. No   iii. Don't know

    Details: _____

44. Do you or your family own a motorbike?

  i. Yes   ii. No

  Details: _____

45. Do you think that students and senior citizens should be given a concession on the rent?

  i. Yes   ii. No   iii. Don't know

46. In your opinion what steps are required to improve the public transport system?

_____

_____

47. What is your occupation?

_____

48. Your monthly salary/earnings?

_____ Rupees

Interviewer's name: _____

Date: _____

Time of the interview: _____

Conclusion/Summary/Preview: _____

_____

_____

ANALYSIS OF QUESTIONNAIRES FOR TRANSPORT RESEARCH (MARCH 2014)

The survey forms part of research carried out by Arif Hasan and the Urban Resource Centre. The objectives of the research was to document the economic and social problems and opportunities provided by Karachi's six main commuter transport modes (and their relationship to urban form), to explore the policy implications, and to provide the basis for a film on this topic.

For the purpose of the survey, a total of 150 respondents were interviewed in different parts of Karachi. The places where the survey was conducted include FB Area, North Nazimabad, University Road, Bahadurabad, Saddar, Lyari, Defence Housing Authority (DHA), Korangi, Jail Road, North Karachi, Baloch Colony, Drug Road, Baldia Town, Junejo Town, Rehman Colony, Shadman Town, Nazimabad, Umer Colony, Gulistan-e-Jouhar, Surjani Town, Orangi Town, Moriya Khan Goth, Malir, Gulbahar, Gulshan-e-Iqbal, Shah Faisal Colony, PECHS, Landhi, Manzoor Colony.

Each form of the structured survey took somewhere between 30 to 40 minutes and approximately 80 hours were spent in administering 150 forms. Each form comprises 47 questions. The questions are structured in a closed loop manner, but a couple of queries also seek opinion and further details in the responses.

The findings of the survey are divided into the following three broader categories:

1. Preferred and availability of conveyance
2. Woes of commuters
3. Recommendations by the respondents

1. Preference and availability of conveyance

The preference and availability of the mode varies in normal and unusual days. The unusual days refer to strike calls by various political religious and ethnic parties and groups. The unusual days also signifie CNG shut down days. Moreover, as per respondents, the situation also varies as availability during the daytime is different compared to night.

In normal days, the majority of the respondents (32.7 per cent) use two modes of conveyance for commuting; bus and rickshaw, while the second largest group (19.3 per cent) travels only by bus. Coach is the third major option as is used by 16.7 per cent and the least used mode of conveyance is the rickshaw which is 1.3 per cent. Contract buses are also deployed by 1.3 per cent of commuters who took part in the survey.

Nearly half of the respondents, 50.7 per cent, own a motorcycle while just under half (48 per cent) do not. Motorcycles are considered a better means of public transport by 60.7 percent of the respondents, whereas 34 think otherwise. 19.3 per cent think that it is fast and safe, while 16.3 per cent think that it is a dangerous mode of conveyance. The QINGQI, as mentioned by 60 per cent, was a helpful addition to the modes of conveyance, while 34.7 percent did not think that way.

90 per cent of the respondents mentioned that it is hard to find transport on strike days. 48.7 per cent of respondents avoid going to work on strike days, while 22.7 per cent find rickshaws to take them to their work place. Another 12.7 per cent ask for lift from somebody in order to commute.

In unusual circumstances, as is the case with CNG shut down days, 86.7 per cent of the respondents mentioned that it is difficult to get a bus/van and only 5.3 per cent mentioned that they do not face any difficulties. On CNG shut down days, rickshaw is the alternate transport for 38.7 per cent of the respondents, whereas another 27.3 per cent rely on 'lifts'. A substantial number, 16 per cent, mentioned that they do not go to work on these days.

It is interesting to note that during the night, 62.7 per cent of the respondents cannot find a bus or van easily, while 16.7 per cent mentioned that this varies, while another 18.7 per cent said that they can find these easily. It appears from the survey that most of the respondents (82.7 per cent) do not consider it safe for women to travel at night, whereas 14 per cent think otherwise.

2. Woes of commuters

The difficulties mentioned by the respondents range from a lengthy time spent travelling and waiting for buses, overcrowding on buses, standing when travelling, travelling on roof tops, suffering injuries, leaving the bus half way through the journey for one reason or another, harassment of women commuters, damage of attire, dangers of faulty installation of CNG/LPG cylinders, and non-standardisation of bus fares.

Commuters spend a considerable time on the roads. Exactly 35.3 per cent of the interviewees spend 41 to 60 minutes on the road, daily and each way. Another 13.3 per cent spend 81 to 90 minutes of their time on the road and only 6 per cent mentioned that they spend 11 to 20 minutes for a one-way commute. The waiting time at bus stops for 48.6 per cent varies from 5 minutes to 20 minutes. Woes of travelling as mentioned by the respondents include long travelling hours (32.7 per cent), to long waits for the buses (31.3 per cent) and changing buses (20.0) per cent. Also, most of the respondents (68.7 per cent) are of the opinion that drivers stay quite long at transit stopovers, whereas 28 per cent think the contrary.

The majority of the respondents (36.7 per cent) were concerned about overcrowding on buses, and 26.7 per cent expressed their unhappiness about noise pollution, broken seats/interiors. As a result, only 13.3 per cent of the respondents get a seat while travelling by bus. Another 6 per cent mentioned that they travel on the roof and 27.3 per cent mentioned that they travel standing up.

A considerable percentage, 49.3 per cent, opined that passengers 'sometimes' are dropped half way and another 24.7 per cent mentioned that this is done frequently. Another 14.7 per cent responded to the question with 'never'. Reasons for this include disputes on fares, cited by 54 per cent of respondents, while 16 per cent mentioned running out of CNG/LPG, and 2.7 per cent cited mechanical problems. 'Sometimes' was the frequency of bus route changes by 72.7 per cent of the respondents and another 20 per cent mentioned that the bus routes are never changed. The law and order situation was the reason cited by 56.7 per cent.

While getting on or off the bus, 47.3 per cent of the respondents mentioned that they suffer injuries 'sometimes', whereas 36.7 per cent mentioned 'frequently'. Only 6.7 per cent mentioned that they never sustained any injury. A considerable majority, 60 per cent, mentioned that the footrests on the buses are not in a good condition, while 32.7 per cent think otherwise.

There is also a gender dimension to add to the woes of commuting. The majority of the respondents, 46 per cent, were of the opinion that women are harassed regularly on the bus or in vans, while 37.3 per cent mentioned the frequency as 'sometimes'. It is interesting to note that 11.3 per cent mentioned that women are never harassed.

It appears to be a widely shared belief among the respondents that CNG/LPG cylinders are not installed safely o the buses as 79.3 per cent answered 'no' to the question.

A slight majority, 50.7 per cent, are sceptical about the bus fares being standard.

Apart from the above-mentioned difficulties, a considerable number of the respondents, 60 per cent mentioned that they were robbed either once or more than once on public transport, whereas 36.7 per cent mentioned that they were never robbed.

3. Recommendations

Recommendations by commuters include expanding the seating arrangements, increasing the number of buses, having women-only transport and facilitating transport for the elderly. Most of the respondents, 66.7 per cent, are not satisfied with the measures taken by the government to improve the transport system, though 26 per cent mentioned that they were satisfied. A considerable majority, 73.3 per cent, of the respondents considered the traffic police to be an asset, while another 13.3 per cent are not so satisfied with the reputation of the traffic police.

An overwhelming majority, 86 per cent, are of the opinion that there is a need to increase the seating arrangements for women in buses and only 10 per cent denied the need for it. The need for separate women-only transport was agreed by 76.7 per cent of the respondents, whereas 18.7 per cent do not consider it necessary. 28 per cent mentioned that it would enable women to travel at ease, 22.7 per cent mentioned that it is good for women and another 19.3 per cent think that it is usual practice that women's seats are occupied by men, hence it is better to have their separate buses for men and women.

Bigger buses are the solution of the transport woes for 30.7 per cent, while another 38.7 per cent think that the transport issue could be handled by increasing the number of buses. The majority, 82 per cent, of the respondents believe that a better transport system would help in securing better job opportunities.

An overwhelming majority, 92 per cent, think that the elderly should be given fare discounts.

Conclusion

With an average monthly income of Rs. 13,482, the respondents spend on average Rs 1,500 per month (Rs 18,000 per annum), and approximately two hours daily on a round trip (624 hours per annum) while commuting, which is much higher than the world average commuting hours. The time spent on commuting by the respondents in one year is equivalent to 78 working days (assuming there are eight working hours in a day). According to a study, the world average commuting time is 80 minutes a day. Thailand is considered to have the longest commuting in the world, while Malawi has the shortest. A 2007 Gallup survey (in the USA), indicated that on a typical day, a worker's average round trip commute takes 46 minutes. Similarly, according to the UK Office of National Statistics (2011), 75 per cent of workers take around one hour for a round trip from home to work.

Despite all the difficulties of travelling, a considerable number travel by bus, though they consider motorcycles (and previously Qingqis) as better modes of conveyance. Besides all perceived misgivings on transport governance, the respondents' recommendations about the scaling-up of the transport system reflect their pinned hopes on a viable mass transit system, as they believe that an improved transport system will contribute to enhanced livelihood opportunities.

GENDER ANALYSIS – TRANSPORT STUDY, 2014

Total Samples

Male		Female		Total
Number	Percentage	Number	Percentage	
103	68.67	47	31.33	150

Responses

		Male		Female	
		Number	Percentage	Number	Percentage
A.	**Mode of conveyance to office**				
1.	Bus and Coaches	29	28.16	20	42.55
2.	Buses	20	19.42	9	19.15
3.	Minibus	18	17.48	6	12.77
B.	**Travel time – one way and daily**				
1.	51 to 60 minutes	19	18.45	10	21.28
2.	41 to 50 minutes	15	14.56	9	19.15
C.	**One way fare**				
1.	Rs 11 to Rs 20	43	41.75	19	40.43
2.	Rs 21 to Rs 30	30	29.13	13	27.66
D.	**Woes of travelling**				
1.	Long travel time	31	30.10	18	38.30
2.	Long waiting time for buses	35	33.98	12	25.53
E.	**The internal environment of buses/ transport**				
1.	Overloaded buses	38	36.89	17	36.17
2.	Overload, noise, broken seats and window glasses	26	25.24	14	29.79
F.	**Difficulties with travelling standing**				
1.	Yes	85	82.52	41	87.23
G.	**Condition of buses/ transport**				
1.	Bad	57	55.34	28	59.57
2.	Normal	42	40.78	16	34.04
H.	**Visibility of route numbers of buses**				
1.	Yes visible	78	75.73	34	72.34
I.	**If route number is not visible, what to do for identification?**				

		Male		Female	
		Number	Percentage	Number	Percentage
1.	Have to ask other people or conductor	30	29.13	14	29.79
J.	**Do you find seats during the journey?**				
1.	Sometimes yes and sometimes travel standing	32	31.07	21	44.68
2.	Travel standing	29	28.16	12	25.53
K.	**Attitude of bus conductor and driver**				
1.	Normal	52	50.49	26	55.32
2.	Bad	29	28.16	13	27.66
L.	**Maintained speed of bus**				
1.	Normal	42	40.78	20	42.55
2.	Slow	38	36.89	11	23.40
3.	Sometimes slow sometimes fast	7	6.80	8	17.02
4.	Fast	13	12.62	4	8.51
5.	Very fast	3	2.91	4	8.51
M.	**Does the bus always stop at the bus stop?**				
1.	Sometimes	46	44.66	30	63.83
2.	Always	44	42.72	14	29.79
N.	**Are elderly, children and women taken care at the time of dis-embarking?**				
1.	Sometimes	59	57.28	33	70.21
2.	Always	27	26.21	8	17.02
O.	**Do passengers get hurt while embarking?**				
1.	Usually	35	33.98	20	42.55
2.	sometimes	51	49.51	20	42.55
P.	**Do women face harassment in public transport?**				
1.	Usually	45	43.69	24	51.06
2.	Sometimes	40	38.83	16	34.04
Q.	**Are passengers dismbarked half-way by the drivers?**				
1.	Sometimes	58	56.31	31	65.96
2.	Usually	26	25.24	11	23.40

		Male		Female	
		Number	Percentage	Number	Percentage
R.	**Do drivers change route by their own free will?**				
1.	Sometimes	74	71.84	35	74.47
2.	Never	22	21.36	8	17.02
S.	**Is difficult to get conveyance on strike days?**				
1.	Yes	95	92.23	40	85.11
T.	**How you got to your job on strike days?**				
1.	Do not go to job	48	46.60	25	53.19
2.	Rickshaw	23	22.33	11	23.40
3.	QINGQI	11	10.68	5	10.64
U.	**Is it easy to find conveyance at night?**				
1.	No	64	62.14	30	63.83
2.	Sometimes	16	15.53	9	19.15
V.	**Is it difficult to find transport on CNG-off days?**				
1.	Yes	87	84.47	43	91.49
W.	**How do you go to job on CNG strike days?**				
1.	Rickshaw	36	34.95	22	46.81
2.	Do not go to job	16	15.53	8	17.02
3.	Lift	34	33.01	7	14.89
X.	**Attrition of attire during travel**				
1.	Usually	80	77.67	36	76.60
2.	Sometimes	16	15.53	10	21.28
Y.	**Are you satisfied with government measures for improvement of public transport?**				
1.	No	63	61.17	34	72.34
Z.	**Should the number of seats for women be increased?**				
1.	Yes	91	88.35	41	87.23
AA.	**Need for separate transport buses for women?**				
1	Yes	72	69.90	43	91.49

		Male		Female	
		Number	Percentage	Number	Percentage
AB.	Is it safe for women to travel at night?				
1.	No	83	80.58	41	87.23
AC.	Do buses stop for a long time at inter-route bus stops?				
1.	Yes	69	66.99	34	72.34
AD.	Are CNG cylinders safely housed in the bus chassis?				
1.	No	79	76.70	40	85.11
AE.	Foot rest appropriate?				
1.	No	61	59.22	29	61.70
2.	Yes	33	32.04	16	34.04
AF.	Should fares be the same for all public transport?				
1.	Yes	45	43.69	24	51.06
2.	No	53	51.46	23	48.94
AG.	Do you like music in transport?				
1.	No	54	52.43	24	51.06
2.	Yes	47	45.63	23	48.94
AH.	Satisfaction with traffic police				
1.	No	76	73.79	34	72.34
2.	Yes	9	8.74	8	17.02
AI.	Did you ever face theft/ robbery in public Transport				
1.	Never	32	31.97	23	48.94
2.	Once	28	27.18	15	31.91
3.	More than once	39	37.86	8	17.02
AJ.	Can a good transport system facilitate securing a better job?				
1.	Yes	81	78.64	42	89.36
AK.	Are QINGQIs better modes of conveyance?				
1.	Yes	59	57.28	31	65.96
2.	No	37	35.92	15	31.91

		Male		Female	
		Number	Percentage	Number	Percentage
AL.	**Are motorbikes better modes of conveyance?**				
1.	Yes	59	57.28	32	68.09
2.	No	40	38.83	11	23.40
AM.	**Do you think that the elderly and students should have a discount fare?**				
1.	Yes	95	92.23	43	91.49
AN.	**What needs to be done to improve the public transport system?**				
1.	Increase the number of buses	32	31.07	26	55.32
2.	Big buses should ply on the roads	33	32.04	13	27.66

Appendix 3.4: Stakeholders in the Transport Sector in Karachi

GOVERNMENT INSTITUTIONS

- The Federal Government of Pakistan: Initiates projects through the planning and development commission, in collaboration with the government of Sindh and the CDGK.
- The Government of Sindh: Coordinates between its various transport-related departments and the federal government.
- CDGK: Its role varies depending on the local system in vogue at the time. Previously, it had a major role in the UTS as its designer and implementer.
- Transport and Communication Department (formerly the Traffic Engineering Bureau under CDGK), Karachi Metropolitan Corporation, Karachi: It researches, designs and implements engineering projects.
- Sindh Mass Transit Project (formerly the Karachi Mass Transit Cell of the CDGK)
- Karachi Urban Transport Society; A federal institution preparing the Karachi
- Transport Improvement Project. Pakistan Railways has 60 per cent of shares in the society, the Sindh government has 25 per cent and the KMC has 15 per cent.
- Regional Transport Authority; Regulates traffic as per Motor Vehicle Ordinance 1979; allots routes for public transport vehicles; looks into transport-related safety issues; runs training programmes for transporters/ drivers; looks into provision of public washrooms and waiting spaces at transport terminals.
- Deputy Inspector General (traffic) Police; Issues driving licences and manages traffic.
- Sindh Environmental Protection Agency; Monitors environmental conditions and develops plans and proposals to mitigate the adverse effects on the environment. It also operates a vehicular emission control programme.
- Karachi Public Transport Society: A government NGO that operates about 150 small buses in the city.

TRANSPORTER'S ASSOCIATIONS

- Karachi Transport Ittehad (an organisation of which all modes of public transport, except for Qingqis, are represented)
- President Muslim Minibus and Coach Owners' Association
- All Karachi Qingqis and Rickshaws Association
- Karachi Taxi, Motor Rickshaw and Yellow Cab Association
- All Pakistan CNG Association
- Minibus Drivers' Association

THE COMMUTING PUBLIC

- Registers its demands and concerns through the print and electronic media and through demonstrations.

Appendix 3.5: Transcripts of Full Interviews

A. INTERVIEWS WITH GOVERNMENT OFFICIALS

A-01. Muhammad Athar, Director Transport and Communication Department, KMC

Today we are in discussion with Mohammad Athar, who is the senior director of the Transport and Communication Department of the Karachi Metropolitan Corporation (KMC). They have a brilliant system in place, they monitor the problems of transport in Karachi very closely and have introduced and are introducing new plans to solve the transport issues. We welcome you on behalf of the Urban Resource Centre (URC).

Q: The issue of transport in Karachi, a mega city with a population of 2 crore, is huge. According to you what are the main reasons behind the problem?

A: First of all, I would like to thank you for giving me an opportunity to talk about all these issues. I have been associated with URC for some time now. URC is playing an amazing role in the transport matter. Now before I answer your question let's first discuss the transport infrastructure of Karachi. The road network of Karachi has spread over an area of 10,000 km and comprises major roads, minor roads and access roads. Major roads make up barely 20 per cent of the total. The rest are access and local roads. These roads have corridors and there are 29, as notified by KMC. These corridors are maintained by KMC. I will also share the list of them with you. As you also know that signal free corridors are also in the planning stages, out of which five have already been designated. The first signal-free corridor is from Karsaz to SITE area, the second is from Sharah-e-Minhas to Surjani town, the third one is the university road, and the fourth one is the Shahrah-e-Faisal corridor. They also have interchange facilities. Currently there are 32 lac registered vehicles in Karachi, if you look at the trend over 10 years it has grown exponentially. If you translate this into numbers, almost 500 cars and motorbikes are entering Karachi every day! The motorbike industry has grown rapidly and is almost uncontrolled. We have factories in the interior part of the province too and with the collaboration of China, the industry has grown a lot. The same goes for the induction of cars. This is happening because we don't have a proper transport system in the city. People have found a solution to this problem themselves as they don't have any other alternative. They are bound to acquire their own transport. This is why those who can afford cars, buy cars while those who can afford motorbikes, buy motorbikes. If you look at the composition of the growth, 46 per cent consists of motorcycles, whereas registered cars make up 36 per cent. The remaining 14-15 per cent is made up of other vehicles. Public transport only accounts for 4.5 per cent of the growth. This 4.5 per cent serves 60 per cent of the population! That is exactly why overcrowding occurs. There exists a gap between the provision of service and needs of the public; this gap is not being filled, resulting in overcrowding on public transport. On the one hand, private vehicles are increasing in number, whereas on the other hand, public transport is decreasing. There are many reasons for this decrease. Firstly, new large buses are not being inducted. This is a primary requirement of a mega city. The reasons why they are not being inducted are their capital costs and their operating costs. Secondly, private transport is not affordable to everyone. Public transport has diminished. The Sindh Road Transport Corporation (SRTC) also catered for 1-2 routes only. But now they are not being run as they should be. The Karachi Transport

Commission (KTC) was closed down in 1997. After that, minibuses and coaches were rapidly inducted in Karachi. KTC was regulated by the government of Sindh. It was really practical and covered more than 100 routes. They had a vast network of university routes as well. It shut down due to various reasons such as fare revenue leakage, improper maintenance of buses and mismanagement. From KTC's experience it was clear that public services cannot maintain/manage the transport service. So, the private sector took over. Minibuses and coaches were inducted but their operating cost was too high. Also, the diesel price rose rapidly. Fares are regulated by government but if they were increased at the same proportion, they wouldn't have been affordable to the public. So, the fares remained the same and were controlled, however because of that it has become difficult for the transporters to maintain the quality of their services. In 2001, when the city district government was formed, they introduced Urban Transport Services. I was part of that plan too. The entire scheme was approved by the Sindh cabinet. The 70 per cent loan mark up of that scheme was supposed to be subsidised by the government to the extent of 6 per cent. Above 6 per cent was to be paid by the operator and below 6 per cent was to be reimbursed by the government. Then work began on this scheme. 300–350 buses were inducted, and finance came from the banks. The government did not continue its patronage. To date no subsidy has been given to the operators involved in that scheme. We had to file claims for the companies. A few companies are still running their buses. They are around 12 in number and being run on Shahrah-e-Faisal. The government of Sindh constituted a committee and we filed claims for two companies. We verified their operations and completed the entire process and forwarded the claims to the finance department for a refund. But this was all in vain. When we launched this service the diesel prices were Rs 19 and now they have increased exponentially. The fares remain the same. The UTS buses exited from the system. In fact, they have exited from Karachi. We wrote letters to the Punjab government that these buses are part of the Karachi scheme and should not be running elsewhere. But our requests were of no use. This project failed badly. Everywhere in the world, public transport is being subsidised by the government. In fact, this is happening in Lahore as well! A rapid bus system is being subsidised by the government. Keeping this in mind, the federal government approved a project of 4,000 CNG buses for Karachi as well. Initially it was approved as a policy in 2007. It was decided that 2,000 buses were to be given to Karachi and the remaining 2,000 were to be given to other large cities in Pakistan. The debt ratio was 80:20 instead of 70:30. The remaining model was the same as UTS. They had a fix subsidy for this project that 6 lac will be given as a per capital cost to the operator. Then local banks were instructed to extend loans to the operators. The National Bank was approached first. They refused to provide loan services because of the past experience of UTS of non-payment of instalments in a timely manner. The matter was taken to the highest level but remain unresolved. Then in the regime of Mayor Mustafa Kamal, he suggested that a pilot project should be initiated to fill the gap of transport to demonstrate that we can make it work. A model was developed that the buses will be procured by the government and outsourced to the private sector. Also, the operators will only be responsible for the operation of the buses so that they will have no relation to the fares and finances. For fares an e-ticketing system was to be introduced which a separate private company would handle. For CNG, we directly contacted CNG stations. We directly paid the CNG stations, the responsible staff used to verify the CNG filling in the vehicles and we would pay money accordingly. Our policy clearly stated that the fare revenue will not be sufficient to meet the operating expenses and the government had to subsidise to the tune of Rs 5 million per month. It was subsidised for two years and the service continued. We had e-ticketing systems, e-ticketing booths with closed doors and comfortable services, and the system continued. But there came a time where the city government was unable to deliver the funds then there was no other option but to reduce the operating cost of the buses. We then had to close the e-ticketing system and introduced conductors in the buses. This resulted in overloading as we couldn't control the number of passengers. It went out of our control. The revenue also decreased. We had a checking system in place and we evaluated and concluded that there was a 10 per cent leakage in the revenue generation from the conductors' side. But despite this there was an off-set. We tried to minimise it as much as possible. Then when the time came to change the tyres of these buses after four years, repair the engines of a few, the contract of outsourcing had also changed by that time. None of the private operators participated in the maintenance of the buses. We invited tender but no company came forward. This was in February 2013. Since then these buses are parked in one place. We tried hard to get funds to maintain these buses and resume the service but we have had no support. We have sent a proposal but they haven't responded.

Q: Out of the 73 buses, how many are in a working condition?

A: Our overall estimate for the maintenance of the buses is Rs 40 million. Some cost around 8 lac while some cost 5 lac, depending on the condition of the buses. One bus now costs 70 million. When we bought them, they used to cost Rs 4.4 million each.

Q: What is being done about it now?

A: First these buses need to be brought back. We are discussing whether to convert them to LPG because supply and pricing of CNG is also an issue. We wrote a letter to the Oil and Gas Regulatory Authority (OGRA) asking for permission of at least one CNG station that would provide us with CNG even on a holiday. They responded that they have nothing to do with this and we need to contact the Ministry of Petroleum and Natural Resources. We wrote to them and we still haven't received a response. Even the Secretary of Transport wrote to OGRA and they got the same response. We cannot write directly to the federal government. We have to go through the provincial government. We mentioned two issues in the letter: (1) Supply of CNG (2) Repair of the buses.

Q: What is your take on the infrastructure of the city including flyovers, underpasses, etc. To what extent are they proving to be beneficial for the city?

A: If we had a mass transit system in Karachi, we would not have needed flyovers. 70 per cent of the transport which you see on roads is private. You only see one or two minibuses. So, under these conditions if flyovers had not been built, the city would be at a standstill. In the absence of a mass transit system, this was the only solution. If the flyovers hadn't have been built, we couldn't even begin to imagine the trouble we would been in.

Q: Where do we require such flyovers and intersections?

A: JICA Japan International Cooperation Agency carried out a comprehensive study in 2013. They developed a master transport plan, with a proposal for a mass transit transport system, including two railways and MRT lines, six rapid transit lines for buses, one Karachi Circular Railway (KCR) loop and a bus network system. They proposed flyovers in 53 different locations. They divided the construction of flyovers into phases. Also, they proposed 43 different road improvement and road building projects and bridge construction. Furthermore, they included 53 intersections along with an intercity bus system. The plan is targeted to be completed by 2030.

Q: You have been associated with transport for some time now and must've participated in different sessions including with other transporters. Do you think there could be plans and schemes in which we can include the existing transporters too?

A: The CNG bus network plan was constructed keeping the existing transports in the loop. They gave consent for the plan too. But since there were no funds this plan couldn't be completed.

Q: Did they back out because it would affect their current business?

A: No. It was never part of the plan that this project would go to any specific group of people and it was they who had to run this project. It was and is open for all. The only objection they had was from where they would get the loan. Also, another concern was how the payment of fares would work because we do not have control over the operating costs, neither do the operators themselves. The diesel prices have increased so much and the financial plan is not stable.

Q: But the transporters are still running their vehicles?

A: Minibuses are working as double-decker buses. They used to be operated seat-by-seat and they also used to earn a profit. But now they are being overloaded to such a great extent. Even with Qingqi rickshaws, we often see 12 people in one rickshaw.

Q: Do Qingqi rickshaws have any policy?

A: Not as yet. They have not been included in the current transport plan. Action was taken against them, but they are still running.

Q: What is your take on them? Are they able to solve the transport issue of the city?

A: Yes, they are solving the transport issue of the city in the absence of public transport.

Q: Are they secure?

A: No, they aren't.

Q: Should they be continued?

A: Yes, but with a proper plan and design. Their design should be approved by the relevant transport department. They should be properly maintained and registered with the fitness department which determines if a vehicle is road worthy or not. But they should be running on small/link roads not main roads. Even rickshaws with six seats did not previously run parallel to the bus routes. Now these Qingqis are running on highways, Shahrah-e-Faisal, the national highway and this goes beyond a violation. Even the enforcing agencies are not doing anything about it because they are at least providing a public service. The public has no other option, where would they go? A public transport only survives if there is demand for it otherwise who would want to overload their Qingqi with 12 passengers at a time?

Q: The CNG buses which you talked about, what is going to be their fare?

A: It will be between Rs 20–25. Previously it was Rs 15–18.

Q: According to you what can be done about the current problems/situation?

A: First of all, we need extensive support by the city government and policies to encourage the induction of buses in the city. Public transport policies have to be encouraged. This needs to be done by the federal government. Secondly, the 200 buses currently in planning by the government have to be bought as soon as possible. These buses will be run on inter-city routes. We require transport on urban roads.

Q: How can the problem of traffic jams in the city be solved?

A: Traffic jams are occurring because we do not have a proper public transport system which is why private cars have increased in number. The second issue is the misuse of road space. The roads should be only be used for the movement of traffic. Also, irregular parking is an issue. This has occurred because of the increase in the number of private cars. The rationale of demand and capacity has lost its meaning. Moreover, as a road user we have some responsibility as well. Until we realise and fulfil that responsibility, the system won't improve. Religious events should be held in open areas rather than on roads to avoid traffic jams. There should be a policy at a national level for this.

A-02. ARIF HANIF, DIG, TRAFFIC POLICE

On behalf of URC we are extremely grateful to you for having agreed to meet us and discuss the situation of traffic within the city, especially the causes of traffic jams and the steps being taken by the traffic police. We will also discuss the increase in the number of fatal accidents in the city.

Q: How many traffic police officials are there?

A: On the streets of Karachi and in administration, duties are being performed by 3,300 officials. These 3,300 officials work in three different shifts. They don't carry any weapons with them.

Q: How are the traffic police officials in the city affected by the air pollution? What are the common illnesses which are found?

A: You must have seen that now the traffic police officials wear masks these days. With the number of vehicles increasing within the city, our officials are easily affected by the smoke and pollution. Most of the illnesses which they suffer are flu, asthma, constant cough etc.

Q: In the event of a VIP duty, there must be a high demand of traffic police officials.

A: Yes definitely. But we still try to continue the flow of traffic in the city.

Q: What are the main reasons for traffic jams in the city?

A: This is mostly because the number of vehicles in the city is increasing, especially small cars. Ever since the banks have started giving loans for cars and motorbikes, people are solving their own issues of transport by buying cars or motorbikes according to their convenience. Also, the problem is parking which is getting worse day by day. At every signal you can see loads of cars. Then there are extensions on the roads causing more traffic jams and whenever the government takes any action against these extensions, the shopkeepers protest. Parking is a problem as whenever a new building project is made they don't provide adequate parking facilities. Moreover, people park their cars in front of the shopping centres on the main roads. This causes further traffic jams and it is difficult to maintain the flow of the traffic in such cases.

Q: Are Qingqi rickshaws a problem in the city?

A: Yes. Currently 60-70 Qingqi rickshaws are operating on the main roads of the city. They were meant to operate only on link roads, but now they can be seen everywhere in the city. They have made their stops on the roundabouts of the cities. When we wanted to take an action against them, their owners got a stay order from the High Court. But until we remove them from the roads of the city, the problem won't be resolved.

Q: What roles have underpasses and flyovers played in controlling the traffic flow?

A: They have provided the public with temporary relief. If there were no underpasses or flyovers, then the traffic situation would be much worse. Wherever corridors are constructed, the traffic flow is rapid.

Q: How does one get a licence? There are stories about corruption in the licence branches, how can this situation be resolved?

A: The licence branch is an entirely different department and we have no official relations with them for any administrative purposes. If there is a problem them, you'll have to contact them. I have to leave now. There is a situation at Numaish roundabout which I need to take care of.

A-03. Fazal Karim Khatri, DG, Mass Transit, Karachi Metropolitan Corporation

We are going to talk about mass transit; what it is, what is its role, why and when was it established, and what is its function.

Mr Khatri: If we talk about the history behind mass transit, then I'd like to tell you that it began in 1987 under the Karachi Development Authority (KDA), then in 1994 it was transferred to the National Mass Transit Authority. In 1995, it faced a problem and went under PMD; the salaries were controlled by KDA. In 1997, administrative control was handed over to the transport department and only our salaries were still on KDA's payroll. After that, in 2002, when KDA was dissolved, it again became a part of city district government. In 2011, it became a part of KMC. Then in July 2013, restructuring of the government departments was carried out and we were told that now we are part of the transport and mass transit department (formerly called the transport department). This change has been made in schedule I only, schedule II is still pending. The situation is that if we look at it from the ownership perspective, keeping the public interest and the importance of mass transit in view, we are taking care of both systems, i.e. we are responsible for the transport system and at the same time answerable to KMC. This is because we are getting a salary from KMC, so we have to respond to them as well. But it is still undecided where we stand.

Q: Why is mass transit required?

A: Initially, when the population of Karachi was 4 lacs, the system of mass transit used to exist. And now we have a population of 2 crores and not a single mass transit system exists in the city! This is a dilemma and our bad luck. You've seen the city conditions. Qingqi and rickshaws have taken over the transport system. Karachi is a mega city and we are moving towards operating only Qingqis, it's a downward regression, instead we should be moving towards mass transit projects like sky trains or underground metro buses. We have further degraded from these. The current situation is that the regular traffic in our city, motorcycles consist of 46 per cent of that traffic, whereas cars make up 36 per cent, and public transport is merely 4.5 per cent! And it may even have decreased. This 4.5 per cent carries the load of 42 per cent of the population! This is the seriousness of the problem. People have to travel on the roofs of buses, why? Because of the lack of a proper public transport system. Some time back, CNG buses were introduced and they served the purpose to an extent, but subsidies were eliminated, and the project ended.

Q: In 1987 the mass transit system was introduced, now we are in 2014, the position of Karachi is the same, if not worse. We had a railway system too, and in 1999 it was discontinued. Do you think there is a solution to all this after mass transit is introduced?

A: If there isn't any mass transit, then we won't be able to solve these problems. Nobody is coming to the fore and owning this project. Until we restore this ownership I don't think we'll be able to solve this problem.

Q: What's the future of the mass transit system?

A: We think positively about the future—that the democratic vision and the federal government both support a mass transit system. The provincial government has also committed to this project. We can see their harmonisation to an extent towards this project, including our local government. That is why we believe that one or two of our projects can be initiated. For the yellow line's Bus Rapid Transport (BRT) corridor, the advertisement is already out, and we have received the invitation for that already and hopefully on 25 February 2014 we will receive the final date and then the evaluation will start, and within six months hopefully permission to build will be received. We have invited internationally; the international billing process has been adopted.

Q: What about the present transport system?

A: Consultation with the stakeholders is needed. We don't want a conflict or a controversy, we wish to harmonise the system. We all earn from this system and if we don't resolve it without controversy, this project may not be successful. We have planned that we'd take them with us and sit with them and give the service road to them so that they can earn a livelihood too and they are able to harmonise with the system.

Q: What are the existing plans for mass transit?

A: The master plan that currently exists recommends six BRT corridors, out of which three are priority corridors. One of them is the yellow line, which we have already initiated, the second is the red line, this would start from Model Colony, pass Safoora Chowrangi from the University Road and end at Chowrangi which is at Quaid-i-Azam's Mausoleum. This connection will touch the yellow line. The third one is going to be from Surjani town, which is the most viable BRT corridor, and will pass from Nazimabad all the way up to Patel Para, Numaish, and end at Jama Cloth. It is almost 21 km long and it is our priority corridor no. 2. Apart from this, we have plans for three other BRT corridors—they are orange, purple and aqua lines.

Q: What is the meaning of these colours?

A: They are only for identification purposes. I can provide you with the entire plan so that you can get an idea that where these lines operate. These are all routes. Green, red and yellow pass from Korangi area. We have two other Mass Rapid Transit (MRT) lines, this is the blue line (pointing out on the map) this starts from Sohrab Goth and goes as far as Jama Cloth. The second one is the brown line. The brown line runs from the Power House and connects to Shahrah-e-Faisal ultimately, also very viable. All BRT corridors interconnect with the KCR. The extension of the KCR has also been proposed to connect it from the airport. This is our master plan which we are currently working on.

Q: Are bus terminals a part of this plan?

A: Bus terminals have a separate plan. They are very important that's why we are tackling the issue differently. We have numerous illegal bus terminals we are not taking care of those, we have a separate department which is responsible called the transport and communication department of KDA. We have identified two sites which are at the entrance to the city.

Q: Which are the two sites you have mentioned?

A: One is the Regional Cooperation for Development (RCD) highway's bus terminal by the city district. The second one is the land identified on the super highway, near to the northern bypass, our plan also entertains that. We will start working on them soon and we'll soon receive the ad for it. We need a centralised bus terminal. One more area of land has been identified on the national highway, we may build a bus terminal there too.

Q: Do you see any risk in the process of the completion of these bus terminals?

A: Given the trend which we have seen in the past, yes I do see a risk. But hopefully, this project will take two years to complete.

Q: Are the BRT and MRT projects separate? Or have they been merged into one?

A: The BRT is a separate project and we still haven't even started MRT since it costs a lot and we don't have any funds at the moment. We'll first run a pilot of the yellow line to see if we get investors or not.

Q: What is the estimated cost of both these projects?

A: The estimated cost of the yellow line is around Rs 13 billion and the green line's cost is approximately Rs 14–15 billion. These are the priority corridors. The red line would cost around Rs 8–10.

Q: What kind of a future do you see for the mass transit system?

A: The city government initiated the Mass Transit Authority. When we have the authority, the draft which is with the secretary, will go to the chief minister and we will get it in the form of a bill, with all the functions clearly set out. Automatically we'd also become a part of that authority. We'd all come under a single umbrella.

Q: Is the government planning a separate plan for the mass transit system?

A: Yes, I think they are and the transport department have given an ad for the buses as well.

Q: How do you judge the status of KCR?

A: We have already worked a lot on KCR and have a recent plan with us too. Now, we had some pending issues which we have almost resolved, and hopefully we'll start working on it again. Even now the issue is of sovereign guarantees because the cost is around six billion US dollars and has now increased. The government of Pakistan is not in the position to support it and give sovereign guarantees. We have still worked a lot on it. The people will be given homes and resettled in Goth and an amount of Rs 50,000 to move. They'll be moved into already constructed homes.

Q: But this clause is not mentioned here?

A: This was actually decided by the Karachi Urban Transport Corporation which looks after the KCR.

Q: What is going to be the fare for travelling on the mass transit system?

A: For the yellow line we are planning to have an affordable fare of around Rs 30–31. Nobody would pay more than that or the subsidy would increase, which the government cannot afford, and the project may backfire again.

Q: How would you describe the impact of signal free corridors?

A: The problem is that they are not the solution to the actual problem. This is the mandate which the government received during its term, if they had taken mass transit option the amount of traffic in the city would not be there. These signal free corridors are good, but once you get out of them you get stuck in the bottlenecks, this issue still persists therefore I don't think that these are the solutions. No matter how many flyovers, you construct when you come down you again get stuck. This is not the solution. Mass transit is the only answer to this. Lahore has already come up with this. We should now too!

A-04. GHAZANFAR ALI QADRI, SECRETARY REGIONAL TRANSPORT AUTHORITY (RTA)

Today is 12 February 2014 and we are present with Ghazanfar Ali Qadri who is a factory RTA. We will talk about the role that an RTA plays in the transport business. So, on behalf of the Urban Resource Centre I welcome you. We are grateful that you took the time to speak with us and we will try our best to understand what exactly it is that you do for this city and we are also hopeful that through our efforts we are able to bring some improvement to this city.

Q: First tell us exactly what is an RTA?

A: First of all, I am also very thankful to you that you came and have shown an interest in the common man. All these functions that are related to the RTA and those of the government's public transportation, these are all for the welfare of the common man. Another thing is the initiative of new routes which have a separate portion for women…now I am telling you all this as it is all interlinked. The basic function of an RTA is to facilitate public transport and serve the public and regulate traffic according to Motor Vehicle Ordinance 1979. There are 3-4 things that need to be observed in this. One is maintenance of a standard such that if we are putting a stand/stop somewhere, we should provide public washrooms, waiting rooms and public lobbies.

Q: You are saying that provision of a stand requires there to be restaurants, toilets, seating areas and places for the public to eat and drink…is this what RTA basically looks after?

A: Yes, we provide training for this too and this is only for standing points. Then we take care of route allotments that is to say that we allot any routes—XYZ or ABC. If a route links Sohrab Goth to Kemari, RTA has to make sure that these routes don't overlap with any other routes. Or for example, if a vehicle has moved off its main route where there is no public that needs it, or to avoid the occurrence of say ten routes on one road as this creates congestion, our governor and the RTA commissioner take the initiative to streamline the routes. There are similar conditions to those in Saddar, so they want to regulate traffic by keeping incoming traffic in one direction and outgoing in another. And also there should be a public transport free zone where the public can be facilitated. The second thing about route allotment is that we need to set routes that are feasible and lawful…3-4 things come under consideration whilst deciding such things. We take the views of traffic policemen in this as well as KMC's traffic department, we take non-objection certificates (NOCs) from them and the third thing is that we take an objective view through print media. Through this we figure out the alignment and approval of routes. The third thing that comes into play is the regulation of vehicles. This is also done through route permits. Route permits involve three to four different departments. First is us, the Road Transport Authority along with the coordination of the traffic police, and third is the excise department that does the registration. Now if there is a new car on the road and a company has issued the device, he will bring his NOC and come and ask us that he wants to drive this car as a public transport vehicle. Then we give him the NOC and it is registered as a commercial vehicle. The second is that the vehicle has to go for traffic fitness for which it goes and issues a certificate according to its roadworthiness and then comes to us. Then there are inspections from time to time according to specifications, because it is not permissible if a car doesn't have rear view mirrors or the seats are missing, etc. So we also look after maintenance issues. And a new thing that has been introduced is the checking of CNG cylinders. This is very important because those innocent people who are travelling on these vehicles have their lives at stake, especially if the cylinder is not placed in a proper place. Sometimes it is kept behind or under the seat. If the windows are up and someone decides to smoke a cigarette in the vehicle it could cause a blast. So, the recent development in the transport department as well as in RTA is that whosoever violates the rules regarding the placement of CNG cylinders will be punished by taking away their route permits, and a heavy fine will be charged. This would result in impounding the car and seizing the CNG cylinder and storing it with the traffic police department. So, this is our third function, i.e. the proper inspection of vehicles. The fourth function is the collection of revenue. We have to see to it that no car should be travelling without a route permit. If the government is not receiving its taxes, we have to see to it that they are paid. Every three years we re-issue a route permit. This is our highest priority at the moment.

Q: What is the approximate amount you recover in taxes?

A: This month's recovery is Rs 4,963,000.

Q: What is your yearly target?

A: Our yearly target is Rs 500 bn. Based on this bifurcation it's Rs 41 lakhs per month. So now we have almost touched Rs 50 lakhs so our efforts are directed towards increasing government revenue...that is collection of government revenue and proper placement and reimbursement of it. The main two functions I would say are issuing vehicle NOCs and managing routes.

Q: Can you estimate how many routes are operating on a monthly basis?

A: A few days back we took out a document which revealed that there are 239 minibus routes. Out of these 111 are non-operational and 129 are operational.

Q: What about coaches?

A: There are 60 routes in total out of which 49 are operational and 11 are non-operational.

Q: You said earlier that a fee is charged for the route permit...what is the fee?

A: The fee has been Rs 700 for 3 years. But there is a condition on this that if the vehicle is late in reissuing the permit, say late by a year or so, then an additional fee of Rs 2400 is charged. So, reissuing is strictly enforced.

Q: So, if the police stop your vehicles, they will ask for a route permit?

A: Yes, and it is necessary to have a valid permit as it is a violation of traffic laws not to have one. The police charge a fine of Rs 2000 for violating this rule. The commissioner has recently set up a committee in which the Secretary RTA, Secretary PTA and concerned assistant commissioners and a member of the HDRP will all be responsible for checking the violation of CNG cylinders and route permits.

Q: Are these violations of the vehicle ordinance?

A: Yes.

Q: Actually, we have interviewed other people and women particularly were scared by the positioning of the cylinders behind the driver's seat.

A: Yes, and the thing is that they are supposed to keep it outside the car where the spare tyres are kept, not on the roof or under any seat. We have identified this proper placement of the cylinders and along with that we also have to see that the vehicle is maintaining a proper standard and following the given procedures for placements or whether they are risking the lives of the passengers.

Q: Have there been any cases where you removed the cylinders?

A: Yes, there have been 1000s; you will get a better idea from Adnan Sahib in the traffic police. They can give you the details of how many transporters are lying to them. We have also collected fines in lakhs for this violation.

Q: What are the requirements to get a route permit, say, if I am a driver?

A: First you have to fill out documents for the registration process, stating whose name the vehicle is in and a copy of their NIC is needed for that. Second part is the application and the third is as you said the Rs 700 that you have to deposit in the bank.

Q: Since you are involved in this department, what problems would you identify in the transport sector? Every day you see people travel, where they travel to, some literally hang and travel and you see how the city is full of traffic jams...what do you suggest as the solution to all this?

A: There is not just one issue. For instance, if I say traffic is an issue, it is interlinked with a lot of other issues. If there an event or if there is a rally or a strike, then traffic gets diverted from one route to the other. Consequently, heavy traffic gathers in one part of the city. If there is terrorist activity people run from that area to other areas and this includes the public transport. Now the problem is that public transport is following specific routes which get disturbed. The second problem is an increase in the number of vehicles. Day by day you can see how many banks open up to hire purchase and other schemes to buy cars on convenient loans etc. and due to this the common man, who could not previously afford to buy a car was also able to purchase one.

Q: Are you talking about an increase in public transport or private transport? Because our private transport has definitely increased.

A: Increase in both public and private. If a road where one person was previously driving is now occupied by four persons and their cars it will obviously exert pressure on the city's roads.

Q: Whenever there are big cities such as Bombay, Tehran, Bangkok, Tokyo, Delhi etc, there is always big transport such as big buses, a circular railway, and mass transit systems. These motorcycles etc are not really the solution to the problem we are facing...

A: Yes, you have stated it correctly that we should have big buses according to international standards along with proper regulations that will help us come out of the problems that the public is facing. Now day by day we see the exponential rise in diesel and petrol prices. Even those buses that we have converted to CNG are stuck because of the long lines in which they have to wait to refill their CNG tanks. Now the pressure we have is to convert the buses into carriers or trucks.

Q: A lot of them have already converted to CNG haven't they?

A: Absolutely a lot of them have converted but now based on 138 votes, the commissioner has banned such conversions. Moreover, based on these votes it was decided that the old vehicles, that is, those that are older than or are the 80 model, will be allowed to be converted. So, the problem that is occurring is that the increase in the price of fuel and difficulty in filling CNG is affecting the profit margins. Now it is all coming down to small vehicles. For example, a rickshaw costs about Rs. 2-3 lakhs.

Q: And is there no organisation that provides funds etc. to purchase vehicles?

A: There are none and no government subsidies or anything else. All these factors are discouraging transport, especially heavy vehicles. Thus, there is a shift from heavy vehicles to small vehicles.

Q: How do you view this…as in what are the solutions or possibilities?

A: For this I think that organisations should come forward, awareness programmes should be launched, and banks should provide loans or schemes to facilitate the purchase of public transport vehicles. As far as CNG goes, for at least our new green bus project, there should be a particular terminal where these buses can fill up their CNG tanks, whether CNG is running or not. So if such significant steps are taken or there is a public-private partnership or such a mechanism is made…

Q: Why did the PTA fail? The one that started the metro bus system?

A: That was the UTS (Urban Transport Scheme) and that is still running. There is not just one issue; they are all linked, for example, if there is any trouble the first thing is to burn a mini-bus not any other cars.

Q: Law and order is also a big problem that is interlinked?

A: Yes, the law and order situation is also a big issue.

Q: The city's streets are an issue, the law and order situation is an issue and subsidies are a problem.

A: Moreover, the ease of availability of CNG is also an issue. So, these are 3-4 things. Plus as I told you terrorist activities play their part, as well as strikes and protests and illegal encroachments. If we look at the encroachment problems it's like half the road is covered with encroachments and half has a bus parked on it. If drastic action is taken then this will also help clear congestion. Number 4 is that this needs to be properly regulated.

Q: It took me 5-7 minutes to reach the Abbottabad flyover from here. From there it took me 35 minutes to reach the No. 10 flyover.

A: If you go anywhere in the world, firstly, there is the law and then there is the human behaviour. Over here, maybe you and I abide by the law but if no one is watching it is a given that the car behind you will keep honking if there is less rush or no one watching at a signal. This reflects the level of civic sense of our people. This civic sense needs to be highlighted. Our society is like a social network, it is a social fabric which is made by each individual. Even if 5-6 friends are sitting somewhere their behaviour, as social scientists have said, makes a mini society.

Q: Now there are these premises called the civic centre. Inside there is one floor for the mass transit system office, one for the transport and communication office, one for the RTA, one for roadworthiness and one for excise. So, these are the five offices in the same building. So, this raises two questions, firstly, how do they coordinate among themselves? And secondly, can this be a one-window operation?

A: With regards to your first question, the answer is yes. Our commissioner holds a meeting every fortnight or every month in which the representatives from each office are present. This includes the KMC director, myself, that is Secretary of the RTA and the traffic police department along with others. We sit down and discuss the collective progress as to what goals we have achieved and what the responsibility of each department is. So the coordination is very much there. As to your second question, a one-window operation is not possible. This is because the revenue collection is a full process…until you have registered you can't get a route permit, and as long as you don't go through roadworthiness testing you can't go to the next step. Say, for example, we do set up a centre for a one-window operation; this process still has three stages. First the invite for the NOC will come to us, then it will go to excise for registration and then come back to us. Now suppose that one part of the process gets held up, say the roadworthiness people don't approve the vehicle as roadworthy. In a one window operation, the individual will have already given the full payment for the whole process…now the problem will occur as to how we can refund this part of the money he has paid. So, every process has its own method of analysis. The KMC, RTA and excise department are coordinating but to mix these processes you need a higher authority to control everything.

A-05. Tahir Ahmed Khan, Secretary Transport

Today we are in discussion with the secretary of transport, Tahir Ahmed Khan, on the 16 February 2014 at 1030 hours. The topics which we will be discussing with him are: The issues of traffic in Karachi, traffic jams, new schemes, the government's view on these and what steps are being taken currently for all these issues. We are really grateful to you and your team for taking the time to do this interview.

Respondent: We are grateful to you and URC as well since they have shown concern for the issue of transport in our city. Karachi comprises of a population of almost 2–2.5 crore, it is a metropolitan city and when we compare it to other metropolitan cities of the world, we can see that the population growth rate in Karachi is higher and the length of constructed roads is shorter than they should be as appropriate for the population. Moreover, public service vehicles are scarce for this size population. Also, rapid bus transport, which should be a part of a metropolitan city's basic transport system, is lacking in Karachi. Keeping all these things in mind, the government of Sindh and the Secretary of Transport have shown a great interest in this regard. With their collaboration, we've already launched a new rapid bus transport, based on international standards, called the yellow line. It starts from Korangi Industrial area and stretches over an area of 26km, covers Korangi road, Shahrah-e-Faisal, Shahrah-e-Quaideen and ends at Saddar. Furthermore, we have also put one more plan into action which is going to be for 100 buses, both within and outside Karachi. It is called Benazir Shaheed 100 buses and is a part of the international tender. It will link Karachi to the other divisional headquarters in Sukkur, Mirpurkhas and Larkana. Also, there is one more project to link Sharah-e-Faisal, Malir Cantt and Tower, which is currently in the pipeline. Moreover, to tackle the problem of traffic congestion and its related problems such as pollution, for that Sindh is the only province that has formulated CNG laws and debated them with the government, and they are already in the process of implementation. We have also worked on school buses, about which, nobody has given a thought before. We have planned to work on the rules/ laws of school buses based on discussions with the stakeholders and have published them as a public notice in the newspaper and this too will soon be completed. Apart from this, we are also working on the regulation of Qingqi rickshaws.

Q: Apart from what you have told us, can you please tell us about the situation of the circular railway in Karachi?

A: The circular railway is actually a project of the federal government of Pakistan through the Karachi Urban Transport Company. 60 per cent of the share is of the federal government, whereas 40 per cent is of Sindh Government of Pakistan. Sindh government's share is further divided into 25 per cent of commission government and 15 per cent of city government. The project plans to cover 43 km with a circular railway and has been initiated by a loan of 2.6 billion dollars by the Japanese government. As soon as the Japanese government gives us the green signal, the project will start. The contract has 45 different conditions set out by the Japanese government which the federal government, Sindh government and the provincial government have to fulfil. Most of the conditions have been fulfilled already. Most important was to make all the machinery and equipment for the circular railway, which is to be imported, duty free. This has already been done by the federal government, our cabinet and the Sindh government has also approved it. So now we are just waiting for the Japanese government's consent. There are no restrictions or delays from the Pakistani government.

Q: What about the fare of these circular railways? We wouldn't want that we spend so much on it and it is unaffordable for the people of Karachi.

A: The fares would definitely be affordable. They are probably going to be around Rs 35. Fares are calculated per kilometre and would not be excessive. Also, the rent of the rapid bus transport would also go from the existing structure. If the operational cost is more than the ticket cost, then the government will pay the subsidy. The same goes for the circular railway. It will work on the subsidy of the city government, Sindh and provincial government.

Q: What are the steps being taken by the city government for the traffic situation in Karachi?

A: As the traffic increases, traffic jams are inevitable. Nothing can be done about that. The best solution is that, for a 2–2.5 crore population, a mass transit system should be introduced. If a mass transit system is there, automatically the capacity of the city to incorporate more and more vehicles will increase. Also, our plans for BRT and MRT in the upcoming 5-6 years will substantially improve the traffic conditions in Karachi.

Q: When do you think people will get some relief from these issues?

A: Hopefully as soon as we launch the BRT project, it will create a huge impact on the traffic situation. It'll be completed in the next 2-3 years, including the red, green and yellow lines. The yellow line is being implemented through an international tender. For the red and green lines, we are negotiating with the Asian Development Bank. These lines will complement the circular railway system and will definitely improve the flow of traffic. The ratio of public vehicles to the population of Karachi is really low. 4.5 per cent of the vehicles are used for public services including rickshaws, buses and taxis. This 4.5 per cent caters for 47 per cent of the total population. Metropolitan cities cannot function like this. Even in India they have progressed to a better railway system. And there is not much difference between the population of Bombay and Karachi. If the population of a city is high in number and the infrastructure is weak, then plans like mass transit are necessary. By law, if the population of a city is more than or equal to 6 million, then a mass transit system has to be in place. With a population of 20 million, we still don't have a mass transit system! It will definitely end in chaos. It makes it difficult for the traffic police to control the traffic too especially during peak hours. The road width is too narrow to accommodate our traffic. There also should be parking plazas in the city.

Q: What happened to the UTS system which was introduced by the government a few years ago?

A: The commitment which was made by the government was not fulfilled. No compensation was paid. Also, this system was developed on the basis of CNG supply. The availability of CNG then became unpredictable. Secondly, pricing was an issue since the cost of CNG increased regularly. The fleets of buses were divided into groups of 25 buses each. Initially, these were run on CNG at low prices, but as the price of CNG increased, it became difficult to run them. And the rates of CNG were regulated too. The CNG prices doubled and tripled over time. Because of which it was no longer feasible to operate the system. Even private sector organisations were unwilling to take it over.

Q: What is its current status?

A: Negotiations with the Sindh government are being carried out to operate it on any route on Shahrah-e-Faisal. NGOs such as the URC are also helping us in this progress.

Q: What role can an NGO play in this regard?

A: Draft a proposal for the government of Sindh to allocate resources to such projects. We have many needs and we need resources. The population is high in number and resources are low. There is a huge resource gap. We need to fill this gap. People like you should come forward and highlight such issues.

A-06. Syed Iftikhar Hussain, District Officer, Transport and Communication Department, Karachi Municipal Corporation

As you know, pollution in Karachi has exceeded its usual limit. Keeping that in view, everybody decided to come up with a solution for this. The government of Pakistan decided to take an initiative and introduced CNG over petrol and diesel. A proposal to take care of the environment was prepared by the city government and the project director; Syed Mohammad Athar designed the project and presented it to the mayor for approval. Initially it was approved for 50 buses. This project was designed, proposed and approved in 2009 and 50 buses were funded by the city government. Out of these 50 buses, 25 were Daewoo buses and 25 were Hino and were following two routes: (1) Surjani to Tower (2) Surjani to Korangi. When this project was introduced, the mayor replicated it as it is run in other countries, for example a ticketing system was introduced, a bus operator was hired, and maintenance was the responsibility of the city government. The bus drivers were hired on contracts and recovery of finances was not the issue to end the overtaking and racing each other, usually done by bus drivers. Booths and machines were constructed to facilitate the public, men were hired for safety, a local private company was given the contract to take care of all these things, a ticket system was introduced and a proper set-up was built. This project started in June 2009 and the incumbent mayor's tenure was about to end and any losses were taken care of by the city government. As long as the mayor was there, this situation was under control but when he left, this system was discontinued. This led to problems in the maintenance of the system and in the meantime, the contracts of the operators who were hired for the period of two years ended. KMC informed us that we should complete the subsidy and renew the contracts ourselves. Based on that, we had to end all the contracts since the government was paying for it, including the salaries of the men which were hired and the payment to the companies. We then changed our plan so that the operators had to handle the ticket system and earn their fares themselves and also take care of the maintenance and CNG. The department would not compensate for anything. The contracts were also for a shorter duration but it was not viable. At that time the price of CNG was low too, but gradually it was increased. The contractors did not find the work viable anymore and left in between contracts. We then had to recover all the funds of the existing contracts and pay for the maintenance of the buses. The buses were then not being used for some while, it was decided then they will be operated through the department itself. For some time the department was running the system and it worked fine. We were able to run it without any glitches and recovered the finances too. Instead of going into loss, we were able to balance the books. But that too lasted only for 3-5 months. Then again we started the contract system so that the operators operate the system, pay for the maintenance themselves and also hand over some of the amount to KMC as well which was agreed as Rs 10 per day. During this process, continuation of the gas supply was also halted, the timings of gas supply were changed, and the prices rose too high, causing a dent in the viability of the contract and the operators were unable to pay any revenue to KMC and again the contracts were ended and the system was handed over. After this, many tenders were proposed for different operators but nobody was ready to take over this system and ever since the buses remain parked at the bus terminals. Many meetings and discussions were held between the accounts and the finance department and it was proposed to KMC that they should take over the system, but they also refused and ultimately it came under the department. But since the buses were being used and not being maintained, the tyres of a few have busted and we need money to get them repaired to make them viable again and put to use. This matter is pending with the finance department to date.

Q: Were the buses imported initially?

A: No, the buses were not imported but were taken directly from the local company and Daewoo.

Q: Who invested in this system? And how much money was invested?

A: City District Government Karachi invested in the system and one bus costs around Rs 4.4 million.

Q: What about the booths? Were they paid for by a private company?

A: Those who built them used it as advertisement for their work and recovered the amount invested from that revenue.

Q: Currently how many buses are parked at the terminals?

A: In 2010, 25 more buses were inducted and routed from Orangi to Malir. Those buses were part of the same project and currently remain parked and unused.

Q: You shared that the project catered routes from Surjani to Tower, Surjani to Korangi and Orangi to Malir, did these routes cause any problems for the project?

A: Firstly, the maintenance of the buses, Secondly, CNG. and thirdly was that when we lost the operators, buses were being overloaded and drivers were difficult to get a hold of and overtaking resumed. The buses were not being controlled and regulated properly, we lost track of time usually and mainly Daewoo were the first to go off-road. Because of that the gap in the time schedule widened and continuity of the schedule was not being met, causing problems for the passengers too. People then looked for other ways to commute. Initially, everybody used to wait for these buses and many used to prefer travelling via these buses instead of their own cars but soon policies changed and these buses degraded to the level of all other buses and the situation became worse.

Q: Are the buses parked at the terminals in this condition so that they can be re-introduced onto the roads? Or does investment need to be done prior to this process?

A: The buses have been parked at the terminals for three to four months. We did ask for money early on to get the buses, in particular the tyres, repaired. The batteries are flat as it has been a year since these buses have been used, but some of the tyres are still in good condition. But some work e.g. maintenance of clutches and brakes and tuning still needs to be done.

Q: When the company and the government ended the contract, did it affect the employment rate?

A: Employment was not an issue in this project as the operators used their own resources during their tenure and when we took over, we paid the staff daily wages.

Q: What about the booths which were constructed?

A: Those are still there on the sites and are now the property of CDGK. They aren't being taken care of but are still there and some were removed due to security issues. Some are lying around at the terminals.

Q: If we go back in time a little, UTS buses were introduced and were also discontinued. Why aren't big buses continued for a longer period of time in Karachi?

A: The commitment of transport is done by the government. They don't want big buses to run on our roads, if you give benefits, have duty-free on buses and give some sort of attraction / reward, then only someone will bring such buses. Currently one bus costs 80 lacs, now who would spend so much, also there is no security in our city, previously our two buses were torched, are now useless because of all this. One was torched at Jahangir road and the other in Orangi town. In Karachi, green buses were also very notable but the city conditions are unpredictable.

Q: Have you tried collaborating with the transport committee?

A: They also refused to take over it. There is not viability in it. Transport is a service to the public; it is the responsibility of the government to a provide service to the public. But the government doesn't consider it as a service, which is our biggest issue. Since it doesn't regard it as a service, it formulates policy accordingly. Everywhere else in the world, governments provide such facilities with subsidised rates as not everyone can afford it. This is not a profitable project. But here nobody considers it as a service.

Q: This means that currently there is no policy?

A: I can't recall any policy at the moment. There is not much emphasis on policy.

Q: What, according to you, is the solution to this entire transport problem?

A: The best solution is a circular railway. It can cater for 1,000 people at one time and will reduce pollution, the number of accidents and congestion. Everywhere in the world, circular railways, whether underground or above, are being operated successfully. In Bombay, India, millions of people travel for their jobs, they have a wonderful system. Nobody has realised how important a looping system could be in our city and there would be no reason for people not to travel on this system. It is also a cheaper way to travel.

Q: Is there anything being done on the circular railway?

A: JICA showed an interest in it and even requested a loan from the government of Sindh. We read in the newspaper that negotiations are being carried out but then there was silence and we don't know what is being done about it.

Q: What can be done to introduce bigger buses in Karachi? Can we make the routes safer?

A: There are no safe routes in Karachi. The main requirement for this is financial support. If we don't have that, you know about the high prices of diesel. If we charge rent according to the price of the diesel then nobody would travel on these buses and when it comes to subsidy, the same question arises about who would pay for it. The government is paying subsidies for health, education, sewerage system, and no one is making a profit out of it, this is part of the service. Until the government accepts transport as a part of the service, nothing can be done about it. The transport situation in Karachi is becoming worse with time instead of improving. The few big buses, despite their conditions, were on the road, but now they have ended too. There is no effective law and no implementation of it. Neither there is any continuity in our policy. When the mayor left, more could've been done on this system as we were informed that we have an approval of 200 more buses, but it has been abandoned. He had to appear in court too because even though everything was done transparently, the authorities believed that corruption had been done. Inquiries are still being carried out!

Q: Are there any other terminals, other than in Surjani?

A: We have terminals in Orangi too where the buses are currently parked. We have other terminals such as 7A (Surjani), which is also deserted.

A-07. Shams-ud-Din Abro, Director, Karachi Public Transport Society

Public transport is available all over the world, both in the government and public sector. It is running in England, Saudi Arabia and India. The problem in Pakistan is that it is running at a loss, but it is still running. Pakistan International Airlines (PIA) is also running at a loss and a subsidy is provided to the public sector. If PIA is nationalised, air fares will be so high that people won't be able to afford them. If it is privatised, the present facilities provided to the passengers will also be not available. Likewise KTC and SRTC were not partners but as soon as Pakistan came in to being, these two started running for public service. KTC's head office was in Tibet Plaza. Later on the office of the RTI was also accommodated there. Karachi city's population is increasing in leaps and bounds. Settlements like Khuda Ki Basti and New Karachi are examples. If transport is provided in the public sector, it will be as a business even if the government also provides transport to public and facilities to the poor; so the matter has stopped here.

And if the transport sector is privatised it will create more problems such as the Qingqi which is neither reliable nor durable. This is a rickshaw with the 70 CC engine of a motor bike which carries 10 to 12 persons. This is not a permanent solution—a permanent solution is the mass transit programme.

In London, the largest system of mass transit is working very well. If there is additional government provision, it will be much better. Another place is Sao Paulo in Brazil where our officers also paid a visit arranged by the World Bank. London, Brazil and Argentina are good examples of this system.

In 1999, SRTC's service stopped and in 1997 we also stopped the KTC. Prior to this Mr Bhutto suggested that KTC should not be separated; this was also a public transport system and the government would be responsible for its running. The buses which are plying in the cities are running at a loss, therefore the federal government said they would subsidise them. The cities earmarked for this purpose were Islamabad, Lahore and Karachi. These buses were to ply under the federal government and Brig. Qasim was made the head of this programme. He made 9 depots on 25 acres each. The floors were not cemented and in case of rain, it was very difficult to pull buses out of the depot—a lot of time was wasted. Therefore, cement flooring was laid. Later on Gen. Saeed Qadir supported Brig. Qasim in this connection and insisted that facilities should be provided to the public. The reason of closure of KTC is less fare, plus corruption. Moreover, the technical staff did not have the required skills. For example, when fixing a gear, the bearing broke. Many losses were borne because of these technical faults. The drivers and conductor made mistakes and these can be corrected but the ones which occurred due to technical negligence cannot be corrected. The service should have not been stopped.

Since 1997, seventeen years have passed and this property of billions of rupees is lying useless—some portions are being grabbed. An example is Korangi's depot. There are 8/9 more depots where the cemented floors are never used. In Peerabad and Orangi Towns the police chowkies have been established. No institution can work if it is not properly maintained, etc.

The management of Daewoo is ready to take over it but the fare will be beyond the capacity of the public. This is some 15/20 years before the prime minister had a vision of running trolley buses but it was not put into practice, the reason being the exorbitant fare of Rs. 50/- per passenger.

People have now switched over to motor cycles. People need transport—the well-off lease cars, others resort to motorcycles and rickshaws. Then the Qingqi arrived—and our people are very innovative—they converted a rickshaw from a two-seater to a 9-seater.

A maximum of four persons can travel in a car, whereas, in a bus 100 persons can travel. As such there have been an excessive number of cars, rickshaws and Qingqis.

In 1997, the government invited the public sector with a promise of providing depots, traffic police and other facilities to fill the gap. This was the basis of the creation of the Karachi Public Transport Society which was registered later on.

A similar system is working at Faisalabad also under the auspices of Commissioner Mr Masood Noorani who later became the interior minister also we also tried to work on the same lines but the people were afraid of law and order situations. They were hesitant to invest their money in this regard.

Then Mr Javed Chaudhary purchased 200 buses and started a service called 'metro bus'. We invited him proposing that the fare be reasonable. At that time the fare was Rs 5 whereas that of the metro bus was Rs 7/-. Mr Zia ul Islam was the secretary at that time. The proposal included the following terms and conditions:

Buses will ply on a route and at each stop, will be available every 5 minutes and passengers will sit on seat by seat arrangement. A conductor will be there—buses will not be allowed to race with other buses to access more passengers. A retired army person would serve as a checker. There will be no races with other buses. These buses started on nine routes but the bad luck started because these buses plyed on Clifton and airport routes where bad elements of society started robbing the passengers.

Then we started the metro car service with 150 cars which are running quite successfully 'KPTS' is a society where there are 27 members—18 members are from government including DIG, Traffic, City Dist. government and personal secretary etc.

Among the nine members from the public are responsible persons like Mr Arif Hasan and Brig. Qasim. Some members are from CPLC. If there are any problems regarding fares or changes of routes, they are discussed by the governing body—no single person can decide the matter arbitrarily.

If it pertains to fare, then the transporter's benefit is also considered. The public sector member tends to support the transporter because he is the prime mover and most dependable person. If other institutions are running on such a basis it is expected that there will not be any dispute. There should be a monthly meeting and an executive committee should handle all the matters.

There was a stroke of bad luck. Mr Javed Chaudhary died, he had no son—his wife was the sole inheritor. The subordinates lost the entire investment through mismanagement. His wife ultimately sold the business and the buses which were taken to different cities and provinces. Some 50/60 buses were taken out. Mr Adil Siddiquie objected to this claiming that these buses were registered with the society. He said that either the society should write to the government that either their tax etc. is not paid or there should be a case of change of route etc. This would retain the buses in Karachi and thereby facilitate the public.

At present some 150 buses are registered with the KPTS but only 100 are plied on different routes.

The number of routes has also been curtailed. In the beginning, four routes were provided to the university. Other routes were:

- 9-B Samama to Glistan Johar via Stadium (80 buses plied on this route)

- Sharah-e-Faisal to Malir another to Malir Cannt.

- 15-A Malir Cantonment to Tower

- Shuttle Malir Cantonment to Quaidabad

'OCS' was also the property of Javed Chowdhary. This service met the same fate. People bought the buses from his wife at a throw-away price of Rs 3 lac (Rs 300,000) and later on sold them for Rs 10 (Rs. 1 million) or Rs 12 lac (Rs 1.2 million).

These new owners minted money without taking care of the buses; racing and overloading were the salient features of these buses. Unless we take some strict measures the number of buses will decrease further. People are already traveling on the roofs of the buses.

Q: How many cabs are there?

A: The number is about 160. Now we anticipate that the number may also diminish. They planned for the cabs to go out to the airport and return at the same fare. They have an office near Boat Basin and have provided 400 cars thinking that they would not require any route permits and the charges are also different. In this way some 8 to 10 companies have parted their ways with us. You will be surprised to know that the rent from Karachi to Ranipur was Rs 12,000/- on CNG.

The minister has asked the traffic controller that the problem of all such cars (rent a car), school vans and vans going to Hyderabad/Larkana) should be discussed in the meeting of the governing body of the KPTS. The fares and roadworthiness should be checked. Gas cylinders should also be checked because these are generally not in good condition and burst tyres cause damage to cars and passengers.

The governing body has passed the bill but it has not yet been implemented by the government. We have also in mind to present the issue of the fare of Daewoo owners. If the fare is for Rs. 50/- it will be decided in the governing body as Brig. Qasim had been watching these matters for almost eight years. He is still an expert in these matters. He will consider all the pros and cons.

If the fare is increased people will talk of money grabbing and if the fare is decreased then the transporters will make a hue and cry.

Therefore, each and every aspect is looked at very carefully. It will be appropriate that the matter be discussed in the governing body and whatever plan is made and decided will be acceptable to the transporters.

We receive some money as a 'security deposit'. If they stop running their cars without any valid reason, we will forfeit the deposit.

We have now become quite helpless because no new cars or buses have been registered with us and there are no new cars are coming into the city. The number of mini buses was 20,000, which has gone down to only 5,000.

Qingqi and other means of transport are not a solution to this problem. Qingqi's fare from Surjani to Tower is Rs. 50/-. For short distances, Qingqi is fine, but for the people who cover long distances, this type of transport is not feasible. If big buses are available the passengers will be able to cover long distances at a low fare. If we do not provide a service to the people, the problem will be highlighted by the media which is very active these days. We have the solution for all these problems. We have people like Brig. Qasim and Mr Irshad Bukhari who will never damage the interest of the transporters.

The former Secretary of RT, Mr Shamim, was a true gentleman. He would never listen to any ill-wishing suggestions. There should be a group of four to five capable and expert persons. Two or three people cannot handle this matter. Whatever decision is to be taken, it should be through a committee, not by individuals. This would be a sort of 'inspection team' which would take care of various matters like the uniform of the driver and conductor (no decorations) and the seats which should be comfortable. The doors should be automatic so that the passengers may board or alight the bus easily.

Now a bus is bought by two or three persons together and each tries to impose his likes or style which creates problems. We had started a school called 'Karachi School of Driving'. Later on I completed a course entitled 'Mass transit in London'. It did not only cover driving but other things such as the driver, conductor and distance manager.

The duration of the courses was different. Some courses were for one month, some for three months and others for a week. I gathered some useful material. The World Bank has provided material such as cassettes etc. But here, sheer bad luck, the 'Karachi School of Driving' is closed. I tried my best to revive it but vested interest came in my way.

Corruption is our worst enemy. It may be KTC, SRTC and KPTS or any such institution, which will be destroyed by this uncontrollable enemy.

Q: In 1997, one institution was working, buses were also available so why was it closed? How many buses were there in KTC?

A: When we came there were 700/800 buses in KTC. There were 51 routes and only 50/60 buses were plying. KTC was closed in March 1997. In 1995 SRTC was closed. The solution is that the government should reopen it. Experts should be hired to manage it. Depots should be taken back. The high court has given the verdict that the depots cannot be sold. These depots were meant for the buses—any other kind of factory or residence would not be erected on them. It is a crime according to the verdict since our future generations will require more buses and means of transport—when there is no land / place for the vehicles, what would they do?

Q: Were the buses of SRTC only for Karachi or were they plied outside of Karachi also?

A: There was an institution with the name of the 'West Pakistan Transport Corporation'. When one unit was done away with, SRTC was there. In 1977, SRTC was for the interior of Sindh and its buses used to come to Karachi from other cities. Then KTC was formed so that the buses could go out of Karachi. It was assumed that the federal government would develop it and it would flourish—just as Brig. Qasim had done in the past. As soon as he took over the charge he stated that it was a challenge.

He instantly prepared nine depots, a central workshop, training schools and stores where all necessary material was available. He used to visit these places every month. Depots were under scrutiny as if these were under the control of the army then an officer (having affinity with MQM; later on he was assassinated) came and took control of the situation. During his tenure the income of the KTC increased so much that there was no need for the subsidy from the government, I am not a spokesman of any political party yet it is true that an institution flourishes only when it is kept under control. If some commendable work is done by a person, he should be given the credit for his good work. Mr Azar Siddiqui also did a good job and Mr Manzoor Wasan, who was minister for transport at that time, also did a fair job. The minister for transport who came after Mr Wasan did not take any interest and the KTC was on the brink of destruction. Depots were changed from one place to the other and the material which was given by the World Bank was a feast for the thieves.

Benazir Bhutto's tenure also met the same fate. 30 crore were taken and the amount was not traceable. The officer was shifted from one place to the other so that no documentary evidence was left. To keep the matter untraceable the RTI was also destroyed. The real work demands that government should start it by itself. Legally, SRTC is not closed. It could be restarted which would procure employment and students would also benefit.

Q: What steps did you take to improve the situation?

A: I sent the proposal to the secretary of transport and a copy to the chief minister. I belong to Larkana and I have been serving here since 1972. During this time a person with the name of Akhtar Jadoon, who was transport minister was in place for a short period but he sold almost every thing and went back. Later on he became director. It is highly surprising how he reached the top slot from grade 18. The furniture of the office in a very bad condition and when he left the office he took the car with him worth Rs 15 lac. He did all these things because he had strong connection with the government of that time.

Q: What is your opinion of the UTS service which was started in the days of Mr Naimatullah?

A: During the time of Mr Naimatullah, UTS was started as the green bus. It plied from Safoorah to Keamari and Tower to Clifton. The buses could run on both CNG and diesel, but CNG was not started so it was run on diesel only. It plied for only 5/6 months. The green bus is still there but it is different. One or two green buses are still parked, out of order, as a token of that time. The 4 K Bus stop also had a KTS terminal. There was a dispute between the two parties. Then UTS was started with a subsidy from the government and also a loan from the banks. They spent a lot of money and had to suspend the service because they were unable to pay back the loan.

Q: How many buses did they have?

A: There were 200 buses plying on 13 routes. About 8/10 buses are still plying. It is a separate matter. They have taken a depot at Landhi but have not paid its rent. Nothing is left. There has been a deal between the city government and the UTS that whatever losses occur will be borne by the city government. Now the losses are increasing and the government has refused to make up the difference as they have no reason to do so. Then the city government bought 75 buses but these plied only for 6 months. They received half of the CNG from the city government and half from Daewoo. They had technical expertise. 80 buses are parked up out of order, some have no engine, some have no brakes, some have no radiators. Now they have received Rs. 34 crore for repair. If they fit genuine parts, these buses will be okay but if not, the same fate will be met.

Q: What you have to say about mass transit?

A: The answer is with the secretary of transport. It has not yet come into being. They have pointed out the blue and green lines which will have a BRT system, as in Lahore. Its fare will be different and people are ready to go to the court because of illegal encroachment. There must be some system to remove the encroachment and provide neat and clean space for the buses. Some measures have been taken. The road from Dawood Chowrangi to Mill area is quite broad. There is no such road anywhere in Karachi. One can reach Qayyumabad easily and from there to Regal Cinema. From there one can go up to the Tower. The second route is that of North Nazimabad. It is in very good condition up to the Board Office but its condition is bad near Lasbela. The area of Golimar, where there is a big market of household goods, is a question mark. It is not sure whether the public allows these people to work there or not. If some arrangement, like that of underground subway, is agreed, one is not sure whether the public will get a staying order or not. The solution to these problems is the plying of the big buses which may be brought by the SRTC. SRTC should be revived with a team of persons having technical knowledge. There should be a board of governors which should keep a watch over it. A monthly check and biannual audit should be provided through the members of the board of governors because subsidies given to the public sector are being used for personal interest. The green buses, which are plying from Gulshan-e-Hadeed to Tower were run by the government. But recently these have been handed over to the private sector. A lot of money has been given by the city government for this purpose. Now the private sector will extract the last drop of blood from these buses. Whatever parts are in good condition, they will remove them and the undrivable buses will be sold like garbage. I am speaking of this with great confidence. The fare should be so that cost of running and maintenance is covered. People are prepared to make money from the buses which are plying between Hyderabad and other cities like Larkana, Dadu, Jacobabad, Sukkur and Kashmore etc. There is no route permit for these buses. Regular bus stops have been made for these buses. Buses do not come from Punjab because of the long distance. Several 10/15 seated buses are available near Capri Cinema. Instead of these vans, big buses should be provided. The entire system should be monitored. The owners charge the fare at the cost of diesel but run the buses on CNG. They know that nobody is going to check. There should be a body that represents the private sector whenever we have a meeting. The private sector member complains with the DIG that injustice is being done to them. Likewise the secretary of the RTI is also misinformed and the matter runs between allegation and counter-allegation. This body will be a controlling authority and if it continues checking, corruption will decrease. If a transporter makes a wrong statement, he is stopped and told that he is flouting the system, then his route permit may be cancelled. When 2-B and 4-B were plying, the public sector, members used to come occasionally—they were not permanent members. Mr Irshad Bukhari and Captain Moeed (representative of the chamber of commerce) checked matters on the spot and the governing body brought such people to task. The report was presented before the governing body and permits were cancelled. People knew that in case of any malpractice, their route permit would be cancelled. Fearing this, they did desist, to some extent, from openly corrupt practices. I will tell you some facts about KPTS backed up with evidence, which if published, will reach the public and should make a difference. I recognised one very senior officer, Mr Musarrat Hussain. He asked me how I recognised him and I told him that he had visited our school once. He told us that in 1970 a letter from here was written to Mr Bhutto saying that SRTC should be stopped. At this Mr Bhutto became angry saying that he is trying to provide a service to the masses and also increasing employment, and yet he is being asked to shelve this scheme. He said it was his job to provide buses and that he would increase the number of depots. Then he sent for Bedford buses from National Motors. There was one bus BNF which used to ply from Korangi. He ordered that there should be a depot in every district and at least 50 buses in each district. Mr Bashir Ahmed, who was IG, at that time, was made the chairman as directed to improve the entire situation. Mr Bhutto opined that the lower classes and labourers would travel in these buses, the fare of which was 50 paisas but the buses should be big enough to carry 100 persons or more. Nowhere in the world have big buses been shelved. These should be plied on a one way system because this system is the world's number one system. He further instructed that shops of spare parts should be opened around the depot and hotels should also be there so that traveller may not face any difficulty and the drivers may easily buy the spare parts. So this is the whole situation.

B. INTERVIEWS WITH TRANSPORTERS

B-01. Syed Irshad Bukhari, President, Karachi Transport Union

Today we are in discussion with Mr Irshad Bukhari, who is the president of the Karachi Transport Alliance/Union. This organisation is working for the issues of the transporters who are currently working in the transport sector of Karachi. For several years Mr Irshad Bukhari has been associated with this sector. In today's interview we have Zahid Farooq, Rizwan-ul-Haq and Mansoor Raza with us. The Urban Resource Centre (URC) Karachi and Arif Hasan are researching the problems of the transport sector in Karachi. We have been trying to find a solution to this problem for a long time now, but the situation doesn't seem to be getting better. Both the buses and the travellers' needs are not being met, nor are the problems of the transporters being resolved. Today we are going to talk about the issues of the transporters.

Irshad Bukhari: Zahid Farooq, I am grateful to the URC who have been working with us over the past 20-25 years. Mr Arif Hasan has given us ample support and it is because of his patronage that our organisation is undeterred, along with the support of the chief secretary and the secretary of transport of the government.

Q: How long have you been associated with the transport sector?

A: Almost 15 years. Since 1962—the years just passed by—I have been a member of the alliance/union for the past 40 years. Then in 1978, I became the vice secretary of transport, in 1981 I was appointed as the general secretary of transport, then in 1988 we formed the Case Alliance Transport Action Committee and I was the chairman of that committee and after a year Karachi Transport Alliance/Union came into being where I am currently working.

Q: You have been working in the sector for some time now, what are the major issues that the transporters have to face?

A: There are many problems! 50 years ago there were very few buses—only 30-40. Vehicles which had urban use were utilised more and in the event of strikes they used to torch our vehicles even more than now. Vehicles costing 20-50 lacs were destroyed with a mere matchstick. The government has not provided provide us with anything—except in Benazir Bhutto's regime; in return for a burnt 20 lac vehicle, we received only 2 lacs. We are offered no compensation from the government. A new vehicle costs 20 lacs. Secondly, we are not able to get insurance for them. Thirdly, the fares are less in other areas such as in the areas of Punjab where it is Rs 28 per 20 km; here we charge Rs 14 per 20 km. Moreover, people now travel in their personal cars because there is no other viable transportation. The problem is that our tyres are expensive. So is the engine. Also, the diesel costs a lot and our good drivers have left. We have a lot of problems.

Q: Do the roads need to be fixed as well?

A: Yes! The roads need to be fixed as well; they are in a really bad condition and travelling becomes difficult; the tyres get damaged which causes more problems. Moreover, people tend not to like transporters.

Q: If you want to buy buses, how will you buy them? Do you pay for them out of your own pocket?

A: It is difficult to buy a vehicle costing 50-80 lacs but we give advance payments and buy our vehicles. We don't buy inter-Karachi buses, it is almost impossible to even think about it. First, the diesel prices went up so we increased the rent of the buses run on diesel; we then converted our buses to CNG, then CNG prices went up. If we don't solve all these problems, we can't run the transport system in Karachi.

Q: In your opinion how much rent should we charge, keeping the current scenario in mind?

A: Naimatullah Khan introduced UTS buses in his time; they charged less rent and they failed. Then Mustafa Kamal introduced 50 green buses, then 25 more vehicles and now 75 vehicles are parked idly. They have requested us to take those vehicles but the rent of those vehicles is Rs 10 to 15 less than what we charge. If we are investing 2 lacs in a vehicle, we have to pay that amount in instalments. If we are buying a Mazda for 10 lacs, then we need to pay 20 lacs in a year.

Q: What was the transport policy during different governments?

A: Those who come to power have no interest in the transport policy. If you look at the policies of the Punjab government, they provide their transporters with every kind of subsidy. But the chief minister in power has no interest in this. So now we have Qingqi rickshaws.

Q: What objection do you have to the Qingqi rickshaws?

A: They are ruining our business!

Q: Who funds or gives loans to buy new vehicles?

A: Banks and transport companies do not provide us with loans. We told these companies that if they provide credit for the purchasing, we'll be able to introduce more and more buses onto the roads of Karachi.

Q: Do you have any suggestions of how to improve this?

A: The government body should provide us with loans and the transporters' community should be given loans so that the transport sector can prosper in the city.

Q: What do you think is the reason behind traffic jams in the city?

A: There are two to three reasons why a traffic jam occurs. People have now starting buying cars on lease and motorcycles on instalments, so the number of cars has increased leading to traffic jams. Qingqi rickshaws also add to the jams.

Q: Have flyovers and underpasses affected our city and how?

A: Yes! These underpasses and flyovers were constructed by Mustafa Kamal, the former mayor of Karachi. We welcome such advancements. All the development work that happens in Karachi is valued as it improves the state of transport in the city. Thanks to the flyovers, the distance which used to take an hour to cover, now only takes 30 minutes.

Q: What is your take on the signal free corridor development?

A: They have proved to be very beneficial—from Metroville to the last stop you will not have to face any delays or hold-ups.

Q: What is the role of the city traffic police?

A: When we give the traffic police money, they take it and those vehicles on the street whose engine isn't working or the body needs work are overlooked by them. If vehicles are stopped by the traffic police, the drivers give them Rs 50 to 100 to avoid any penalties.

Q: What is the monthly deal with the traffic police?

A: One vehicle costs Rs 1,500-2,000 monthly in bribes to the police. You must have heard the story about the motorway. The police stopped the minister's car and charged a challan from him too. Traffic police earn between Rs 15,000-20,000 monthly, In Punjab, the motorway police earn up to Rs 40,000-50,000. Here the traffic police have inadequate accommodation—officials' quarters consist of two rooms only which makes living conditions difficult.

Q: When the city conditions get worse, why are public transport vehicles targeted whereas banks or houses are not torched?

A: Keeping God as my witness, I do not belong to any specific group, but there is ethnic conflict. Most of the drivers are Pathans/Pashtuns. Two years ago, 40 of our Pathan/Pashtun drivers were killed.

Q: Which areas do you refrain from sending your drivers to when there is violence in the city?

A: Liaquatabad, Lyari and all those other areas which are highly sensitive. You must know by now that Muhajirs and Pathans/Pashtuns are confined to the areas where there is a Muhajir majority and Pathans/ Pashtuns majority, respectively. It now means that if the vehicle belongs to a Pathan/Pashtun, he can't go in the Muhajir's area. City conditions are such that people are dragged out of the cars and killed. It is our bad luck and what could be worse than this. When I came to Karachi city there were no Muhajirs or Pathans/Pashtuns and all were brothers. [As if the politics of ethnicity were not there. All the ethnicities lived like brothers].

Q: Are you satisfied with the road transport?

A: How do we focus on the road transport? We already have too few buses. We had 100 operational vehicles before and now we only have 20.

Q: What do you want to change? What change do you wish to see?

A: Most of our vehicles head towards Saddar. Many shopping malls have emerged now and the population has also increased. If we resettle then we can bring about a substantial change.

Q: Are you satisfied with the facilities at the bus terminals?

A: Bus terminals should be located at multiple sites. They are only present at two sites so far and can't be used as yet.

Q: Why do these drivers not care about the law?

A: Because Irshad Bukhari, who is the owner of the transport, has their back. We take care of their fines, bail them out of prisons, and arrange for lawyers in the court for them. What else can we do other than take their guarantees, as it is our responsibility to take care of them.

Q: Why has the ticket system been dissolved?

A: The ticket system should be there but it was dissolved because no profits were made. The transport sector was in a crisis, we were not able to save much money, and now we save the money which was previously used to buy tickets to sell.

Q: Currently, how many buses do the transporters have?

A: We have 1,500 buses. 1,150 are minibuses and we have coaches, out of which 6,000 are coaches and 5,500 are minibuses.

ADDITIONAL INTERVIEW WITH IRSHAD HUSSAIN BUKHARI ON 12 MARCH 2014

Q: What is the structure of the Karachi Transport Association?

A: The structure of Karachi Transport Association is: president, senior vice president, four vice presidents, general secretary, deputy general secretary, joint secretary, publicity secretary and treasurer.

Q: What are the problems and difficulties being faced by Karachi Transport Association?

A: They are numerous problems and it would not be wrong to say that these problems have limited the activities of the organisation. Firstly, nobody is ready to have a discussion with us at the government level. Everybody notices the problems with the transport system but no one is ready to solve them. We are not involved in any planning and our opinions are not taken into account. We have put forward so many requests to the former Transport Minister Akhter Jadoon, asking him to hold a meeting but he never did. He didn't take any steps to improve the transport system in his tenure, in fact he was known for corruption. I must say that operating buses in Karachi is a skill. Ayub Khan had introduced KUTC buses in his tenure which operated for some time and were then shut down. Then KTC buses came, then UTC and then CNG buses but nobody could manage them. They have still been operating somehow over the past 35 years. The experienced transporters are not calling for any help or contributions [no request for subsidies, they just want the fares raised so that they can function with a reasonable profit which is not available today]. Our biggest problem is the fare. No increments have been made in bus fares over the past three years, whereas inflation is rising. Diesel, spare parts and maintenance prices are constantly increasing but bus fares are not increasing.

Q: Who is in charge of increasing the fares? How does this increment take place?

A: To increase the fare a request has to be given to the secretary of transport. This request is then forwarded to the chief secretary then it goes to the secretary of RTA, then we receive a notification. There are many issues which we are facing regarding our bus and coach fares, whereas Qingqi and rickshaw owners increase fares as they wish. These days, rickshaws and Qingqis take Rs 40-50 for a ride from Surjani town to Tower whereas our fare is still Rs 20 which is not enough. The fare should be Rs 25 or 30. If we only even think about increasing the fare, chaos breaks out in the city, but nobody looks at our problems and how we are taking care of the expenses. We receive less fare, our buses our torched, and we are labelled as mafia, it is a weird system.

Q: In your opinion, what kind of a role could the Karachi Transport Association play in the mass transit system?

A: When Zaheer-ul-Islam was part of the mass transit project, he would involve us as well but after he left, nobody bothered to call us or involve us. We really want a mega city like Karachi to have a mass transit system just like other foreign cities and we are ready to play our role as well if they consider us important enough. We want a better transport system too. We want to give the people of the city who, despite paying the fare have to travel on the roofs, better travelling facilities, but we cannot do this on our own and require the government's cooperation.

Q: What kind of cooperation do you require from the government?

A: The government should provide us with loans so that we can buy new buses. Individual loans are hard to get. We would tell the government to give the loan to the Karachi Transport Association and we would further distribute it and will take the payments from the transporters and give back to the government. The government only has to show trust in us and we guarantee that the loan payment would be given back with a proper mark-up. One restriction should be put on this system—that no one should take their buses out of the city or sell them to someone outside the city. In the past, many people have done this, resulting in a scarcity of buses within the city. If government talks to us, we will ensure that we would give back the money, faithfully.

Q: There was a time when we could see numerous buses in the city, where have these buses gone now?

A: Because of the constant city crisis, many people have moved their vehicles out of the city. Some now operate them on inter-city routes, while some have sold them. According to Mahmood Afridi, many people have sold their buses in Dubai and have started their own business now. They are selling our capital in Dubai and running a business there. Five trailers, owned by Mahmood, operate from Dubai to Saudi Arabia. Many people have wrapped up their business here and have moved to South Africa, Dubai and Saudi Arabia for business purposes. It is highly disappointing that people, who should be running a business here, are running it outside the country and investing our capital in other countries. But they've been forced to do so because of our city conditions. Prosperity is not possible without peace. We are constantly in the state of decline. Previously, in this same city, Ford buses used to run, then Mazda buses were introduced and now it has come to rickshaws and Qingqis. We don't know what kind of a transport system would be introduced in the future.

Q: Have you contacted any Insurance companies?

A: We did discuss with an insurance company in 1993 that the buses should be insured, but the company deceived us. After that, nobody showed an interest in insuring public transport vehicles. Our vehicles our not insured and nobody is ready to insure them either. There exists a third-party insurance which is only there in name and is just a way of making money.

B-02. Shabir H. Sulemanjee, Chairman CNG Association

I welcome you, Sir Shabir Suleman, Chairman of the CNG Association, on behalf of the Urban Resource Centre. Today we are going to talk about the issue of CNG in Sindh, especially in Karachi, about the problems that the CNG Association has, and how and who can help us in resolving these problems. CNG is playing a very vital role in all the activities and businesses currently working in this city. Thank you for your time.

Q: How many CNG stations are there in Sindh? How many CNG stations and vehicles are there in Karachi and how many problems are there?

A: Thank you very much for giving me this opportunity to talk about CNG. There are a total of 3,300 CNG stations in the whole of Pakistan. Sindh has 600 CNG stations. When this plan was initiated in the 1990 by the government of Pakistan, there were two reasons behind it; Foreign exchange—one of our top imports is oil and CNG helps to reduce the energy bill (since CNG is locally available) and pollution. In addition, we create jobs. Pakistan is currently at the lead of all the countries that use CNG, ahead of Italy.

Q: Any specific reason for it?

A: The government has come up with such policies that for our gas resources, which are 25–30 years old, we build CNG stations. They give you a license and most importantly, the import bill has been reduced. The government has introduced a state policy based on this. You have seen here that every government has introduced their own policies. When the CNG stations were built, the number of vehicles which were converted to CNG were approximately 40-45 lacs. Private cars, rickshaws, taxis, Mazda buses in Pakistan have been converted to CNG, particularly in 2005, when the order issued by the supreme court was that vehicles running on diesel were to convert to CNG so that environmental pollution could be reduced. In this regard, the transport sector working in Sindh, Punjab and the whole of Pakistan, spent billions of rupees to get CNG kits in the buses. One CNG kit costs around Rs 1-2 lac.

Q: Where did the shortage start from?

A: Domestic users, fertilizers, cement, power generation, industrial power, and power captive are seven different sectors that consume CNG. The total amount of CNG used by these sectors is 4,000 mmcfpd (millimetre cubic feeds per day) which is our current shortage. The demand is about 5,500—6,000 mmcfpd, today the shortage in this is 1,500 in Punjab, whereas the shortage of CNG in Sindh is 100-200. From the total production or extraction of gas, 72 per cent comes from Sindh, out of which, 27 per cent is produced. 17 per cent of the gas comes from Balochistan and 11 per cent comes from Khyber Pakhtunkhwa and we supply gas to Punjab. Balochistan produces 10-15 per cent of the gas. In Punjab, 6 per cent of the gas is produced. Since it's a huge province, the consumption of gas is more and the demand for gas in winter increases in the domestic sector. The geyser is used more in winter along with other things. In winter, the demand for gas increases by up to 300 per cent. This causes a shortage or crisis. Now how does the shortage occur? The raw material for CNG is gas only and we don't have any other raw material for it. The total amount which we use in Sindh accounts for 2 per cent of the production; Pakistan uses up to 60 per cent of CNG. But the media is misguiding the public that the entire CNG is being used by the CNG transport sector only. This is completely untrue. The real facts reveal the opposite to this. Sindh uses 2 per cent of the gas while the whole of Pakistan uses 7 per cent in the CNG sector. The loss occurred when back in 2008-2009 and 2010 the oil prices rose resulting in an increase in the price of petrol and diesel. Now gas is used by domestic users for cooking, but the people who live in big areas such as Clifton and Defence run their generators on diesel when the electricity goes out. They have now converted the generator kits, which used to run on diesel, to gas. Now if you go to the market, you'll find generators ranging from 5KB to 20KB. 4,000 mmcfpd of gas is being produced in Pakistan. Many generators which run on gas have been imported and the government should put a ban on them. They are solely being used by domestic users. The shortage which we are facing today is because people want gas to cook food; if they can't tolerate load-shedding then they should produce their own electricity and if they want to use the generator use the one which runs on diesel. Due to the low price of gas in the domestic sector, the income is almost nil. It should not be misused. The shortage is such that the percentage increases and diesel is pricier than petrol. Diesel has become expensive and now costs Rs 117 per litre. Load-shedding used to occur in industries, now if you look at the SITE area of Korangi, you will find gas generators everywhere. When the electricity goes out, they use these generators despite having generators which run on diesel too! It is because the gas costs less; diesel is Rs 40 per unit and electricity costs Rs 17 per unit, gas costs Rs 6 to 7 per unit that's why its use has rapidly increased. The second reason is captive power. It is very dangerous. The thing is that whoever now has an electrical connection, also has a generator which runs on diesel. When the electricity goes out, in Site area and Korangi KESC only does load-shedding for an hour, despite the fact that they run their factories on gas.

It is not benefitting anyone apart from those who are earning a profit out of it, and this is causing a crisis. The common man is not getting any gas, people are unable to cook food in their homes. Thirdly, the CNG which we buy costs Rs 650 per unit of gas, whereas, other sectors pay Rs 200 or Rs 400 per unit. Most tariffs are for CNG prices, and despite that CNG load-shedding occurs. First justify the tariff and the gas being provided to others should be at the same price as the CNG so that it can be used in a permissible way. In the industrial areas gas is being used instead of electricity because it costs less. When they get gas and electricity at the same prices per unit, then they will use according to their consumption. Fourthly, there is the unaccounted for gas (UFG), the gas which is being stolen, so it does not go through the gas meter. There is an international standard followed all over the world that UFG gas should not exceed 4-6 per cent. This is also mentioned in the bylaws of OGRA (Oil and Gas Regulatory Authority). Unfortunately, it has increased over the time from 4 to 4.5 per cent, then 12 per cent, and has now gone up to 13 per cent.

We prepared a report on CNG and there was a report which was prepared by the MD of Sui Gas who stated that the billing is 99 per cent, whereas, when you step out of Karachi towards Larkana or Hyderabad, the UFG there is 10-12 per cent. 10-12 per cent would mean what? 4,000 mmcfpd gas is being produced in the country. The crisis in Sindh is 10 per cent, which means 400 mmcfpd, and a crisis of 100 mmcfpd exists in Karachi. All the things which I have shared with you, if we control them, then the crisis in Sindh can be resolved. This is only because of an agenda which, due to gas in the CNG sector, affects the transport sector, whereas all the other seven sectors receive gas, when they have an alternative energy system in place, yet CNG pump owners don't even have an alternative energy system. Instead, they are shutting us down and ruining the transport system because there is no option to use diesel in transport. Once vehicles have been converted to CNG, they cannot be reverted back to diesel or petrol. When the CNG stations are closed, vehicles are not taken out on the roads and remain parked on the bus stands. The public becomes worried and the transportation system of the entire city is affected. You know that how important a transportation system is in the city. Since diesel costs Rs 117, petrol costs Rs 107 and CNG costs less, everybody wants to take advantage. If you count everyone who either travels by bus or by car, that means that around 3-4 crore people are associated with CNG. If you shut down CNG then everybody is affected by it. It also disrupts the ambulance service of the hospitals along with the vehicles which drop the students off at schools. It disrupts the entire city system. The use of CNG in the whole of Pakistan equates to 2.3 billion litres of petrol! If you think about it, if CNG shuts down permanently what will happen? In order to import 2 billion litres, we need at least 5 million or a billion dollars! If Pakistan spends 5 million dollars on importing petrol then the deficit will increase as import will be more and export less, and the demand for the dollar will also increase. Unemployment will also rise, and the economy will be weakened. The law and order situation will worsen, and poverty will further increase. I have just shared with you about the foreign exchange. We pay almost 32 billion of taxes and our government literally begs the economic experts/super powers for loans. Every child who is born in Pakistan has a debt of 500-600 dollars on him. If this country defaults, then every person will have to pay 600 dollars so instead of shutting this sector down, we should find solutions.

There should be long-term planning. We should have fundamental rights in Sindh. According to Article 158 whichever province produces gas they are entitled to it first. So, if Sindh produces 72 per cent of the gas and uses only 2 per cent, then why does load-shedding occur in Sindh? First fulfil the gas needs of Sindh then move to other provinces, this is the only solution to this problem. First provide gas here! Khyber Pakhtunkhwa is able to extract 10 per cent gas, which is 300-400 mmcfpd of gas. None of the industries have to face load-shedding problems there, but CNG stations do. Domestic users receive gas throughout the week, and whatever gas Khyber Pakhtunkhwa produces, it gives it to its own province first.

Even in Balochistan, whatever gas they produce their first supply is within their province and the amount which is left they then supply to the other provinces. Our province Sindh, which is like a gas basket, produces 72 per cent gas, and if we are still facing a shortfall then, according to the Law, 100-200 of the gas should be made as a part of SSGC Network and the remaining should be supplied to Punjab, this is the first solution to it. Another solution is that the gas which is supplied to the industries is cheaper. It should be costly, so that the CNG prices should be levelled with the other sectors and gas is used in its true means. Even in the decision made by the Supreme Court on 17 December 2013, given by former Chief Justice Chaudhry Iftikhar Ali, on page 36, it states that power captive should receive gas at the prices of electricity. Gas should be given to those industries which use boilers, or which need gas for their processes. But just because you wish to make one factory, a rickshaw maker or a transport company who wants to increase their number of buses, stronger, you shouldn't weaken the rest of the nation. It is not a solution to keep increasing the prices and not controlling theft. Thirdly, if we want to reduce load-shedding then everyone should work together and not penalise the CNG sector. Captive, CNG, and industry, if all these three sectors decide on one day to close CNG, then it is my guarantee that the domestic users would not have to face any difficulties. CNG is shut down for 3-4 days here resulting in increased traffic on the roads. We don't get to meet the minister or the prime minister because we are limited to the roads only. The people in the other sectors are crocodiles, they sit with the ministers, so they listen to them immediately. We'll be old by the time they'll listen to us. This system is not good, but we are trying to call a strike in the transport sector. We are trying our best that we make ourselves heard in front of the leaders with the help of the judiciary so that we can get justice.

Q: How is a CNG station set up, what is its cost and how many people does it give employment to?

A: To set up a CNG station, it costs a capital of Rs 7-8 crore which includes the land, compressor unit, dispenser, green tower and other material and an effort of 1.5 years goes into setting it up. It also includes NOC and a fee which we pay to the government. This is our investment and the other investment comes from the public. The public is exploited too. Converting small vehicles to CNG costs around Rs 30-40 thousand and for buses it costs around 2 lacs. Likewise, the public has invested billions and trillions of money. Vehicles belonging to the people have been converted to CNG. As far as the owners are concerned, their investment for this conversion is Rs 185 billion. If we combine both of the investments, it is a huge amount! Where employment is concerned, the CNG sector employs over 4 lac people. If the CNG stations are shut down, then many families will have no food to survive on. By using CNG a person can save up to Rs 10,000-15,000 monthly. But if there is no CNG then it increases the expense to Rs 10,000-15,000 for a person. In an ordinary man's income, if we add an extra expense of Rs 10,000-12,000, just imagine how high the poverty rate will be then!

Q: How do you see transport and CNG working together?

A: Just as I shared earlier, CNG and transport are like the wheels on the same vehicle. Before vehicles were converted to CNG, the vehicles run on diesel or petrol, and because of the immense amount of smoke people used to return to their homes with tanned skins. Since the transport sector has shifted to CNG, environmental pollution has also reduced. Now people have to queue for 4-5 hours on the roads to get CNG filled in their vehicles and when their turn comes, the pressure of the gas has already reduced, which is a sheer injustice. If there is no transport sector, there won't be any CNG sector either. The rent has not been increased due to the CNG sector. The rents were increased in 2011 whereas, diesel prices have gone up. If the vehicle was being run on diesel then imagine how high the rent would have been, it would have been difficult for anyone to travel.

Q: How many CNG stations do you own in Karachi?

A: I own four CNG stations in Karachi.

Q: What steps has the government taken for the CNG sector?

A: The steps taken by the government were truly unfair, especially those of the former government. This government is still somewhat positive. The federal minister of petroleum, Shahid Khaqan Abbasi says that the investment made by the public should not be eliminated. The lobby mafia which exists has such an outreach and such strong roots which is why we are not being heard and only the CNG sector is being affected by it. After distributing the gas everywhere, the CNG sector only gets what is left of it.

Q: What is the difference between LPG and CNG?

A: CNG is a natural gas. LPG is a mixture of carbon and gas. LPG, just like petrol, is in liquid form. LPG is not our produce, whereas CNG is. LPG is very expensive and its supply decreases in winter because those who can't find gas in their area use LPG. LPG is also used in industrial areas. LPG costs Rs 170-180 and is more expensive than petrol, so who will buy it? CNG is cheaper so people buy CNG.

B-03. MEHMOOD AFRIDI (PRESIDENT) AND TAWAB KHAN (VICE PRESIDENT), MUSLIM MINI BUS COACH OWNER ASSOCIATION

We are gathering information regarding the transport situation in Karachi. This is for research purposes and will be published in an international magazine. We've seen Bombay and Delhi; they are mega-cities too. There is no country/city in the world which solely runs on Qingqis and rickshaws. How will people travel if you don't provide them with proper transport? We want transport to be considered an industry and issues should be looked into. People pinpoint the transport issues but we wish to see what problems the transporters are facing. So we are going to discuss that today. URC is grateful to you for your time today. URC is doing a research on the transport system of the city. We will ask you some questions pertaining to that research. We also want to discuss the problems which you are facing.

Q: How many coaches and Mazdas are currently running in the city?

A: Approximately 14,000. The number has reduced from 22,000 and is still reducing. They are transformed into mini trucks and coaches and are then moved out of Karachi to Hyderabad and other cities.

Q: Are they utilised as Mazdas and mini-buses or are converted into mini trucks?

A: Both. The biggest benefit is that the fare over there is pretty good. The biggest problem that we face in Karachi regarding transport is the torching of all these buses. I refused to believe that there is any city in the world facing this problem to such a great extent as we are. The existing transporters should protest against this.

Q: Does the government give any compensation for these cars?

A: Yes, but after tedious efforts and hesitation. For a vehicle which costs us 15–18 lakhs, the government only gives a maximum of 2 lakhs for it.

Q: Are these buses insured?

A: No insurance company covers a mini bus or a bus running in Karachi.

Q: When a vehicle is torched, do you give the member who runs that vehicle, any compensation? How does that work?

A: Yes. We have two different kinds of members: From the union and from the committee which we have constituted. Our rule is that the payment has to be done per day, but the operators usually give them per month.

Q: What is the per day charge?

A: Rs 30 /day.

Q: How much does your association give to them as compensation?

A: We don't have any resources to give such compensation. We give them from what the government gives us.

Q: If anyone is hit by one of your vehicles, who takes care of it?

A: The vehicle owner himself. They try to settle it on their own.

Q: How do you pay for the vehicles?

A: The payment is done in three different ways. One the person who can afford to pay by himself. Or you can buy in instalments. I can then also sell it to someone else too.

Q: How does the payment process work? Through the bank?

A: That can be done but banks usually finances new vehicles which are not inducted anymore. But not everyone can go through the banks.

Q: If somebody is buying these vehicles in instalments, who do they pay it to? Who takes the down payment?

A: If I manufacture vehicles and you buy it from me then you would pay me the down payment. It is usually Rs 10,000 per month.

Q: Does the manufacturer/bank issue a funding letter to the buyer? What if he is selling a 5 lakh vehicle for 10 lakh?

A: Depends on the bank you are dealing with. Every bank has different interest rates too for the loans they give. Obviously the manufacturer won't sell the vehicle at the manufacturing price.

Q: What is the lowest and highest price for a vehicle?

A: Even a vehicle which is not in a good condition would cost 5-6 lac and maximum 15 lac.

Q: What are the problems which you have to face while buying/operating a vehicle?

A: Road permits and roadworthiness are not an issue for us. After 2002, the company which was manufacturing and supplying these Mazdas stopped operating. We cannot afford the new one; they are too expensive for us.

Q: Does a road permit cost anything?

A: No.

Q: Who issues the road permit?

A: The secretary of RTA.

Q: And what about the fitness certificate?

A: The motor vehicle department.

Q: How much does it cost for one vehicle running on one route?

A: Rs 100-200. The total expense for the permit is between Rs 1,000-2,000.

Q: Do you encounter any problems with the traffic police?

A: I think they are really good. Our vehicles are running in the city without any glitches.

Q: What about your department head?

A: Well, whichever laws and rules there are regarding traffic etc., all apply to us. Even our fares are approved by the government.

Q: But we don't get tickets in the buses anymore, how do we make sure that the rules are being followed?

A: Nowadays nobody gives tickets.

Q: When did the ticketing system stop?

A: Sometime after 1992-1993.

Q: Did this benefit anyone?

A: It's our loss actually. When the ticketing system was there, there was a limit which we could give to the contractors. Now we can't.

Q: How much money in a month do the Mazdas and coaches currently running on the streets give to the traffic police?

A: It is between the driver and the traffic police himself. But it isn't that much. It's usually between Rs 2,000–3,000. It is according to the route not according to the vehicle.

Q: What is the role of a vehicle inspector?

A: He checks the vehicle. In the case of an accident he takes the witness' account. But in most cases we get the blame for hitting the person.

Q: What are the fitness charges?

A: Between Rs 1,000-2,000.

Q: For how long have you been associated with this field? How do you think the transport system can be improved?

A: The first and foremost thing is security. Then the matters of the fares have to be resolved. Fares should be according to the cost of the vehicle. The transport industry needs to be recognised as an industry by our government. We pay the highest taxes.

Q: What should be the fare according to you?

A: For the current vehicles which we have, at least Rs 50 per passenger. If someone is paying 10 lacs for a vehicle and if he dies, under a strike condition it is torched down within minutes.

Q: What is your take on signal free corridors?

A: It is a progression. The problem is that in our country/city policies are formulated but not implemented. We don't have CNG, we don't have petrol, we don't have diesel but vehicles from all over the world are being inducted in the city and are being registered on CNG. We don't have petrol but if you at Sohrab Goth trucks loaded with numerous motorcycles can be seen. If a man has guests coming over to his place, he'll arrange for things accordingly for 20 guests or 5 guests. I discussed these issues with the secretary of transport especially about Qingqis, he informed that they are formulating a policy for it but what is the point of registering them if these vehicles are loading 9 passengers on 3 seats? He wasn't then sure if the Qingqis are being registered or not. You are in a certain position in an institution and you aren't well informed. Such issues do exist.

Q: Who should be taking care of the transport issues?

A: We've written complaint/request letters to everyone in the government and the chief minister must have a drawer full of our letters by now.

Q: What is your take on the circular railway?

A: We will agree anything which would benefit this city. But it should not merely be limited to paperwork because these plans are expensive and take up resources.

Now we are in discussion with Syed Mahmood Afridi who is the President of Karachi Muslim Mini Bus Coach Owner Association.

Q: How long have you been associated with this organisation?

A: Since 1966 when four-wheelers and small vehicles used to be seen on the roads of Karachi.

Q: How many people/members are there in your association?

A: We have at least 8,000-9,000 members. We have a cabinet too.

Q: What is the structure of that cabinet?

A: First is the president, then the vice president, then a chairman, general secretary, finance minister. Then we also have a cabinet in the district. It follows the same structure.

Q: What is the role of the district cabinet?

A: To solve the problems of that district for e.g. if a problem has occurred in the Malir district, we do not have to travel all the way to Malir for that, the Malir district can take care of it. If they are unable to resolve it, then we have to go.

Q: How many organisations/institutions do you have to be in touch with e.g. traffic police, transport committee etc.?

A: RTA secretary, commissioner of Karachi, traffic police etc. We deal with many institutions.

Q: What is the usual attitude of government institutions towards your association? What do they take you as, problem creators or problem solvers?

A: Well I think they may have some complaints against us too. I am the president here and the general secretary of the Karachi Transport Union. I am thankful to God that I have earned a lot of respect over the years. I think one of the main transport issues is the fare. Every association charges the fare according to their wishes and not according to the policy.

Q: What kinds of complaints do the travellers/ users of transport usually have?

A: They must have complaints from us maybe because some of our vehicles/buses are not in good condition. Until we fix them, they will of course complain. They are completely unaware that even transporters have certain complaints. Transporters are now just getting by because it's their job.

Q: How much pay does a driver get?

A: The ticketing system was perfect for us. It was easier to keep a check on the earnings of the drivers as well. We could also then calculate that how much we've saved. Now there is no accountability. Both the conductors and the driver are involved in this because at certain times the drivers won't drive our bus if they is not accompanied by a conductor of his own choice.

Q: How much money do they give back at least?

A: Depends on the route and isn't fixed—it can be Rs 800, 900 1,000 etc.

Q: What does the operator do for his driver?

A: It's us who do everything for them from challan to bail to food to the cigarette they smoke.

Q: What is the solution to all this?

A: The government should support the transport department making sure that Karachi and the public of Karachi are benefitting from the steps which we'd take. Secondly, the city conditions should be taken into account and improved.

Q: Are you satisfied with the roads and the bus stops in the city?

A: The city is nothing compared to the rural areas, you should visit them. Baldia town, Rasheedabad, Banaras, Qasba colony Manghopir etc. have terrible roads. Some tribal areas might be in better conditions then these areas.

Q: Are there broken roads?

A: The roads don't even exist there, let alone be broken. They damage our vehicles.

Q: What do you think is the solution to the traffic jam in the city?

A: The traffic police are not doing their job. They are more concerned about their earnings (through bribes). We don't have a proper parking system. We had such a good time in Karachi in the old days. The police and rangers do not follow the rules themselves so traffic jams are inevitable.

B-04. Akbar Khan (Finance Secretary) and Syed Khattri (President), All Karachi Qingqi Welfare Association

We are in discussion with Akbar Khan

Today we are here with Mr Akbar Khan, who is the finance secretary of the Qingqi Rickshaw Association, Karachi. We are going to talk about how Qingqi rickshaws help the people of Karachi in commuting when they are already facing so many transport issues. Also, to what extent are Qingqi rickshaws fulfilling their roles and responsibilities?

Q: For how long have you been associated with this association? Also, please tell us how Qingqis came into being?

A: Qingqi is a Chinese motorcycle company, it's a brand. It was initiated in Punjab and then moved to Sindh and has been a part of our transport system for 20 years now. In Karachi, they were introduced in 2002. I was the one who introduced them in Karachi. The route which was first experimented for Qingqis was from Askari Park (Old Sabzi Mandi) then to Liaquatabad. And now because people have appreciated them so much that in the past 13 years, ever since their inception, over 40,000 Qingqis are on the Karachi roads. Now we have CNG, which has been introduced due to Qingqi, so we have both motorcycle and rickshaw Qingqis.

Q: How many people can Qingqis accommodate at a time?

A: According to the notification issues by the government, 4+1 people but it can accommodate 6 people easily, 3 on each side.

Q: How many people do you have in your association?

A: 7.

Q: What about the Qingqi drivers?

A: Numerous. We have their information along with their photographs.

Q: Do you call them for meetings?

A: Yes, frequently, especially if someone encounters problems. Both parties are invited and the problem is resolved.

Q: How much does one Qingqi cost?

A: A new Qingqi of 100 cc which the government has approved costs Rs 115,000. Chinese ones cost around Rs 90,000.

Q: What about the rickshaw?

A: Around 2 lacs for the ones with 6 seats.

Q: Apart from this, what other expenses are there?

A: Mechanic fee, starter's fee, contractors and jets. Contractors take Rs 500. If someone is experienced, they even charge Rs 600.

Q: What role does a contractor play?

A: He manages the registration of all the Qingqis, makes sure that they have number plates and if we wouldn't have contractors, drivers would argue amongst themselves about their tasks. Contractors organise their turns and tasks.

Q: How do you pay these contractors?

A: We pay them through the rent which we get from the rickshaw stands.

Q: And how much is this rent?

A: Rs 120. But it varies between Rs 110 and Rs 150. This for the Qingqi rickshaws. I had initially introduced these Qingqi rickshaws in the city and there was no trend of rickshaw stops/stands. So, I tried to establish the system. But just introducing them wasn't enough. I needed drivers, mechanics. I had to put in a lot of effort to make this work. I hired drivers on a fixed rent/ pay including food. I continued this for 6 months even when nobody was using the

Qingqis, I had to pay the drivers their rent/pay. Initially, people also had trouble with getting on and off the Qingqis. But now people know how to travel on them.

Q: What is the lowest and the highest rent of these Qingqis?

A: For Qingqis it is between Rs10–15. We raised it to Rs 15 recently due to inflation. I received a call from someone saying that he was paying Rs 10 and now we have increased it, whereas the petrol prices have decreased/will decrease! I replied that if the prices were set according to petrol and diesel prices, they would've gone up 3 years ago. And the petrol prices rise every 15 days but our rent is the same. But now there are requirements like oil, tires, maintenance of the Qingqis as well, so we have raised the rent.

Q: How much salary do you give to the drivers?

A: They only pay the rent of the Qingqi, the rest of whatever they earn, they get to keep it.

Q: How much does it come out to be?

A: Rs 200.

Q: And contractors?

A: I pay the mechanics, the contractors, and the starters from those Rs 200.

Q: What about the challans?

A: All the police challans are also included in those Rs 200.

Q: So, what is the estimated expense for one Qingqi?

A: Around Rs 3,000–4,000. Can also go up to Rs 5,000.

Q: Who pays for it?

A: The owner of the stands. In this case, Me.

Q: You are paying for everything; you pay the drivers, the mechanics, the starters, and the contractors?

A: The driver only pays for the stand rent, which includes the challan.

Q: Is the Qingqi system affected by any of the political parties?

A: Not as such. We don't even have to pay anything to them, there are just rumours. You can ask the drivers too.

Q: Do you buy these Qingqis on instalments/loans?

A: At times, we deal with people in Gulistan-e-Johar. The usual rate is Rs 30,000–40,000 if we buy them in instalments. They take Rs 30–40,000 in advance and hand over the vehicle to you.

Q: When hiring the drivers, do you take their age into account as well?

A: We do. We have also caught kids who took the rickshaws from their uncles/fathers and drive them themselves. They say that their uncle/father's unwell and they had to work on their behalf. We have asked them not to do this.

Q: How are the routes designed and how do you get permits for them?

A: The issuing of permits requires a lot of effort. We are still in discussion with the government regarding our road permits. At the moment we have designed routes in such a way that we target places like markets, hospitals where more people use our service. They can get dropped off at the nearest place from where they can get a bus.

Q: Can you tell us about the matter which we had heard about regarding Qingqi rickshaws and motorcycles?

A: The government claimed that we are using stolen motorcycles and rickshaws.

Q: Did you or are you negotiating with the government for the regulation of this system?

A: We want to have proper regulations and laws for our system. So that the revenue we generate can be put to proper use.

Q: So, you want motorcycle Qingqis to be used to generate revenue?

A: Yes, why not. You could see that they are playing a role in the transport system of Karachi and CNG.

Q: What kind of a role, according to you, can the Qingqi rickshaws and motorcycles play in providing service to a population of a mega city?

A: I think the situation which we are in is only due to the lack of proper law and regulation in our city. If we'll have law, we can regulate this system easily. Since we don't have anyone to look after this system currently, the situation is going from bad to worse.

As we have informed you previously, we are part of an NGO called the Urban Resource Centre, and we are not connected to the government in any way. We just wish to see that what exactly is happening within the city.

Now we are in discussion with Syed Khatri

A: My name is Syed Khatri and I am the president of the All Karachi Qingqi Association. We founded this association in 2010 with the aim of regulating the system of Qingqis in Karachi. We've been fighting for regulation, permits, and registration since 2010 and it is now 2014 but we're still where we started. Promises were made but it is now February 2014 and we haven't received a legal status as yet. We wanted to form a system as you can see that now the public has to face a lot of issues, but the system which we had developed initially for Qingqi, is in form to date and inshallah we'd be able to keep it this way. We hope that the government regulates this system at its earliest, but it doesn't seem much interested in it. In October 2013, an order was passed by ADIG to shut down Qingqis, whereas we had met them only 2 days previously They didn't listen to our arguments and asked us to abide by the order. We are ready to discuss every matter with them. We are just saying to the government that if they have any issues with us, we are here and willing to discuss them. It is supposed to be a give and take system. We request a law and a legal status so that we can also form and maintain a proper system. People who deal with and have the knowledge about the transport issues, such as you people, know very well that in Karachi transport is one of the biggest issues and people who use public transport need it badly. The government should take care of it. Instead we are doing it. Even the commissioner agreed with us that yes transport really IS an issue. We have even written a letter to them that we wish to have a meeting/discussion with them.

Q: Do you follow a system for monitoring your members, your vehicles and complaints by the public?

A: We have a proper system in place. Mr Bakshi takes care of it. If somebody registers a complaint, it goes via Mr Bakshi to the operator.

Q: How many routes are currently being operated in the city?

A: More than 100. But they are also being run in other areas such as no-go areas, super highway, Gulshan-e-Aziz, but they are not registered with us. The ones being operated on the national highway do not come under us.

Q: What is the process of getting registered and operating a route, with your association?

A: For route operating, firstly you require a plan for which you need to submit a request to our office. We then have a separate union committee, which makes sure that the new request for the route is not overlapping with an already existing route for a Qingqi or CNG rickshaw. If not, then the committee formulates a route for you which is then approved by the government. Then we issue an NOC and based on that the operators then operate the routes.

Q: Do they have to submit a fee as well?

A: First the registration committee will visit that route and then issue the NOC accordingly. After the NOC is issued, a one-time payment is required which is Rs 5,000.

Q: Keeping the scenario of Qingqis in view, what do you think are the major transport issues which we are facing?

A: Karachi, even though it is a mega city, lacks a proper system of categorisation of heavy traffic, small vehicles etc. We, the public, are also to be blamed for it as we don't follow the rules e.g. now that U-turns locations have been clearly located, people still violate them. They blame Qingqis for it as well.

Q: Weren't Qingqis allowed on smaller routes only in the beginning?

A: If we had a proper law, we would have properly followed it. Once the law is provided to us, we will abide by it for sure.

Q: Have you prepared any kind of presentation for when you get the chance to have a meeting with the authorities?

A: Yes, we have. Also, we have already submitted every detail including pictures, documents to the authorities. We did this in 2010 only but still we haven't received a response. We have also proposed that we get a separate lane on the main roads. If somebody from our members bypasses it, they have the right to confiscate that vehicle.

Q: What other ways monitoring can you suggest?

A: First we get the permit, and then we take care of all the vehicles. To make sure that everybody follows that law, we would implement it strictly. We initiated this system to get the status of mini-public transport and we put this request in front of the government too. The motor ordinance which was passed recently does state we have the permission to carry 1+4 in Qingqis, i.e. 1 driver and 4 passengers. But they complain that instead of 4, we accommodate 6 passengers. But we don't have a proper law to follow. Even a Mazda with 25 seats, how many people actually sit on them? You see people hanging from the doors, sitting on the roof and we accommodate 2 extra people and they complain about us.

Q: We have interviewed several people regarding your service, and people really appreciate it.

A: Yes! Even the commissioner has given us his appreciation.

Q: Have you corresponded with the secretary of transport on this matter?

A: We are sorry, but all former secretaries were on really good terms with us. But the current secretary only circumvents our issues.

Q: According to you, what is the solution to all this?

A: People think that the public transport i.e. buses, trains will shut down in Karachi because of the Qingqis, and this is not the case. We would never want to shut down the big transport. The big transport system is closing down because of the decreased CNG supply. Don't treat us unfairly. If we are making mistakes, sit with us and tell us. We can discuss it. Regulate us. A circular railway system should be introduced as well. Don't harm/damage the green buses. And if you look at the past records, Qingqis have not had, so far, any huge accidents. Until all these efforts are appreciated and welcomed, the situation won't change.

B-06. Hafeez-ul-Haq Hassan Zai, Karachi Taxi, Yellow Cab and Motor Rickshaw Association

First of all, on the behalf of Urban Resource Centre, We welcome Mr Hafiz-ul-Haq on the 10 February 2014, who is the President of the Karachi Taxi Yellow Cab Association.

Q: How long have you been associated with this association?

A: My uncle Mr Haji was the former president of this association, after him, I took the responsibility of it and have been in post almost 15 years. This is a social service which runs in our family. All the people who drive rickshaws are like my family members. We have around 52,300 rickshaws which the government has forcefully banned and no public institution is helping us regarding this, despite our plea and arguments. They only help us when they are gaining something from it. I'll give you an example. First, they put a ban on rickshaw stops, stating that they create noise and air pollution. The institutions who complain about pollution should understand that rickshaws are not the only ones causing it. There are other reasons too. We then met with the environment committee. The previous minister of that committee is really good friends with my uncle too. The committee has supported us throughout and unfortunately we don't have many people like Mr Ishrat-ul-Ebaad. Whenever we had a problem, they helped us out for three years, this is extraordinary. He understood our complaints which the city government did not. After his tenure, Mr Jadoon took over. This is a different story where profit is more important which is understandable.

Q: What sort of problems do the rickshaw members come to you with?

A: They came to me with all sorts of problems such as incidents with the police, accidents and any emergencies. They discuss all issues with me including diseases. We even complained to the government that if they aren't providing people with jobs, why are they making them unemployed? These rickshaws used to previously sell for 1.5 lacs and because of certain policies these rickshaws now cost 40 lacs and people would rent them; they would also sell them if they needed cash for treatments, or for their children's wedding. This is the mistake on the government's part. Secondly, it doesn't solely give us profit, we earn labour from it. The government charges us so much tax e.g. taxes for permits, taxes for fitness, taxes for Exide battery kits, all these taxes directly go to the government, and these were also ended.

Q: What kinds of resources are required to run one rickshaw?

A: Route permit, fitness, insurance and vehicle tax.

Q: How much is a vehicle tax these days?

A: Around Rs 400. And Rs 550 is the cost for permits whereas Rs 50-100 is the cost for fitness.

Q: Are all the other expenses covered in these amounts?

A: No. We do want the government to take tax, but where is all the tax going? It is disappointing that we are paying our taxes, but the government is not ready to listen to our problems. They say our vehicles emit smoke into the environment, but smoke is emitted by all sorts of vehicles, buses, motorcycles, factories as well. They say we are ruining the environment but the shops also create huge amounts of waste. These are thrown in the sea. They want to stop 1 lac 4,000 drivers but won't close down those 3,200 shops.

Q: How much does a rickshaw cost these days?

A: It ranges from Rs 180,000 to 2 lacs. This is separate from the cylinder and the expense for the kit.

Q: How much does it cost to convert a rickshaw to CNG?

A: We tried to negotiate with the companies from which we buy these rickshaws to have CNG pre-fitted into the rickshaw. But they said it isn't possible. We reasoned with them that since they are constructing these rickshaws themselves then why can't they convert them to CNG? We believe it is because it won't bring any benefit to them. I talked to the governor of Sindh as well that this can be done. He said okay then we should give it a try ourselves. We agreed to it.

Q: How much did it cost you to construct one CNG rickshaw?

A: I only created a prototype. I don't own a factory and I certainly do not have the resources to construct one. The cost doesn't matter. It's like war. It doesn't matter how many people are being killed, it's just a matter of winning and losing. We created a successful prototype and after this, the governor published an ad in the newspaper asking a company to come forward that wished to help us in this regard. 10-12 companies came forward and agreed to this proposal. After this, again an ad was published in the newspaper that we are registering our company. I then went to the governor stating that we aren't registering our company but merely working on the conversion of rickshaws. Then a third ad was published in the newspaper. This just confused people. The government said that we should construct rickshaws. I told them that this wasn't our job.

Q: You talked about renting rickshaws. Could you please explain this in more detail?

A: We can buy rickshaws on loan/rent/ instalments. There is no fixed payment for this.

Q: All the rickshaws which are being run on certain routes, do they come under your jurisdiction?

A: This is a fairly new system. It doesn't come under our registration. The transport in this country is for the rich not for the poor.

Q: So, are these being run on any political parties' orders?

A: You are an educated man; I think you already know the answer to this.

Q: There was a time in Karachi where we used to see huge buses on the roads, now these are hardly seen; they have been replaced by rickshaws, taxis, and Qingqis. In your opinion, what kind of transport system should a mega city with a population of 2 crore have: huge buses or small rickshaws?

A: Green buses were introduced, but the government could not sustain them. We are still running the old buses and wagons. The governor of Sindh did not want people to travels on the roofs of the buses, but with such a scarcity in the number of buses, what else they can do? The second issue is the strikes. It is not secure to run huge buses on our streets. People torch these each time there is a strike. Every new project which the government introduces, ends. We don't have electricity, petrol, CNG etc. You have seen the route from Gurumandir to Numaish. There are so many CNG stations in one single line. We told with them that closing down petrol pumps is bizarre. The supply of CNG is unpredictable and it is only being supplied every other day. We have to put up with the trouble. They suggested we convert our rickshaws to CNG. What do they think? That it is so easy to pay for all these conversions? It costs 2-3 lacs per rickshaw. And now that CNG supply is low, they say to convert it back to diesel. You know the diesel prices, they are so high. We have seen the days where people used to park their cars and preferred traveling in buses!

Q: In old days rickshaws and taxis used to run on meters. Why don't they do it anymore?

A: It is a strategy of the government to make the institutions of transport and the public, fight amongst each other. Instead we should be taking care of these rickshaws. They don't treat them well. It is all about connections here. The government was unable to manage this service and hence the system of meters finished.

Q: If the roads of a city are not properly built, what kind of consequences can it lead to?

A: Many. If the roads are not built properly it damages the cars. The contractors take money and yet are still unable to fix the roads.

Q: The rickshaw drivers which you have hired, how much amount of money do they give you from their earnings?

A: Rs 80–100. Nothing fixed.

Q: How much do they earn in a day?

A: They don't tell us that.

Q: How much do the taxi drivers give?

A: Around Rs 100-200.

Q: Is it per day or per hour?

A: Per day.

Q: The taxis have reduced considerably in number. Is there anything being done on it?

A: As I mentioned earlier as well, the governor stated that taxis are now mundane. New taxis cost 8-12 lac. The government will have to pay for it. This is not in the government's policy. We are running them on loan.

Q: What is the structure of the taxis and rickshaws association?

A: We have general secretaries, president, chairman etc.

Q: If a rickshaw is destroyed in any incident, do you help your drivers/members?

A: We do as much as possible. But the government doesn't pay anything and we don't ask for it either. We give as much money as possible.

Q: What is the solution to all these problems according to you?

A: I believe we all should start from small deeds. We all should do our bit. There is no planning. Also, implementation of policies is important. Accountability is also a vital factor. Nobody asks that why a certain thing is occurring. They accept it without questioning it.

Q: We see small children driving rickshaws, is there a solution to it?

A: We have to protect them from the police since most of them are driving without a licence. Also, you would see that children are driving motorbikes, rickshaws, cars and I believe they are innocent children. Everybody is responsible for city's workings and problems.

C. INTERVIEWS WITH THE PUBLIC

D-01. Amjad Ali, Saiban Office, Khuda-ki-Basti

Q: What is your name?

A: My name is Amjad Ali.

Q: Where did you live before?

A: In Liaquatabad Sindhi hotel.

Q: How long did you live there?

A: We lived almost 35 to 40 years I was born there my parents were there when it was just being cultivated.

Q: When did you come here?

A: When plots were being cut but we hardly lived here because there weren't any facilities such as water, gas or electricity. As time passed we got these things except water which we still have to buy.

Q: Why did you come here?

A: Because our house was very small and only one family could live in it. Me and my elder brother got married we couldn't adjust there so our parents forced us to buy a plot here.

Q: But why didn't you buy house in Liaquatabad Sindhi hotel?

A: Because houses are too expensive we didn't have resources to buy a land or any house; we had to buy as cheaply as we can that's why we came here.

Q: What difference do you feel here as compare to that place?

A: The city is very far from here that's why we face problems getting work but there we easily got work.

Q: Where did you work?

A: I was an employee at Liaquatabad furniture market.

Q: And what about now?

A: I sell children's clothes at the market now.

Q: How many years have you been doing this work?

A: Almost two years.

Q: When you were working in the furniture market how did you travel?

A: By bus, but I arrived late everyday that's why my owner got a bike for me.

Q: What were the expenses when you travelled by bus?

A: Almost Rs 100 because I had to take 2 modes of transport—there wasn't any straight route, so I took the Qingqi and gave Rs 35 then took another because the distance was too much and he took Rs 10 to 15 which means Rs 50 each way totalling Rs 100.

Q: Why did you leave that work if your owner gave you a bike as well?

A: Because the shop closed.

Q: How much money did you earn and what about now?

A: Both are same just a little bit different for travelling and lunch. I can save this money now because I work here and have lunch at my house. Suppose if I earn Rs 500 and include Rs 150 in it so the total money is Rs 650 but as I earned Rs 500 and spent Rs150 for travelling and lunch then I saved Rs 350.

Q: How much money do you earn in a month?

A: Around Rs 10,11,14,15 thousand but in a season I earn more than that like Rs 20 to 25 thousand. In the off season I earn less than Rs15 thousand—more like Rs 8 to 10 thousand

Q: What difference do you feel in your expenses?

A: The only difference is that if we go outside for work it wastes our time and money

Q: Where do you get things for your children?

A: We get things from the city we go once in a week not everyday

Q: How much time and money is required to go once in a week?

A: I get things from the empress market at Saddar. It takes one and a half hour and Rs 50 to 60 for travelling, but when I go there I become very tired and aren't able to do any other work.

Q: How do you go to marriages?

A: We can only go with our own conveyance. If I would go alone I would prefer to go by bike, but if my family is with me then I have to get a taxi for them.

Q: How much expense is required if you hire a taxi?

A: Rs 500 to 600 if I go to Liaquatabad but when we come back we hardly find any conveyance and it would cost more than Rs 600.

Q: What are the circumstances when you travel?

A: It's dangerous late at night because my mobile and money got snatched before near Rivulent. I was on my bike; that's why I don't take the risk after 12 a.m.

Q: How many children do you have?

A: 5. Masha Allah.

Q: Are they studying or working?

A: Three are studying and two are still small.

Q: Are they studying in this basti?

A: Yes, they are studying there.

Q: What are the expenses for children's education?

A: They are studying in the government school so their total expenses are Rs 2 to 3 thousand per month.

Q: How do you pay the Rs 3 thousand?

A: Rs 150 for each and tuition fees also then the expense of stationery etc.

Q: Is there any hospital or dispensary for health here?

A: Baqai Hospital is here where treatment is better. They don't take money, but I prefer to go outside for treatment.

Q: Where do you take your family for treatment?

A: I prefer to go to Nagan for my younger children especially.

Q: In case of emergency?

A: I am thankful to Allah that no emergency occurred I always take them on bike either day or night.

Q: As you lived in Liaquatabad among your relatives for many years is your relationship still the same?

A: The relationship is better but I don't meet them often.

Q: What is the reason?

A: Because they are far away.

Q: Is this right or wrong?

A: It's good to often meet them but it's our choice that we meet less because it takes so much time and money as well, so we save time and money by meeting less frequently.

Q: You met them every day but don't see them now for more than a week so how do you feel?

A: We all understand each other terms and conditions, so it's better to be in touch by mobile phone.

Q: Do you feel like going there to live again?

A: No, not really the only time I feel like that is when we have no water. But since I have spent so much time here, my children were also born here and their schools are here, if I go back they would get disrupted.

Q: Have you maintained relations here?

A: Yes, I have made relations here because of my children. If I left, they would get disrupted.

Q: What are the issues of transport here?

A: Two buses run—55 or Masood at daytime if the whole family comes.

Q: What about the Qingqi rickshaw are these also included in the transport?

A: Yes, it is but they cost a lot of money. If we were to go to Nagan, it would cost Rs 35.

Q: How much does Mazda cost?

A: Almost Rs 15 to 20 for both ways but the Qingqi costs Rs 35 for one way only.

Q: But why do people like the Qingqi?

A: Because they save time. Buses run every 20 minutes. Buses are fewer than Qingqis that's why people prefer Qingqi to save time. They don't care about the money.

Q: You can go to Saddar for Rs 50. If large buses ran it would take Rs 35 to Saddar or Talwar, is that ok?

A: It would be better if large buses run for long journeys for less money because we pay Rs 35 to Nagan so it would be better if we paid Rs 35 to Saddar.

D-02. JAWED SULTAN, SAIBAN OFFICE, KHUDA-KI-BASTI

Q: What is your name?

A: My name is Jawed.

Q: How long have you been living in Khuda li Basti?

A: Almost 12 years.

Q: Did you come at the beginning?

A: Yes.

Q: Where did you come from?

A: From New Karachi No. 5.

Q: Did you rent or live at your own house?

A: I rented. I am a butcher at day time I am there at night.

Q: Why you come here?

A: Because we lived on rent there but Allah blessed us with our own house here.

Q: Who told you about Khuda ki Basti?

A: It was the effort of my wife. The lady doctor came and told us about it. Shahid Sahab invited us to live here he gave us one room for me and then my family came with all our luggage for one year. After that he gave us a plot whose owner is somebody else, but he cancelled his name and gave it to us. We gave them Rs 25,000 for construction and paid Rs 10,000 to prosecute then we got this plot.

Q: When you came from New Karachi No. 5 these areas are thickly populated and in full bloom at night so how do you feel?

A: I always wished to have my own house where I would live happily with my family. Finally, Allah fulfilled my desire.

Q: How do you go to work?

A: I go to work at 9 a.m. pick and drop my sir then I go home. It is my daily duty.

Q: How do other people go to their work?

A: By rickshaw.

Q: How much fare do they charge?

A: Rs 25 from New Karachi.

Q: Rs 25 for both ways?

A: Yes.

Q: How many children do you have?

A: 5 children—3 daughters and 2 sons.

Q: Does anybody work?

A: No.

Q: How many children go to school, college, or university?

A: My daughters go to college.

Q: How much expense is required for them?

A: Almost Rs 250 everyday Rs 125 for each.

Q: That means Rs 250 for their daily expenses?

A: Definitely I give them.

Q: And what about those who are getting education in school?

A: Rs 80 per month.

Q: How much money do you earn as you are butcher and driver as well?

A: I earn Rs 5,600 for the organisation.

Q: Rickshaws are moving now but before that how did you go?

A: By Mazda van.

Q: Is that more as compared to Mazda?

A: When we travelled by Mazda we also used to go by foot but at least rickshaw save us from that walk

Q: How do you go to marriages or anywhere else?

A: Either I borrow car from my boss or by taxi or rickshaw.

Q: How much do you pay for it?

A: It depends on the distance. If we go to Korangi then Rs 600 for one way so a total of Rs 1,200.

Q: Do you face any problem for travelling at night?

A: I am very thankful to Allah that no incident has happened as I heard people got mugged every time but Allah keeps me save because I earn pure money and I hope that he will always save me like this

Q: If you go to hospital or some issues occurred at night then?

A: No, it never happened to me yet.

Q: Are hospital facilities provided here?

A: Yes, Baqai and two more hospitals are here.

Q: It means you have facilities here?

A: Yes, I am thankful to Allah and his kindness

Q: Where do your relatives live?

A: In New Karachi.

Q: When you lived in New Karachi you used to meet your relatives?

A: Yes, they come here now. When we lived in New Karachi we often met each other on a regular basis, but now we meet once a month or so.

Q: How do you see this difference—is that right or wrong?

A: Actually, we could not get time to meet each other because my daughters went to college after that. Each daughter fees is Rs1,600 and the total is Rs 3,200 for the first and second year.

Q: As you don't meet them often does it impact on your social relations?

A: We meet at weddings because otherwise everybody is busy working

Q: Do you feel like moving back to New Karachi?

A: No, I am thankful to Allah that I got this place

Q: Buses run then Mazda, UTS, CNG bus and after that Qingqi—do you think large buses should run?

A: It should run because rickshaws are more than enough they take Rs 25 usually but when CNG close they take Rs 40 and when CNG closes for 2 days they feel like they have a supreme power like God.

Q: Why do people give them a lot of money?

A: People have to give them money because there are not enough buses.

Q: If large buses were running and charged Rs 35 to Saddar do you think people would use them?

A: They should support them.

Q: Do you think it would be better if 25 to 30 buses run?

A: Buses should run in fact must run because there isn't enough place in rickshaws and they can accidently divert any time but we have no choice than to travel in them.

Q: How did you make house here?

A: We have completed our house in one and a half years. They gave us a plot we constructed it slowly through committees.

D-03. NADEEM BAKHASH, KHUDA-KI-BASTI

Q: When did you come in Khuda Ki Basti?

A: We came here when the basti was being inhabited. That time just a few lanes were inhabited. Selling cold drinks/sweet syrups was our business. Our selling point was located at Sindh Government Hospital UP Morr Karachi. We lived there in a rented house. My friend told me about cheap plots for low income families at Khuda Ki Basti seeing that the area was depopulated we would come here time to time. One day we met with Mr Akhtar Sahib he suggested we buy a plot and save the money which we were spending on rent. Five other low-income families came here who couldn't afford to live in rented places. Six plots were bought at a time now we are paying instalments for the plots. Initially we had difficulties but now we are relaxed due to the available facilities.

Q: Where did you come from?

A: We came here from UP Society.

Q: How long had you been there?

A: We spent our whole childhood there. My father had been living in a flat in Haji Camp since the beginning of its settlement when people were being evicted from the area. He bought a house at UP Karachi and moved there with his family and later his sons bought houses to live separately; then we settled in Khuda ki Basti. We have been living here for 14/15 years.

Q: How did you feel living here in an unoccupied area compared to the saturated UP area?

A: In the beginning we were deprived of water, gas, and electricity. We said that we when we pass away our children would have their own residence. We couldn't afford to buy a house at any other place, when we had saved money the prices of houses became higher than our savings.

Q: What are the benefits of living here?

A: The environment is very calm here but recently the water and electricity supply are major issues. Some sewer lines have been laid but others will be constructed in the future. We say that God will solve our problems and we are waiting for good days and they must come.

Q: Are your expenses the same living in UP as compare with Basti?

A: Expenses have increased now. We use wood for cooking, purchase water from tankers. We have been using wood for 6 years. Vegetables and other things are more expensive than in UP. We have Rs 150 expense daily on buying water at Rs 10 per gallon. People purchase water from tankers with underground storage tanks. But those who had no tanks would buy 3-4 gallons daily and store them. When we settled here there was no water at 50 feet depth but now it exists at 20-22 feet depth. We dug for six weeks with our own hands. We use it and the people from the area carry water from it. It is sweet water so, they are using it for drinking as well and people bear just the material cost. It was our good act (sadqa-e-jaria)

Q: How did you do this work? Did you hire mechanics and labour?

A: We did this work jointly with four friends to help people and to get blessings from God without hiring labour and mechanics. We fixed four rings; two of them were fixed at the bottom of the well and two at the upper level. These rings will provide protection for those who might fall in it. We get water from the well throwing a can on a rope.

Q: Where do you work?

A: I sell goods setting up stalls in daily bazaars in the basti.

Q: How Much is you income?

A: I earn an average Rs 500 daily.

Q: How many family members do you have?

A: I have a son and seven daughters which totals ten family members including my wife.

Q: Are the children all getting education?

A: No, they are not studying anywhere. Some time ago they would go for tuition at someone's home.

Q: What about the citizen foundation school which has no tuition fees?

A: We visited there two or three times for our children's admissions. They took a test and failed. Their official requirements were wrong; they embezzle funds having shown poor children round. I don't trust them.

Q: Do your children want to get education?

A: Yes, they are interested.

Q: Are you the only earning person in your family?

A: Yes

Q: How do you bear home expenses with a very low income?

A: It is very difficult. I do embroidery work

D-04. MUHAMMAD YASEEN, KHUDA KI BASTI

Q: What is your name?

A: M. Yaseen

Q: Where did you live previously?

A: We lived in Lal market, Khameeso Goth, New Karachi. We moved to the Goth from Shikarpoor district in the interior of Sindh during ethnic violence between the Sindhi and the Muhajir after having sold our 80 yard built house for Rs 40,000. We came here for our safety. We sold the house at a very low price and didn't claim because we were to pay Rs 500 as bribe for it but my 110 year old father wouldn't pay the hush money.

Q: When did you sell out that house?

A: In 1992 during ethnic violence, people were being killed on both sides so we were forced us to move to a safer place and people left their houses without selling them. I studied up to fifth grade. My father died in Shikarpoor. I came here with my younger siblings because I was the only person to look after them.

Q: How long did you live in Khameeso Goth?

A: For 14 years.

Q: Did you have your own house at Khameeso Goth?

A: No, We didn't; we lived there in a rented house.

Q: Why did you come here in Khuda Ki Basti?

A: Because we bought our own house. I bought here at a very low price. We couldn't afford to buy a house in any other part of Karachi.

Q: What is the difference between living here and the Khameeso Goth?

A: We don't have to pay house rent here but we purchase water.

Q: How much do you spend for water in every month?

A: We buy two tankers of water for each Rs 1000 every month. There are also power shortages here. I sell pakoras and samosas at the daily bachat bazaar taking a stall for Rs 100 per day. It was Rs 50 in 2006. I sell in these bazaars which are at different places on fixed days. Every Tuesday and Saturday it is fixed in the basti. The stall rent is Rs 50 for a Saturday here because it is a small bazaar.

Q: Where do you sell in the evening?

A: At the main bus stop.

Q: How much is your daily income?

A: Rs 500-700 is my daily sales income; sometimes it reaches up to Rs 1,000-1,200 per day. Now my average is Rs 300 per day.

Q: How many children do you have?

A: I have six children

Q: Are your all children studying or working?

A: All three daughters are studying but the three sons have given up their studies now they are learning to recite the Quran. My elder son works in a refrigerator and deep freezer repair shop and is learning the work and earning Rs 100-150 weekly.

Q: How do you bear your expenses on such a very low income?

A: I sell fried fish in the winter season but I earn very little because I buy ice for Rs 100 to use daily to keep the fish fresh. There has been no electricity for two months due to the disconnection of illegal connections. I don't have any savings. I work hard daily until late at night to cover all my expenditure.

Q: How do you go to the city?

A: I have a motor bike and I transport fish and other things on it. We could not afford Rs 1,000 per day for the rickshaw fare so I bought the bike. We use this for visiting relatives as well. My family doesn't go out together as we do not have a big vehicle.

Q: Where do your relatives live?

A: Some live in Orangi, Some in New Karachi and mostly in the interior of Sindh.

Q: How often you visit to relatives?

A: Our visits have reduced due to not having a big vehicle. They come to meet us. We visit only to attend marriages, funerals and if someone is sick.

Q: Do you want to live again in your previous place?

A: Yes, in Shikarpoor where I was born. My business of making Peshawari slippers was good there. It's my fate to live here. God will also give and bless us here but there is an electricity and water shortage which is a headache. If I could save the Rs 2,000 per month that we are paying for water, I would easily afford the plot instalment.

Q: How many ethnic groups are there in Shikarpoor?

A: Urdu speaking people are in the majority. Sindhi and Gujrati people also live there.

Q: Which relatives are there?

A: My in-laws live there. Two months ago I visited to attend a marriage ceremony.

Q: What are the issues of transport here?

A: There are no buses except two mini buses (Mazda) CNG rickshaws are available here which demand fares of Rs 15-25.

Q: What health facilities are available here?

A: There is one hospital named Baqai where doctors treat sick people like animals and do not give any medicine. They just write on papers. Those who opened private clinics are not qualified. They charge high fees. Most of them opened their own medical stores. They prescribe unnecessary medicines.

Q: Why did you move here in absence of facilities?

A: We cannot afford to live in any other better place. If we live at other place and pay rent who will live in this house? We have a house that we rent to my brother. Now he says it is his house. He is not paying electricity bills although he instaled a separate meter. It is very difficult to retrieve the house from him.

Q: What are the security matters here?

A: There is no security. We should pray to God for it.

Q: Did any incident take place while you coming back house in nights?

A: I don't go anywhere at nights whenever I go to attend marriages I go with my family Thank God no incident has happened with us.

Q: How do you feel living here?

A: In the beginning when the area was under control by the office of Saiban (the housing scheme) we felt better, but now anyone who has political power can stand here.

Q: Did you do any effort acquiring water?

A: We also went to the water board but due to not having political influence we haven't succeeded. We cannot do anything to bypass them. People went to Akhter Sahib many times. Water pipes exist here but there is no water. Electricity has been disconnected for two months. People have paid the electric bills that were received of Rs. 1,000-1,500 last month.

Q: Did you give requests to the parties for this?

A: Yes, they always promise that electricity power will connect soon. Actually, they have electricity all the time in their houses or in offices. They don't see troubles.

Q: How did you sleep in nights without electric fans?

A: We sleep with mosquito coils on hot nights.

D-05. Basheer, Khuda-ki-Basti

Q: Where did you live previously?

A: I lived in New Karachi.

Q: How long did you live there?

A: We lived there for about 20-22 years.

Q: Do all your relatives and friends live there now?

A: No, Some of them live in New Karachi and some live in Baldia Town.

Q: When did you come here?

A: We come here in 2001.

Q: Why did you come here?

A: We lived in a rented house. We heard about available cheap plots being sold to very low-income families through a low cost housing scheme project called Saiban. We wanted to get our own house.

Q: What is your job?

A: I labour in a factory. I installed a stall for first time today because there has been no work for me in the factory for the last four months. The textile factory is disrupted nowadays due to shortage of water and electricity.

Q: Where is the factory located?

A: It is in an industrial area of Gabol Town New Karachi. There are many small factories there.

Q: How did you used to go to the factory?

A: I had used to go by changing 2 or 3 Mazdas every day.

Q: How much would you spent of transport fare?

A: Rs 70-80 per day. When CNG remains shut down we have to pay higher fares for the CNG rickshaws.

Q: You aren't doing work in that factory? How are you running your house?

A: In the beginning of my joblessness I took loans but now I took another loan of Rs 10,000 for a restart of selling slippers.

Q: How many children you have?

A: I have six children.

Q: Are they studying or working?

A: Three of them are studying and a daughter is married.

Q: Are you the only earning member of your family?

A: Yes, I am.

Q: How much was your monthly income in the factory?

A: It was not fixed, I would receive between Rs 10-12 thousand from that work; my work was on a contract basis according to weave fabric availability.

Q: How much time would you spent travelling to the factory?

A: About 1 hour or 11-4 hours daily travelling by CNG rickshaw—time saving but much more expensive than Mazdas. On the closed day of CNG the rickshaw driver charged an extra Rs 5-10.

Q: What is the difference of living between here and New Karachi?

A: New Karachi is in the city. There are many facilities available—hospitals, big markets. There is no big hospital and market here. If we want to buy good things we have to pay much higher prices. Otherwise we have to go to the city markets.

Q: If you need to go to hospital in emergency do you get transport at night?

A: Public transport is not available here in nights we have to hire a taxi or rickshaw which is expensive for us. Taxi or rickshaw drivers charge two or three times the fare. Usually we pay between Rs 300-600 for the visits.

Q: How do you go to attend weddings?

A: Last month I went to a wedding with my family by taxi and coming back home in the late hours of the night. There was no transport available we changed vehicles four times and came back home spending Rs 350 and taking 1 and half hours.

Q: What your children do?

A: I have four daughters. My two sons are younger. One of them is studying in grade six and the other is in youth grade.

Q: How are security matters especially in nights?

A: Transport runs on the roads until the late hours as being a populated Lyari settlement there is no problem of transport in nights.

Q: What are the difference in your expenditures between living here and the New Karachi?

A: We have to buy water here. We had to pay house rent in New Karachi. Due to the remote area we have to pay more amounts in transportation. There are also problems of power shortages.

Q: How do you get water?

A: There are water pipes, but there is no water in the pipes so people buy water. Previously water from the tanker was Rs 700. Now it is Rs 750 [for about 1000 gallons].

Q: Do you want to live again in New Karachi?

A: Yes, it was better living there in a rented house because my work place was near—10-15 minutes' walk. In case of strikes I would come back on foot. Now I own my house and I and my family are facing problems happily.

Q: Do you visit your relatives more or less often?

A: The prices of everything have gone up and we need much money and time to visit them. Most of my relatives live in Baldia town which is very far from here I have a big family with six children. Our visits have been difficult in the absence of our own vehicle. When we lived in New Karachi, transport problems were not as bad as today. It was a cheap period and CNG wouldn't shutdown then. Transport would be available except during strikes and coming back home late at night was easy. Now travelling late at night from any other place to Basti is risky due to muggings and lootings. If I had a late night in the factory I would stay there the whole night.

Q: Would you like to live again in a city renting a house?

A: No, nobody takes any house on rent here because most people have their own houses. A rented house can cost easily Rs 1,000-1,500 monthly. A house rent is high in the city; a single room in a rented house is about Rs 3,000-4,000 which is not affordable for us.

D-06. Dr Qazi Mujahid Ali, MBBS, DIP. DIAB, Family Physician & Diabetologist

Q: What kind of illness are caused by transport, traffic, noise or air pollution?

A: The most common illnesses are divided into two main categories: (1) Diseases related to air pollution (2) Diseases related to noise pollution.

1. Diseases related to air pollution: Studies demonstrate a special vulnerability to air pollution among those with serious illnesses, including asthma, chronic obstructive pulmonary disease (COPD), cardiovascular disease, diabetes, and lung cancer. Hundreds of thousands of Karachiites suffer from these diseases mainly due to living in areas where air pollution is dangerously high. Children, the elderly, those with compromised immune systems, and those with specific genetic traits are at special risk.

2. Diseases related to noise pollution: Noise pollution is not believed to be a cause of mental illness, but it can accelerate and intensify the development of latent mental disorders. Noise pollution may cause or contribute to the following adverse effects: anxiety, stress, nervousness, nausea, headache, emotional instability, argumentativeness, sexual impotence, changes in mood, increase in social conflicts, neurosis, hysteria, and psychosis. It also causes hearing defects.

Q: What kind of prevention is necessary?

A: The transport sector emits a wide range of gaseous air pollutants and of suspended particulate matter (PM) of different sizes and composition. There are tailpipe emissions of primary particles from road transport. Road transport is also the biggest source of emissions of nitrogen dioxide and benzene in cities.

Implementation of technological improvements, such as particle traps, preheated catalytic converters and electronic vehicle controls, may have an impact on transport-related air pollution. Also, stricter exhaust-emission legislation (on PM and nitrogen oxides from conventional diesel and petrol engines) can also contribute to a decrease in transport-related air pollution. Alternative vehicle technologies and fuel substitutes may play an important role in substantially reducing the emission of hazardous air pollutants especially CNG. However, many of the positive effects of technological improvements risk being offset by an increase in the number of vehicles, of the number of kilometres travelled, by a trend towards replacing smaller vehicles with more powerful engines and by an increased use of diesel fuel. That is why technological improvements alone may be insufficient to bring concentrations of transport-related pollutants below levels that pose a threat to human health.

Q: What is the ratio of disease or illness of patients caused by transport?

A: Surely it is very high but the exact ratio is very difficult to describe due to lack of any comprehensive study on this subject. But as a family physician I see an increase in the cases related to this pollution.

Q: What do you suggest to reduce illness caused by the transport issue?

A: CNG in not only a cheaper fuel but also environmentally friendly and CNG vehicles do not emit harmful smoke and gas. It is better to use CNG as an alternative fuel if it is available.

I suggest launching an aggressive programme of tree planting in Karachi—trees are the lungs of any city. Karachi needs millions of trees to make its roads, streets, parks, playgrounds, educational institutions, beaches and public places greener—more trees would ensure that the harmful high levels of air pollution could be offset to some extent. There is also a need to consider measures that influence the amount of travel. For example, integrated urban planning, such as zoning offices, green areas and non-residential functions around urban highways, separating pedestrians and bicyclists from road traffic, and introducing measures that provide disincentives to using private vehicles (such as parking fees and congestion charges) seem to contribute to lowering emission rates. Such measures encourage a shift in favour of public transport and an increase in cycling and walking, which have additional positive effects on health. Moreover, control mechanisms, such as mandatory car inspections, are needed to eliminate polluters and avoid badly maintained vehicles. If we make the public transport system better, develop a mass transit system and discourage encroachment, especially on main roads, and make sure to apply traffic laws effectively, we can decrease this pollution to some extent.

Appendix 4.1: List of Flyovers/Bridges and Underpasses in Karachi

Flyovers

1. Bacha Khan Chowk Flyover, Orangi
2. Sohrab Goth Flyover/Interchange
3. Askari 4 Flyover, Johar
4. Johar Mor Flyover
5. Rashid Minhas Road Flyover, NIPA
6. University Road Flyover, Urdu University
7. Hassan Square Flyover, Gulshan-e-Iqbal
8. National Stadium Road Flyover, Karsaz Road
9. Abul Hasan Ispahani Flyover, University Road
10. Samama Flyover, University Road
11. Jinnah Hospital Interchange, Rafiqi H.J. Road
12. Elevated U-Turn Flyover, University Road
13. Liaquatabad Flyover
14. Jail Chowrangi Flyover, Shaheed-e-Millat Road
15. Karsaz Flyover, Shahrah-e-Faisal
16. PAF Chapter Flyover, Korangi
17. Tipu Sultan Flyover, Sharah-e-Faisal
18. Baloch Colony Flyover, Sharah-e-Faisal
19. Drigh Road Flyover, Sharah-e-Faisal
20. Jinnah Flyover and Interchange
21. KPT Flyover
22. Clifton Overpass
23. F.T.C Flyover, Sharah-e-Faisal
24. Gizri Flyover, Defence
23. Gul Bai Flyover
24. Shershah Flyover, SITE Industrial Area
25. Gulshan-e-Iqbal Flyover, Gulshan Chowrangi
26. KPT Interchange, Qayyumabad, Korangi
27. Shah Faisal Colony Flyover, Shahrah-e-Faisal
28. Nursery Flyover, Sharah-e-Faisal
29. Nazimabad Flyover, Petrol Pump
30. Nagan Chowrangi Flyover, Al Habib Restaurant
31. Nagan Chowrangi Flyover, Shadman Town
32. Afza Altaf Flyover, SITE
33. Quaidabad Flyover
34. PIDC Flyover
35. PAF Base Faisal Flyover
36. Moulvi Tamizuddin (M.T.) Khan Road Flyover
37. Jinnah Terminal Flyover

38. Aisha Manzil Flyover
39. Water Pump Flyover
40. Daak Khana Liaquatabad Flyover
41. Malir Halt Flyover
42. Malir 15 Flyover
43. Korangi Crossing Flyover
44. Manzil Pump Flyover Landhi
45. Abdul Sattar Edhi Intercharge, Board Office, Nazimabad
46. Sunset Boulevard Flyover, Clifton
47. Super Highway Flyover D7 Minibus Stop
48. Super Highway Flyover, Old Toll Plaza

Bridges

1. Gulshan-e-Maymar Link Road Bridge toward Allahwali New Karachi
2. Abul Ispahani Road Bridge, Paradise Bakery
3. Gulshan to Aisha Manzil Bridge
4. Hub River Bridge, Northern Bypass
5. Hub River Road Bridge, Northern Bypass

Bridges on Gujar Nala

1. Ayub Goth Bridge, New Karachi
2. Shafeeq Mor Bridge, Rashid Minhas Road, Gujar Nala
3. Gulberg / People's Chowrangi Bridge, Piyla Hotel, Gujar Nala
4. Tahir Villa Bridge, Landi Kotal Chowrangi, Gujar Nala
5. Ziauddin Hospital Bridge, Gujar Nala
6. Petrol Pump-Liaquatabad Bridge, Gujar Nala

Bridges on Lyari Expressway

1. Al-Asif – Sohrab Goth Bridge
2. Rashid Minhas Road at Moti Mahal Twin Bridge
3. Yasinabad Twin Bridge
4. Essa Nagri Twin Bridge
5. PIB Colony Twin Bridge
6. Teen Hatti Twin Bridge
7. Lasbela Twin Bridge
8. Garden Interchange Twin Bridge
9. Dhobi Ghat Twin Bridge
10. Mewa Shah Twin Bridge
11. Miranaka Shershah Twin Bridge
12. Gul Bai Single Bridge

Bridges on Lyari River

1. Al-Asif – Sohrab Goth Bridge
2. Rashid Minhas Road at Moti Mahal Twin Bridge
3. Yasinabad Twin Bridge
4. Essa Nagri Twin Bridge

5. PIB Colony Twin Bridge
6. Teen Hatti Twin Bridge
7. Lasbella Twin Bridge
8. Garden Interchange Twin Bridge
9. Dhobi Ghat Twin Bridge
10. Mewa Shah Twin Bridge
11. Miranaka Shershah Twin Bridge
12. Gul Bai Single Bridge

Ternals/Crossings

1. Super Highway Daewoo Stand
2. Super Highway Al-Asif roundabout
3. Super Highway under Flyover
4. Northern Bypass Moach Goth No.1
5. Northern Bypass Moach Goth No.2
6. Northern Bypass Moach Goth No.3
7. PAF Museum Ternal
8. Malir Dist. Court Al-Falah Society
9. Drigh Road Cantt Bazar
10. Green Town Dist. Korangi
11. 13D Gulshan-e-Iqbal, KCR Track
12. Chanesar Goth, Main Railway Track
13. PECHS Block-6 Ambala Bakery

Green Line Flyovers

1. Elevated Flyover from KE Power House to Nagan Chowrangi
2. Sakhi Hasan Flyover, North Nazimabad, Green Line
3. Five-Star Flyover, North Nazimabad, Green Line
4. KDA Chowrangi Flyover, North Nazimabad, Green Line
5. Petrol Pump Flyover
6. Lasbela Flyover
7. Elevated Flyover from Patel Para to Guru Mandir

Underpasses

1. Nazimabad Petrol Pump Underpass
2. Gharibabad Underpass
3. Liaquatabad #10 Underpass
4. KPT Underpass, Defence
5. Shahrah-e-Faisal Underpass
6. Mehran Hotel Underpass
7. Golimar Underpass, Nazimabad No.1
8. Submarine Chowk Underpass, Clifton
9. Bahria Underpass, Icon Tower, Clifton
10. Sohrab Goth Underpass
11. Shahrah-e-Quaideen Underpass
12. Bahria Town Underpass, Shahrah-e-Iran, Clifton
13. Bahria Town Underpass, Icon Tower, Clifton

Appendix 5.1: Questionnaires for Research

1. Questionnaire for Research on Commutation Preference of Commuters (For Male Commuters: Also served to 18 Women Commuters)

Total Questionnaire: 100
Number of this questionnaire: 1/100
Place where the interview is conducted:
Date:

1. Name of the respondent:
2. Male/Female/Transgender:
3. Age of the respondent:
4. Where do you live?
5. How far is your home from office (in kilometres)?
6. How much time you spend in travelling from home to office and back to home?
7. How much money do you spend in travelling between home-office-home?
8. If you would have choice to abandon bus and buy motorcycle would you go for it?

Yes/No

9. If yes why and if not why not (Pls. narrate the reasons):

    A. _____
    B. _____
    C. _____

10. If Yes, why haven't you buy one (Pls. narrate reasons):

    A. _____
    B. _____
    C. _____

11. For which of the following ranges you would prefer to invest for the purchase of motorcycle:

From Rs30,000 to Rs40,000
From Rs40, 000 to Rs50,0000
From Rs50,000 onwards

12. Should women also get and drive motorcycles?

13. If yes why and if not why not (Pls. narrate the reasons)?

    A. _____
    B. _____
    C. _____

2. Questionnaire for Research on Commutation Preference of Commuters (For Women Commuters)

Total Questionnaire: 50
Number of this questionnaire: …/50
Place where the interview is conducted:
Date:

1. Name of the respondent:
2. Age of the respondent:
3. Where do you live?
4. How far is your home from office (in kilometres)?
5. How much time you spend in travelling from home to office and back to home?
6. How much money do you spend in travelling between home-office-home?
7. If you would have choice to abandon bus and buy motorcycle would you go for it?

Yes/No

8. If yes why and if not why not (Pls narrate the reasons):

    A. _____
    B. _____
    C. _____

10. Will you be allowed by your guardians to commute through motorcycle?   Yes/No

11. If yes why and if not why not (Pls. narrate the reasons):

    A. _____
    B. _____
    C. _____

12. If Yes, by when you will have one?

13. For which of the following ranges you would prefer to invest for the purchase of motorcycle:

From Rs30,000 to Rs40,000
From Rs40, 000 to Rs50,0000
From Rs50,000 onwards

14. Do you see any moral implications of girls/women driving scoters in public sphere?
Yes /No

15. If yes what are those implications:

    A. _____
    B. _____
    C. _____

3. QUESTIONNAIRE FOR RESEARCH ON MOTORBIKE DEALERS

Total Questionnaire: 25
Number of this questionnaire: …/25
Date:

1. Name of the respondent:
2. Name of the shop:
3. Place?
4. Are you:

DEPENDENT INDEPENDENT

5. Brand(s) available with ranges and C.C:

    A. _____
    B. _____
    C. _____
    D. _____

6. Consumer's Preferred Brand and CC:
7. Preferred Range by the Consumer:
8. Do you sell motorcycles on instalments? Yes/No
9. If Yes, than what is the procedure?
10. Down payment?
12. What is the Price difference?
13. Do you offer insurance?   Yes/No
14. Cost of insurance?
15. Do you offer maintenance / after sell services?   Yes/No
16. What are the major maintenance issues?

    A. _____
    B. _____
    C. _____
    D. _____

17. What are the problems you are facing in this business?

    A. _____
    B. _____
    C. _____
    D. _____

18. What do you think are the solutions to these problems?

    A. _____

    B. _____

    C. _____

    D. _____

19. What do you think is the rate of increment in the growth and sell of motorcycles in the last 3 years?

20. Do you consider Electric motorcycles?   Yes/No

4. QUESTIONNAIRE FOR MOTORBIKE USERS

1. What are traffic and road related problems as faced by you?
2. What do you spend per month for the maintenance and fuel costs of your motorbike?
3. What is the frequency at which your motorbike has to be serviced or repaired?
4. What are the problems you face with the police if any and how much does that cost you?
5. Do you consider a motorbike a suitable transport for a family?
6. Is there a need to change the design of the seat to enhance the carrying capacity?

Appendix 5.2: Use of Pedestrian Bridges in Karachi

Date:
Place:
Male/Female (respondent):
Age of the respondent:

1. How many times in a day you use it?
2. For what purpose
3. Before this pedestrian bridge, how you used to cross the road
4. Do you think that it is placed in the right placed
5. Who use it most
6. Are there any people who don't sue it?
7. If yes why people don't use it, and
8. How do they cross the road then?
9. What difficulties do you face while using this pedestrian bridge?
10. Do you use it in the night as well?
11. If not why not?
12. Any other comments?

Appendix 5.3: List of Pedestrian Bridges in Karachi, Sindh

S. No	District	LOCATION	LENGTH		BREADTH		HEIGHT
1	Central	Near Jamia Mosque Quba, Sir Shah Suleman Road	125'	1"	9'	11"	Varies from 15'-21'
2	Central	Over Ghareebabad Underpass, Sir Shah Suleman Road	171'	6"	9'	10"	,-- Do --
3	Central	At Liaquatabad Stop, 10 no., Sir Shah Suleman Road	134	2"	9'	10"	,-- Do --
4	Central	At Liaquatabad Stop, no. 4, Sir Shah Suleman Road	120'	7"	9'	10"	,-- Do --
5	Central	Near Liaquatabad Town, Hakeem Ibn-e-Sina Road	127'	6"	9'	0"	,-- Do --
6	Central	At Nazimabad stop no.2, Hakeem Ibn-e-Sina Road	126'	0"	9'	10"	,-- Do --
7	Central	Near Golimaar, Sir Syed Govt. Girls College	104'	3"	10'	0"	,-- Do --
8	Central	Nazimabad no.1, Near Urdu Bazaar	140'	9"	10'	0"	,-- Do --
9	Central	Nazimabad no.1, near Inquiry office	128'	5"	8'	8"	,-- Do --
10	Central	Near Baqai institute Of Nephro urology at Nazimabad no. 3	148'	5"	10'	0"	,-- Do --
11	Central	Near Board Office stop, Qaser-e-Sheeren at North Nazimabad	198'	10"	9'	9"	,-- Do --
12	Central	At Hydri stop, North Nazimabad	212'	1"	8'	0"	,-- Do --
13	Central	Near Jamia Mosque, Farooq-e-Azam at North Nazimabad	194'	6"	10'	0"	,-- Do --
14	Central	In between Shahra-e-NoorJehan and Qasbah	82'	9"	8'	0"	,-- Do --
15	Central	At Shadman Stop no.1(BOT)	149'	6"	10'	0"	,-- Do --
16	Central	At Shadman Stop no. 2	168'	6"	9'	0"	,-- Do --
17	Central	Near Nagan flyover, Road 5000	152'	1"	8'	8"	,-- Do --
18	Central	Near Al-Haaj Akhtar Restaurant, Road 5000	170'	4"	8'	11"	,-- Do --
19	Central	At UP More, Road 5000	194'	11"	9'	0"	,-- Do --

20	Central	Near Saleem Centre, Road 5000	149	1"	9'	0"	,-- Do --
21	Central	Near Bara Market, Road 5000	169'	6"	9'	0"	,-- Do --
22	Central	Near Sultan Plaza, Road 5000	175'	10"	9'	0"	,-- Do --
23	Central	Near Café Today, Rashid Minhas Road	127'	4"	8'	2"	,-- Do --
24	Central	Near Masjid-o-Imam Bargah, Shahra-e-Pakistan	160'	0"	9'	0"	,-- Do --
25	Central	At Liaquatabad Super Market, Shahra-e-Pakistan	195'	3"	10'	0"	,-- Do --
26	Central	Near Agha Khan Apartments, Shahra-e-Pakistan	158'	8"	8'	10"	,-- Do --
27	Central	Near Aisha Manzil, Shahra-e-Pakistan	155'	2"	9'	6"	,-- Do --
28	Central	At Naseerabad stop, Shahra-e-Pakistan	166'	2"	8'	8"	,-- Do --
29	Central	At Ancholi stop, shahra-e-Pakaistan	161'	3"	8'	10"	,-- Do --
30	Central	Near Al-Asif Square, near Sohrab Goth	148'	0"	8'	8"	,-- Do --
31	Central	Near Centrum Lawn, Rashid Minhas Road (BOT)	164'	0"	8'	2"	,-- Do --
32	Central	Near Eidhi Center, Rashid Minhas Road	188'	0"	8'	2"	,-- Do --
33	Central	Near Happy Palace School & College, Rashid Minhas Road	132'	0"	8'	2"	,-- Do --
34	DHA	Near National Medical Center, DHA Phase 1, Korangi Road	128'	0"	8'	3"	,-- Do --
35	DHA	Near Eat on, DHA Phase-II, Korangi Road	140'	0"	8'	3"	,-- Do --
36	DHA	Near CALTEX Petrol Pump, DHA Phase II EXT, Korangi Road	141'	0"	8'	3"	,-- Do --
37	DHA	Near West Point Towers, DHA Phase II EXT, Korangi Road	141'	0"	8'	3"	,-- Do --
38	East	Near Shaheed-e-Millat flyover, Shahra-e-Faisal	132'	4"	10'	0"	,-- Do --
39	East	Near Nursery-Fortune Centre, Shahra-e-Faisal (BOT)	129'	6"	7'	0"	,-- Do --
40	East	Near Lal Kothi, Shahrae-e-Faisal (BOT)	153'	6"	11'	1"	,-- Do --
41	East	Near Siddiq Sons Tower, Shahra-e-Faisal (BOT)	172'	0"	9'	3"	,-- Do --
42	East	Near Baloch Colony Flyover, Shahra-e-Faisal(RCC)	133'	0"	8'	10"	,-- Do --

43	East	Near Awamee Markaz, Shahra-e-Faisal	148'	7"	8'	7"	,-- Do --
44	East	Near Karsaz, Shahra-e-Faisal	257'	10"	9'	6"	,-- Do --
45	East	Near PNS Karsaz, Shahra-e-Faisal	105'	6"	8'	9"	,-- Do --
46	East	Near Base Montessori, PAF Faisal, Shahra-e-Faisal	102'	9"	10'	0"	,-- Do --
47	East	Near Drigh Road Station, Shahra-e-Faisal	165'	6"	8'	9"	,-- Do --
48	East	Near Drigh Colony Flyover, Shahra-e-Faisal	111'	6"	9'	11"	,-- Do --
49	East	KCR bridge near Drigh Road flyover, Shahra-e-Faisal	130'	8"	8'	1"	,-- Do --
50	East	Near Colony Gate, Shahra-e-Faisal (RCC-Drigh Road flyover)	112'	0"	8'	9"	,-- Do --
51	East	Near Star Gate, Shahra-e-Faisal	125'	6"	9'	0"	,-- Do --
52	East	Near Shahra-e-Quaideen flyover, Shahra-e-Quaideen Road	148'	9"	9'	6"	,-- Do --
53	East	Preedy Street near mosque Imamia (Imam Bargah), Lines Area	126'	2"	10'	0"	,-- Do --
54	East	Near Nazami Road, lines Area	112'	9"	10'	0"	,-- Do --
55	East	Preedy Street near Allah Walli Mosque, Lines Area	119'	11"	10'	0"	,-- Do --
56	East	Near Dawood Engr. University, New M. A. Jinnah Road	147'	7"	10'	1"	,-- Do --
57	East	At Pardah Park near Jail Chowrangi flyover, M.A Jinnah Extension Road	110'	9"	10'	0"	,-- Do --
58	East	Near Jail Chowrangi flyover, University Road	273'	1"	8'	8"	,-- Do --
59	East	Near Newtown Police Staton, University Road	187'	8"	8'	8"	,-- Do --
60	East	Near Faizan-e-Madina, University Road	182'	0"	9'	1"	,-- Do --
61	East	Near Edhi Home, University Road	191'	9"	9'	10"	,-- Do --
62	East	Near Civic Centre, University Road	166'	4"	9'	2"	,-- Do --
63	East	Near Expo Centre, University Road	174'	3"	10'	0"	,-- Do --
64	East	Near Mumtaz Manzil, University Road	120'	0"	8'	8"	,-- Do --
65	East	Near Bait-ul-Mukarram mosque, University Road	155'	6"	8'	8"	,-- Do --

66	East	Near Urdu College, University Road	121'	10"	11'	10"	,-- Do --
67	East	Near NIPA flyover, University Road	330'	0"	10'	0"	,-- Do --
68	East	Near Sindh Technical Board, University Road	127'	0"	9'	0"	,-- Do --
69	East	Near Ibn-e-Sina Hospital, University Road	165'	6"	8'	8"	,-- Do --
70	East	Near Safari Park, University Road	164'	1"	9'	6"	,-- Do --
71	East	Near NED University, University Road	122'	5"	9'	6"	,-- Do --
72	East	Near Karachi University, University Road	118'	7"	8'	8"	,-- Do --
73	East	Near Megna Mall, Rashid Minhas Road	190'	3"	11'	4"	,-- Do --
74	East	Near Mateen Center, Rashid Minhas Road	127'	4"	8'	2"	,-- Do --
75	East	Near Aladin Park, Rashid Minhas Road	172'	0"	11'	0"	,-- Do --
76	East	Near Raza Square, Rashid Minhas Road	154'	7"	9'	6"	,-- Do --
77	East	Near Dhaka Sweets, Rashid Minhas Road	127'	4"	9'	6"	,-- Do --
78	East	Near Oxford School, Rashid Minhas Road	226'	3"	8'	2"	,-- Do --
79	East	Near Abid Plaza, Rashid Minhas Road	127'	4"	8'	2"	,-- Do --
80	East	Near Navy Gate Dalmia Road (BOT)	108'	0"	8'	6"	,-- Do --
81	East	Near Bahria University, National Stadium Road (BOT)	84'	0"	8'	3"	,-- Do --
82	East	Near PNS Karsaz, Karsaz Road (BOT)	134'	0"	8'	2"	,-- Do --
83	East	Near PAK Marine, Karsaz Road (BOT)	125'	0"	8'	2"	,-- Do --
84	East	Near Bahria Auditorium, Karsaz Road (BOT)	110'	0"	8'	2"	,-- Do --
85	East	Near Al-Mashriq Center, Sir Shah Suleman Road (BOT)	114'	0"	8'	2"	,-- Do --
86	East	Near Kareem Plaza, Sir Shah Suleman Road	177'	8"	9'	9"	,-- Do --
87	East	Near Essa Nagri, Sir Shah Suleman Road	110'	6"	9'	10"	,-- Do --

88	East	Near Fraz Avenue Johar More, Gulistan Johar	98'	0"	8'	3"	,-- Do --
89	East	Near Rufi Paradise, Gulistan Johar	103'	0"	8'	3"	,-- Do --
90	East	Near Darulsailhat Hospital, Gulistan Johar	98'	0"	8'	3"	,-- Do --
91	Korangi	Near Chota Gate, Shahra-e-Faisal	133'	10"	9'	6"	,-- Do --
92	Korangi	Near Kala Board Malir, Shahra-e-Faisal	122'	10"	8'	0"	,-- Do --
93	Korangi	Near Murghi Khana, Laeqabad, Shahra-e-Faisal	112'	0"	10'	0"	,-- Do --
94	Korangi	Near Christian Cemetery, Kala Pul, Korangi Road	132'	3"	8'	6"	,-- Do --
95	Korangi	Near Dar-ul-Uloom, Road 8000 korangi	195'	4"	8'	6"	,-- Do --
96	Korangi	Near KPT Interchange, Qayumabad, C-Area, Korangi Road (KMC)	113'	0"	8'	3"	,-- Do --
97	Korangi	Near Iqra University Manzoor Colony, Express Way	135'	0"	8'	6"	,-- Do --
98	Korangi	Near Manzoor Colony, Express Way (KMC)	129'	0"	8'	6"	,-- Do --
99	Korangi	Near Manzoor Colony Bus Stop, Express Way (KMC)	152'	0"	8'	6"	,-- Do --
100	Lyari	Near KCR Lyari Station Yard, Maripur Road (KPT)	160'	0"	9'	6"	,-- Do --
101	Lyari	Near Crown Cinema, Maripur Road (KPT)	168'	0"	9'	6"	,-- Do --
102	Lyari	Near TCF School Cowasjee Campus, Maripur Road (KPT)	158'	0"	9'	6"	,-- Do --
103	Lyari	Near KCR Wazir Mansion Station, Maripur Road (KPT)	130'	0"	9'	6"	,-- Do --
104	Removed	Near Rimpa Plaza, M.A. Jinnah Road	110'	8"	8'	2"	,-- Do --
105	Removed	Near Jamia Cloth, M.A Jinnah Road	77'	6"	8'	0"	,-- Do --
106	South	Near Regent Plaza, Shahra-e-Faisal (BOT)	128'	6"	8'	0"	,-- Do --
107	South	Near Sea Breeze Plaza, Shahra-e-Faisal (BOT)	118'	3"	7'	0"	,-- Do --
108	South	Near Aisha Bawany Academy, Shahra-e-Faisal	132'	5"	10'	0"	,-- Do --
109	South	Near FTC building, Shahra-e-Faisal	158'	3"	8'	0"	,-- Do --

110	South	Near Faran Hotel, Shahra-e-Faisal	160'	6"	10'	0"	,-- Do --
111	South	Near Jason Trade Centre, Shahra-e-Faisal	154'	1"	11'	0"	,-- Do --
112	South	At IBA, Kiyani Shaheed Road	67'	8"	7'	8"	,-- Do --
113	South	Near Taj Medical Complex, M.A. Jinnah Road	135'	0"	9'	6"	,-- Do --

Index